India By Road and Rail

Diary of an Overland Journey in Nehru's Time

Daniel Griffin

Dedicated to
G. Rama Rao
K.S. Visvanathan
K.S. Venkataraman
William Thomas
Tudor and June Thomas
who helped, with many others, to make it possible

India By Road and Rail

Diary of an Overland Journey in Nehru's Time

Daniel Griffin

Contents

Preface

This book describes an extended visit to India and countries on the way in 1961-62. It is based on letters I sent home with added comments (in brackets) reflecting my thoughts and reading in the ensuing thirty years. Hence, after much spillage of ink, I arrive at the moment where my story is ready for a reader's eye.

Initially, some background may be helpful. The early 1960s were a good time for relations between Americans and Indians, though the politics of Washington and New Delhi were incompatible in some ways. India was the leader of the nonaligned nations in that period of the Cold War. Nevertheless, the peoples of the two countries were actively networking. That led to the hippy invasion of India after I departed.

India achieved Independence in 1947, and the optimism of that time was still present in the 1960s, though not as keen, perhaps, as earlier. Gandhi was revered for his nonviolent leadership and his martyrdom in January 1948. Martin Luther King, Jr. took his major inspiration for the civil rights movement from the Hindu leader. The Indian Prime Minister, Jawaharlal Nehru, was a popular personality in a world leadership role and traveled frequently. The U.S. president was John Kennedy, and Mr. Kennedy toured India briefly during my visit. Our ambassador at the time was John Kenneth Galbraith.

For many Americans, India meant yoga and meditation, and Indian music had a following here. Ravi Shankar gave concerts, including one at Tanglewood in Lenox, Massachusetts. Indian films were shown in American theaters, and it was all assisted by the presence of a common language.

Locally, it was the Cleveland Council on World Affairs' sponsorship of the International Students Group (I.S.G.) that facilitated bringing people from different countries together in congenial surroundings. The council contributed a part-time director of activities to the I.S.G., and every Friday evening a large cross-section of university students, doctors and nurses, and their American hosts assembled for a special program and socializing. These stimulating, enjoyable occasions continued for several years. I was a regular member of the I.S.G. and helped form a subgroup we named the Intercultural Forum. This met on Sunday evenings for discussions led by different members and guests. It proved itself by developing a loyal following among I.S.G. participants.

With all this activity it did not take long before I was forming plans for a new trip abroad. The last one had taken me through Europe and the Middle East. This time I wanted to see India, for I had a perennial urge to travel in foreign places. To visit more countries, see more things, as well as save money, I planned to reach the subcontinent overland from England by ferry, train, bus, and car. In other words the plane or ship would not suit the purpose.

I had a plan and set about saving every dollar possible to finance it. The same plan stimulated me to work hard, giving meaning to what I was about. I knew it was going to be a shoestring affair in every sense. I was prepared, however, to kick my job and go abroad for a year.

I had invitations from several visiting professors and students to stay with them in their country. They described how it would be inexpensive if I used ordinary transportation and lodgings. The route I chose proved to have the advantage of letting me see several countries and regions—eastern Turkey, Iran, Afghanistan, Kashmir, and Sri Lanka—that later became more or less inaccessible to the traveler.

In the last few years, as I remembered the stack of letters written to people at home, it came to mind that they contained interesting anecdotes of traveling days in the exotic East. They form the basis of the account you now have before you.

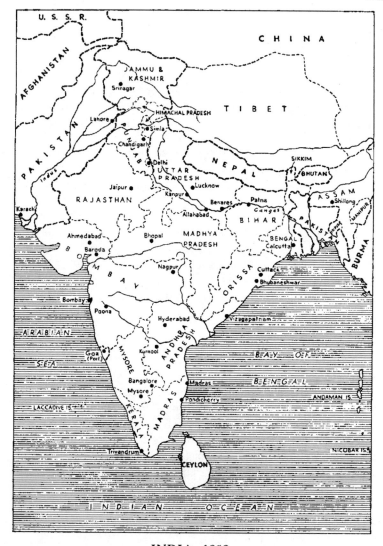

INDIA, 1959

London To Lahore

Headley, Tuesday, June 13

The ship *Groote Beer* docked in Southampton this morning; I sensed the exhilaration of standing on foreign soil again, surrounded by the sights and sounds of another country. I felt freedom in the air as I boarded the boat train waiting on the dock for the nonstop journey to London.

Rolling rapidly through the countryside past villages and towns, we fetched the outskirts of London and soon Victoria Station. One more short rail trip to Leatherhead and I was reunited with Tudor and June Thomas in Headley. They live in a cottage surrounded by Surrey farms and fields.

The following week was filled with trips to London for the purposes of my projected journey to India because I needed information on routes, visa requirements, immunizations, and addresses, as well as maps and guides. Before I set out again, we had an enjoyable evening of dinner and theater in London together. This was my adieu to the Thomases, whose help and suggestions were so valuable. [I would see them again more than a year later—upon my return.]

Paris, Wednesday, June 21

Today I left England behind and entered a more complex phase of the journey. I expected the inevitable contretemps, but was prepared to accept them as part of traveling. As I made the famous channel crossing, I reflected that I would soon be in the midst of many new choices in eating, sleeping, moving about, and sightseeing. In addition, there was the French language to brush up.

In Paris, after some searching on the Left Bank, I discovered a small hotel on the Place du Pantheon that perfectly satisfied my requirements. I had a small room on the top floor with a window looking out on the Pantheon itself.

I took full advantage of the fine spring weather, nearly wearing out a pair of shoes in walking the streets and boulevards and visiting churches, museums, parks, and the Seine. I went to the Louvre to sample its great collections—some of them from countries and cultures I would be visiting.

Several invitations to dinner and luncheon followed. They were from people whom I had met at home or whose names were provided by my English friends. I enjoyed the company of a winsome Parisienne on a visit to the Louvre and the theater.

In a cultural Marathon I attended theatrical performances on seven consecutive evenings. The government provides financial aid to the arts in France and so assures reasonable basic ticket prices.

I always asked for the lowest-priced seat available. My binoculars served well when it was in the high locations.

Economies are possible if you take care in choosing restaurants and accommodations. As long as I was traveling in expensive places, I consumed but one restaurant meal daily and prepared others myself either in my room (breakfast) or in the park (lunch). The nearest *épicerie* (grocery) provided the ingredients. On occasion I ate a meal in a university cafeteria by purchasing a ticket from a student in line. It provided an opportunity to sit with students and engage in conversation.

Verdun, Wednesday, July 5

Yesterday I left Paris and came to Verdun, where the name seems to echo somberly like distant cannons. I found that the scene of that long and terrible battle of World War I reinforced this impression many times.

There being no public transportation, I found a ride with a salesman of farm machinery. In the course of the few miles we drove, he told me how every day relics of the conflict keep turning up. We drove across a scarred terrain of overgrown trenches, shell holes, and decayed fortifications, even vestiges of perished villages. The battlefield is called la Zone Rouge and a kind nature has tried to hide the wounded earth in most places.

The helpful driver brought me to a convenient point to begin a walking tour of a small area near the Ossuary of Douaumont. This hulking monument enshrines the neatly stacked bones of thousands of unidentified soldiers from both sides. The visitor enters a long, dimly illuminated chamber resembling a crypt where every footfall echoes. There are small individual side chambers, also dimly lit, where the bones are stacked by type—one chamber for pelvises, another for femurs and so on, including skulls. Beneath are the cellars where, presumably, more bones lie.

Leaving the Ossuary empty of the living again, I next observed the Fort of Douaumont, which you can enter, though a damp, cold, cavernous and depressing ruin it is. It was first constructed during the Franco-Prussian War. Moving on, I next noticed a revetted trench next to the road, which sheltered strawberry plants bearing ripe fruit, but I could not reach any. Beyond was a monument dedicated to a unit that lost 70 percent of its people on this spot in the course of one engagement. By this time I realized that I had had enough, and I left la Zone Rouge to return to Verdun. The sky, which had been overcast, began to clear and the sun emerged.

Nancy and Strasbourg, Thursday, July 6

Nancy was my next objective. There was opportunity to look around the Place Stanislas this afternoon. The square might be described as an eighteenth-century version of holistic architecture since the buildings surrounding it harmonize in style, period, and height. I thought it made a very attractive ensemble, accentuated by the Hotel de Ville at one end. As evening came on, a son-et-lumière (sound and light show) took place in that edifice and I took the opportunity to go. Such presentations have become frequent in France and tourists like them. By means of music, light, and dialogue, the city's history becomes a kind of operatic celebration, but instead of occurring in a theater the show takes place in a fine building such as the Town Hall of Nancy.

As the celebration ended, I hastened to collect my baggage and board the next train to Strasbourg. Once on board I was told it was the all-first-class European from Paris to Strasbourg. This was a contretemps because I held a second-class ticket. Nevertheless I settled down in a first class compartment and reveled in the unaccustomed luxury. There were six rather than eight places—richly upholstered and provided with arm rests, and the occupants were shielded from the corridor by a sliding door with a panel of decorated frosted class. Soon after the train left the station, a polite and smiling conductor knocked at our door before entering to collect tickets. He requested an additional amount from me to make up the difference in class. I was glad to comply, considering it a bargain.

We fetched Strasbourg in late evening and I found a bus out to the youth hostel.

Strasbourg, Friday, July 7

This clean, municipally operated hostel is a pleasure. A bunk bed costs the equivalent of forty-two cents a night and permits use of the communal kitchen. After preparing my breakfast, I set out to see the city, like a wayfarer, carrying necessaries in my shoulder bag.

Alsace, of which Strasbourg is the principal city, borders on Germany and therefore displays a blend of two cultures and languages. It has become the "new paradigm" for a united and peaceful Europe. It being excellent weather for walking, I tried to visit some of many noted sites. The cathedral, inside and outside, was seen in company with other tourists, with whom I also admired the Pillar of Angels and astronomical clock in action. The romantic tomb of the French general Maurice de Saxe in the Church of St. Thomas fascinated me. I would call it ostentatious but captivating. Albert Schweitzer had played the organ in the same church.

As noonday approached and the streets grew calmer, I located something to eat in my *épicerie*, then sat down next to one of the canals here and had lunch hoping that the vagabond life I was enjoying might go on forever. Ducks gathered around to receive scraps of bread.

In the afternoon I gave attention to La Petite France, several churches, and some museums until it was time to buy something to cook for supper. That turned out to be a type of local cabbage that resembled lettuce, a piece of beefsteak, and Alsatian white wine, which I prepared in the hostel where others were similarly occupied.

Colmar, Saturday, July 8

This morning I traveled la Route du Vin d'Alsace, which connects several wine-growing villages of the lower Vosges Mountains before reaching Colmar. This is a small city possessing a notable group of German pictures, which I wished to see. The master Martin Schongauer was born here, and the cathedral holds his *Virgin of the Rose Garden*. Then in the small museum there is the famous *Isenheim altarpiece* by Mathias Grunewald. It consists of six main painted panels and a carved shrine in the middle which are hinged three pairs of wings. The subjects come from the New Testament. The closed ensemble measures ten feet across; when open, it is twenty-one feet. It could only fit in a large church.

My destination for tonight was Switzerland. However, a contretemps arose because I erred in the location of the small place to which I was headed—Dornach. Purchasing a ticket to Zurich, I boarded the waiting train and sat down but quickly discovered by consulting the map that I should be going to Basel instead. I hurriedly seized my baggage and got off before the train began to move.

Customs and immigration formalities used to be involved, but they are simplified now and at Basel, passengers merely filed past two windows, handing their passport through the first and receiving it again at the second window.

Dornach, Sunday, July 9

At home I had known several members of the Anthroposophical Society, of which Dornach is the headquarters. Everything is contained in a large building that uses reinforced concrete in interesting ways. There is also an auditorium in the Goetheanum, as it is named, and both here and throughout the interior the finish is partly wood, also serving in unique conformations, like things growing. I watched the rehearsal of a play in the auditorium while seated with a group of New Yorkers.

Aeschi, Monday, July 10

As often in the mountains, the weather fell short of ideal this morning as I left Dornach behind and slowly approached the Alps, waiting for it to clear. I did some walking as well as hitchhiking, both good ways to meet people. As I approached Spiez, it suddenly cleared, revealing the finest scenery I could desire. What a difference clear sky and sun can bring, and how quickly! It was as if a curtain had been drawn back.

Consulting my invaluable map for a place to head this night, I selected Aeschi, which would take me up into the foothills near Spiez. It was not too far to reach on foot. As I approached a village, a broad valley spread out in front of me, covered by a meadow scattered with houses, small farms, and Brown Swiss cattle grazing. The village turned out to be Aeschi. A search for lodging led me to a farmhouse where the friendly owners provided a small upper room containing little furniture except a single bed with down mattress and blankets enough to keep me warm. It was charmingly rustic and had once served as winter living quarters for cowherds while the animals stayed below, giving their warmth to the people above.

I found a cafe restaurant serving a supper comsisting of a tureen of home made soup, omelette with flaked cheese, and hot milk. The chunk of cheese exceeded my capacity and I carried away the remainder.

Gemmi Pass, Tuesday, July 11

The cawing of a flock of crows woke me this morning, and soon I set out on foot for Reichenbach. On the road I met early morning milk and bread sellers, who distribute door to door from small carts; They provided my breakfast.

The electric train carried me a few miles up Kander Valley to Frutigen, from where I walked to Kandergrund, farther up the valley. The Alps became loftier and the scenery more spectacular at each mile. The valley is broad and open, making for better views. I boarded another of the frequent electric trains at Kandergrund, which made a large figure eight inside the mountain wall to gain height. This track is one of the many accomplishments of Swiss railroad builders, as is the subsequent nine-mile Lotschberg Tunnel at

Kandersteg. From the latter village I proceeded to take the Stock aerial tramway, which gives access to another alpine gulf with lofty backdrops on both sides. The traverse of this six- to seven-mile gap provided a pleasant and invigorating afternoon's hike because it made a gentle ascent. Few other walkers were to be seen. A marker along the trail contained a dedication in English to six climbers who perished here in 1895.

By early evening I fetched Gemmi Pass, at 7,595 feet, which terminates the gulf and leads to a sharp descent on the further side. A hotel perched at the summit of the pass overlooks Leukerbad 3,000 feet below. A dormitory for skiers adjoins it, and there I took a bunk and dined at the hotel.

By foot and rail to Chamonix, Wednesday, July 12

I was up early and outside in the cool mountain air to observe the sun surmount the ridges to the east, causing the slopes it struck to take on red coloring for awhile. I prepared my simple breakfast in front of the dormitory—bread left from the previous dinner, jam, and instant coffee. By the practice of a few such economies, I spent only $22 for my four days in Switzerland.

As the cable car did not begin to operate until later in the morning and there was no road, I began the walk down to Leukerbad on the extremely steep trail. The effort of descending these 3,000 feet soon brought muscle pain. A narrow-gauge cog railway from Leukerbad follows a narrow defile, which joins the Rhone. Therefore I both rode the little train and walked the picturesque road, which also occupies the confined mountain valley that leads to Montigny. At this point begins a second cog railway, just as pretty, by which I fetched Chamonix in France. It had been altogether a most enjoyable day's journey, one approaching Shangri-la in its scenic qualities.

Chamonix, Thursday, July 13

The Mont Blanc auto tunnel is one-third complete and will eventually offer a quick way to reach Italy from Chamonix. I was able to observe some of the works connected with it because the youth hostel lies in the vicinity.

Climbers of all nations are drawn to Mont Blanc to pit their skills against this ferocious peak where weather is most unpredictable. It is Europe's loftiest at 16,300 feet and in recent days the newspapers have reported five deaths on the perilous slopes.

Chamonix, Friday, July 14

It dawned clear and I seized the opportunity to utilize the highest aerial tram in Europe, the Téléphérique de l'Aiguille du Midi. The string of towers and cables requires two stages to attain the summit station at 13,000 feet. The first of these is a normal ride over the lower mountain slopes; however, the next lap I liken to being plucked up by an eagle and brought to an eyrie among rock, snow, ice, and prevailing winter conditions in which frigid winds buffet the ice-encrusted landing stage facing Mont Blanc. As I was in light clothing, I soon abandoned this wasteland for the heated snack bar and observatory. The upper part of Mont Blanc stands no more than two miles off, snow covered and inhospitable in mid-July. It is possible to prolong the excursion into Italy by connecting aerial cars, but I returned to the halfway station (Plan des Aiguilles), where a trail branches off to the Mer de Glace, a large glacier on which skiers are busy sailing over snow-packed ice. This I started to cross on foot to find a path back to town, but I had to turn back when the way was blocked by a rushing current of meltwater. Instead I scrambled down another rock-strewn way to Chamonix and saved purchasing a tram ticket.

Annecy and Grenoble, Saturday, July 15

My movement at this time was south and east, but I also wished to observe attractive places along the way. For several hours I strayed through the small town of Annecy on the beautiful Lac d'Annecy fringed by hills. A large park containing fine gardens and large trees affords views of lake, hills, and mountains. A small network of narrow canals unites town and lake. The water in these is so clear that occasional litter is clearly visible on the bottom. Vehicles are banned from the old part of the town. I entered a pharmacy to seek relief from painful toes resulting from a new pair of sandals. The benevolent proprietor applied a bandage and asked nothing for the service.

St. Francis de Sales was born and attended school here. I visited the leading Church of the Visitandines, which he helped found. Also, Jean-Jacques Rousseau lived in Annecy for a while and sang in the church choir.

The old spas of Europe interest me, partly perhaps because of their air of genteel living. I stopped in Aix-les-Bains on Lake Bourget, which nostalgically recalls an earlier, calmer period. Alphonse de Lamartine made it the setting of a poem, and the Romans knew the place as Aquae Gratianae. A small Roman arch survives near the modern baths. I enjoyed the well-shaded park frequented by the *curistes* from the baths, and I noticed numerous expensive hotels and shops. A troupe of Soviet dancers were performing in the evening, but the cheap tickets were sold out, so I departed for Grenoble.

I had attended a summer course in French for foreigners at the University of Grenoble in 1954. Therefore the return to Grenoble brought back some memories of that enjoyable experience. In a small restaurant near the station I found a convivial group of dinner guests who engaged one another and the proprietor in conversation concerning the city. It has a young and active mayor, said the owner. "C'est bien pour Grenoble," he added.

Grenoble, Sunday, July 16

Today I retraced steps leading to once familiar locales—the street and house where I stayed and the Place Verdun adjacent, where I found a company of soldiers preparing for a drill. Then I went to Place Grenette, where it was the habit of students I knew to stop at the cafes for coffee, practice French, or study.

The Alps nearly encompass this city, leaving several gaps for access by road or rail. The mountains meet the city on the north, but allow room for growth in other directions, and the place gives signs of being in full development. Educational facilities such as the university are improving, and many cultural features, historic monuments, the old quarter, and parks give citizens enjoyment. The river Isère bisects the city and its embankments are beautiful throughout. All told, Grenoble has many advantages.

Prior to departure I stopped at the Parc Mistral, much developed since last I saw it, and noticed the once familiar Maison des Etudiants. Then, having suitably recognized old reference points here, I left Grenoble by bus, traveling south into Provence. The good weather persisted, and motorists were stopped along the scenic roadway to rest or picnic. Roadside parks have not come to France.

The transition from a temperate to a Mediterranean climate occurs within a short space, and southern plants and trees begin to dominate. The atmosphere becomes clearer, sun drenched, and drier. This is the pleasant world I shall be in the next few weeks as I visit Italy, Greece, and southern Turkey. The thought of this rejoices me and I feel rededicated to travel and seeing new places.

Upon arriving in Aix, I settled in the Hotel Victoire and dined in the park on bread, cheese, salami, wine, and fruit—my standard fare.

Aix-en-Provence, Monday, July 17

In the morning I visited the old town, where many structures were in need of repair. Then I walked out into the country toward Thalonet, most probably the same way Paul Cézanne took when searching for subjects to paint. I came to a small hill whose summit offered a general view of Mont Ste Victoire—the very subject of many of the master's canvases.

One of the obstacles to be faced by a traveler is baggage, and my own inclination is to take too much. The once reliable method was to use a trunk, which could be conveniently handled by others as the thing was sent from one destination to the next, following you dependably. It was either already waiting at your hotel or in the station baggage room upon your arrival. Perhaps I was one of the last travelers to take a trunk because I found it useful for carrying many articles not regularly required. I had mine sent from home to London and from there to Paris, then to Aix. Today it was awaiting me here. After exchanging unneeded equipment for other more suitable, such as my camping gear, I redirected the bulky container to Nice. Another nice thing about shipping a trunk is the reasonable cost.

La Ciotat, Tuesday, July 18

Today I renewed contact with the Mediterranean—not the delightful Rivièra, which begins at Hyères, but at La Ciotat, which does not attract many tourists. I remembered a comfortable youth hostel here and it was a logical choice. The cliffs nearby tower above the sea and are exposed to the mistral, while the coast is indented by *calanques* (coves) separated by sharp hogbacks of gray sedimentary rock. The narrow gravel beaches are difficult to reach. When the mistral is strong, it is prudent to stand back from the cliff edge. The water was cold for swimming. Mainly I sought a place to rest, read, and write my diary, which had fallen behind.

At the hostel they served a good evening meal for sixty cents.

La Ciotat, Wednesday, July 19

Even with constant northwest wind, the weather is good. I did some walking and climbing nearby. La Ciotat has a shipyard, seen in the distance, with ships on the ways. It appears busy and my observations here in France suggest an expanding economy. A speech by Charles de Gaulle on Bastille Day mentioned this. Production has grown by 10 percent in the past year. The average person is still frugal, and shops measure out small amounts of butter and other foodstuffs to customers. I like it, being single and not able to carry much. French farmers regularly face off with the authorities by blocking roads and dumping produce to maintain prices.

Gaou, Thursday, July 20

My design called for moving eastward along the littoral; however, by so doing I could expect greatly increased tourism, and as much as possible I tried to avoid the crowd. By acquiring a Michelin *Green Guide* and a good map of the district, I was able to solve the problem. I found Cap Sicié and reached it today by bus, or more precisely, reached Brusc, where I inquired about the municipal campground on the island of Gaou. I learned that it just fit my needs—it was placed on the far shore of a small island and was not reachable by road. I could not expect better. A staff person escorted me to the camping area and indicated a spot I could use. There were very few other campers about—none nearby—and the site was beautiful, close to the sea and yet sheltered by the maquis. There were some ants, but the authorities provided without charge a magic powder to scatter around my "kitchen" and "bedroom."

Only bathroom facilities and water were provided in this little paradise where the surf produced a gentle cadence to relax by, especially under a clear evening sky. I proceeded to set up a simple camp—air mattress, sheet bag, blanket, and plastic sheet for rain protection. A small stove and several dishes completed it, after which I set out to explore.

Porquerolles Islands and Hyères, Saturday, July 22

After two nights at Gaou, I moved on along the coast. The information led me to the Porquerolles Islands lying off the peninsula of Giens, a half-hour ferry ride distant. So I resolved to seek out the islands and soon found more than I had expected or hoped for.

After landing on the chief island, Porquerolles, I set out walking the tracks and trails beyond the port. The islands are privately owned and protected, though open to visitors (no cars). Only a few hundred residents dwell here, fewer than in former times because some have given up their farms and moved to the mainland. Nature has reclaimed the abandoned fields, and the islands are undisturbed.

I fetched the lighthouse on the south side, then walked through a pine grove and emerged atop a cliff overlooking a peaceful cove. By the cliff trail through the maquis, I reached the port again. A fisherman I encountered said the sea was too calm for him to catch anything today. The sole disturbing presence on these islands might be the navy firing range on Levant. At times the muffled sound of guns is audible.

I tried in vain to locate a hotel room in Porquerolles and gave up to take the ferry back to Tour Fondue on the mainland. A Vespa motor scooter driver took me to Hyères, where I found a room in the Hotel Moderne.

Levant Island, Sunday, July 23

The barber this morning said I would do well to visit the re-maining two islands of Port Cros and Levant. I walked in the attrac-tive town of Hyères before taking the ferry at Le Lavandoau, which called at Levant. My guidebook mentioned the "*naturistes*" on this island, and I assumed they would be protected from the public by fences or walls. I was not a little abashed when the boat arrived at the quai to find *naturistes* and non-naturistes standing there waiting for us to tie up. Nevertheless, I disembarked, knowing that I could camp overnight here but not on Port Cros.

Levant looked unpretentious as I followed the earthen track up to the settlement appropriately named Heliopolis. The partisans of the sun were present everywhere around me. I was spooked and afraid to speak to them and so could not learn anything further. If they have a philosophy they certainly live it.

I found the principal crossroads an unpaved, dusty area with a fountain around which the sun people were washing and brushing their teeth. I took a glass of beer in a cafe before buying some food to prepare in camp; then I found a concealed spot high overlooking the settlement. There I stayed the night—a room with a view.

Port Cros Island and Fréjus, Monday, July 24

I took the early boat to Port Cros. Compared to Porquerolles, it is wilder, although it's not as primitive as Levant. Well-maintained trails take the visitor to the chief beauty spots: La Vigie, Les Falaises du Sud and Vallon de la Solitude. I saw abandoned farms and houses. A small settlement at the port includes several hotels and restaurants. It was five o'clock when the boat returned to the mainland, and I took the bus to Fréjus, where I found a room costing $2.50.

Fréjus and the Corniche, Tuesday, July 25

The large town of Fréjus was a Roman naval station and pre-serves interesting ruins, which I had previously visited. The Esterel begins here, a colorful and picturesque segment of coast composed of a red formation rising sharply from the sea. There is little area for building and so the beauty of the rugged land is protected. The skirting roadway is constructed on a shelf in places. It is named the Corniche d'Or.

I walked the 2.4 miles from Fréjus to St. Raphael, then boarded the bus to Cannes, where the Esterel ends. The sea along the way is limpid blue.

My last lodging in France was in Le Trayas youth hostel, situated in a villa perched high above the Corniche and reached by a twisting drive. It has its own sheltered beach. For two days I rested and read in preparation for further travel.

Rome, Friday, July 28

Yesterday, as I prepared to leave for the Eternal City, I faced another contretemps. My pocket contained only $15 in francs. However American Express in Cannes was holding a check, which was a help. Then I recovered my trunk long enough to exchange various items and redirected this to Rome on my ticket.

The Rome train was full. After a long, sleepless night in a second-class compartment with seven others, we fetched Roma Termini in the morning. I returned to the Pensione Ripetta, lying two steps from the Tiber, where I had put up for six weeks back in 1954 and which I remembered with pleasure. Nothing seemed to have changed except the new, joking sign in the entrance, which said, "In questa casa siamo tutti nervosi." It left me smiling. After dinner with the other guests—all Italians—I set out to renew my acquaintance with this marvelous city.

In the early evening I met an old friend, Lillina Marino, in Piazza Cavalieri di Malta, a quiet square with two old churches and a keyhole view of St. Peter's. I had met her in Cleveland when she was studying social work on a Fulbright scholarship. First we saw her school; then we drove across the city in her small Italian car to the apartment where her sister and a Siamese cat were waiting. A most satisfying supper of cold vegetable pie, beefsteak, salad, and wine followed. Afterwards, we idled away the evening hours on the balcony.

Rome, Saturday, July 29

Because this city holds so many rewarding places to visit, sightseeing is a nearly unending exercise. Therefore, whenever I had the time and strength I was out in the streets, searching out more to see.

The *pensione* serves three meals a day. Following supper at eight, I went to the Baths of Caracalla to see a performance of *Turandot*. The cheap ticket (fifty cents) put me perhaps one-quarter mile from the stage. The sound was loud and full. Floodlights played effectively on the broken Roman vaulting. These outdoor productions are loved by tourists, including me.

Rome, Sunday, July 30

This morning Lillina took her friends Roberto and Lina Prili and me in her car to visit a beach near Fregene, where the sand is fine and the sea clean, but it was too rough for swimming, so we returned to Rome.

The baroque Church of Sant' Ignazio is richly decorated. The wealth of adornment and the frescoes are stunning. Vaults, dome, and apse are covered with technically perfect scenes of saints, virgin with child, and angels floating in the clouds with segments of buildings also suspended in mid-air. In the nave floor a marker establishes the position an observer can take to see these to best advantage.

Compassed within the Eternal City's historic center are the constructions of the ages, which contrast with one another in many ways. For example it is only a few steps from the Church of Sant' Ignazio to the Church of S. Maria Rotonda, which, before consecration as a church by the pope in 608 A.D., was the Roman Pantheon—and still is—although masquerading as a church. But by that inspired papal act the ancient domed building was preserved from the decay and destruction that overtook other antiquities, including the steadfast Colosseum, which was quarried for building material by popes and princes. Several existing *palazzi* are composed of portions of the Colosseum which was so immense that it in large part survived, helped by a papal edict that acknowledged the structure to be consecrated by the blood of so many condemned Christians.

In Paris the view from my hotel window had taken in that Pantheon, and now I had the Roman building before me. The Parisian monument is very large and also memorable, but apart from that it does not particularly inspire me. It is also constructed to the canon of classical architecture. The antique building satisfied me much more, but I cannot say why. It seems presumptuous even to ask. The older building combines several noble features that appear not to have their equal in the French building. In proposing such a comparison I concentrate on esthetics. The low dome, bronze doors, oculus, and light quality in the Roman building require the observer's admiration and they are not equaled in the French Pantheon. Through the Middle Ages and later, the Pantheon in Rome was the one ancient building that remained well preserved. It was on the tourist trail—every visitor to Rome had to see it. Therefore its renown was widespread.

Rome, Tuesday, August 1

One of the delightful amenities that this city offers are her many attractive fountains. They are works of art as well as life-giving oases on a blistering summer day. They offer respite to many sightseers with feet tired from walking and hands aching from holding a guidebook. At certain times of day space is lacking at one of these fresh-flowing sources, so many are the occupants of a fountain's edge.

This afternoon the three large basins of the fountain in the Piazza Navona provided a refreshing place to pause while I read the news in my favorite Italian newspaper, Milan's *Corriere della Sera*, which spoke of Britain's decision to join the European Common Market. This pleases the Italians much because they want more members to act as a counter balance to Germany. My English friends had told me that their government would be compelled to join eventually by economic forces.

Lillina and I ate supper together at the Ristorante Vero Romano in Via Umiltà. This was the same place I had visited in 1954 and it had not changed—they serve good food at fair prices. Subsequently we saw the Trevi Fountain fully illuminated; then we walked along the panoramic way by the Roman Forum, looking down on the illuminated ruins, which were also lit by a full moon. Before ending the evening we had a final espresso near the theater of Marcellus.

Rome, Wednesday, August 2

As I perambulated in Trastevere this morning I was hailed by a citizen of modest height. He wished to place his less than lofty stature next to my own greater height, and upon his friends' observation of the contrast there was a round of laughter.

The morning was as yet young and churches were still open so I scanned S. Maria in Trastevere. Twenty-two ancient columns of varying color, height, and diameter enclose the nave. These were taken from unknown earlier buildings, perhaps churches of still greater age and, ultimately, ancient Roman buildings. The pavement in the church is composed in patterns of colored marble and other stones in a mosaic technique called Cosmati work, which I find attractive and unusual. It is found in a few Roman churches. There are also older and more modern mosaics decorating this church, including a large scene outside over the main entrance.

Rome, Thursday, August 3

The National Gallery in the Barberini Palace seems to contain only a few open galleries of paintings. This morning as I looked around—the number of visitors being small—the attendant must have noticed that I was interested. Therefore he pointed out some particular works of art such as Raphael's *La Fornarina* and the chapel, an architectural work by Bernini. Like a true Italian who appreciated art, he spoke with enthusiasm. It was almost a private tour.

Veii and Cerveteri, Friday, August 4

Lillina, the Prilis, and I drove north of Rome today to visit two Etruscan towns. First was Veii, a green and peaceful site once occupied by a notable Etruscan city, which the Romans took in 396 B.C. following a long siege. We traced the Roman Via Cassia, bordered by several moldering tombs, and then came up to the site of an Etruscan temple. Not much was to be seen by an untrained observer. The attendant provided a description to aid our appreciation. The place had the odor of deep time. As we walked around the sparse remains of the fortifications, we discovered a patch of ripe blackberries and stopped to pick and eat.

Nearby is La Storta, where St. Ignatius Loyola had a famous vision. After Veii we visited the Etruscan necropolis of Cerveteri, where the archaeological zone contains a number of well-preserved tombs, some large with two or more chambers. These are situated on both sides of a main avenue in the "city of the dead," which might be compared to a series of earth covered huts forming a village. Each tomb chamber contains the benches or shelves on which a family placed the sarcophagi or funerary urns of the deceased, and some are still in place. The surfaces dividing the area and the walls are decorated with reliefs. The tombs are partly or fully cut into the soft tufa and roofed over with blocks of the same, then covered with soil. Other tombs are small, single-chambered examples, which cluster together or fill the space between larger ones.

Our walking tour was led by the resident guardian, who introduced the individual chambers and replied to our queries about this strange place. Among the most interesting are the Tomb of the Reliefs, and that of the Sarcophagi and the one of the Shields. Originally the interiors were painted; faint traces of color can be detected after 2,000 years.

At seaside Ladispoli we swam in the Mediterranean before preparing a full spaghetti dinner using my small stove. There was salad, bread, and wine to accompany the main dish.

The coastal plain is fairly flat and sparsely vegetated. You can see the Apennine Mountains in the near distance. I could not help thinking that this region must have been more productive in Etruscan times because the necropolis is extensive, although many graves were destroyed in later times. We tarried at the beach until after seven and as we neared Rome encountered heavy weekend traffic leaving the city.

Once back at our favorite cafe in Piazza Navona, we took espresso with whipped cream while passing the time in this delightfully lazy fashion waiting for the supper hour.

Roberto and Lina are about thirty and lately married after a ten-year courtship. He teaches literature in the gymnasium. Since he can sing, I tried to persuade him to go out into the piazza and show his talent, but he would not. I enjoyed them very much.

Rome, Saturday, August 5

The Museo Nazionale Romano protects a large gathering of fragments of Rome's classical age. It is one of my favorite museums because it is less frequented by the public as well as holding important stone sculpture and works in other media. There is not a great amount of the very best work, but there is some. The objects are displayed in a pleasingly informal though effective way, particularly because of the natural lighting.

The *Ludovisi Throne* (Bath of Venus), the *Discobulus*, and the bronze *Pugilist* are among the outstanding sculptures, yet I probably enjoyed the less-known pieces almost as much. These antiquities and also the Church of Santa Maria degli Angeli are sheltered in surviving parts of the antique Baths of Diocletian. The tepidarium, of imposing dimensions, contains the church Michelangelo designed to fit the Roman buildings. The basilican form of Roman law courts was adapted to Christian churches in early times. The attendant told me of the 40,000 condemned Christians who labored in these baths and the Baedeker also speaks of them.

Most often walking in search of more to see, I arrived at Porta S. Sebastiano, where the Via Appia begins, and I climbed to the top of the gate for a better view over the Campagna, and the famous road to Brindisi and the East. This part of the Roman Campagna has been saved from development. At a distance many-storied apartment blocks line the Via Appia Nuova, hideously spoiling the skyline. When I saw it first in 1950, the Campagna was still open along the modern highway. Now, much the worse for the passage of a few years, it represents one of the sorry results of progress. The heart of the city has been shielded from this development, though not entirely, and here and there are eyesores though not taller than they should be. People are moving into Rome, causing continued expansion, congestion, pollution, and litter. In spite of these insults, however, it is still the Eternal City.

At seven I met Lillina for pizza and wine on a restaurant terrace. Then we picked up Roberto and Lina for an evening at the opera—*Faust* at the Baths of Caracalla. Our places were the best that fifty cents could command, and Roberto, the literature teacher, explained everything as it took place on stage.

Rome, Sunday, August 6

As Lillina begins her vacation tomorrow, we made it the occasion to dine at a garden restaurant in Trastevere, in a poor neighborhood "across the Tiber." Our meal was first rate as well as economical. It also provided the setting to enjoy the life here on a summer evening. Roberto was born in this old neighborhood of the city, and he completed the picture with some of his recollections of Trastevere. Later we strolled through the same streets, too narrow for a car in most places. Some restaurants extend to both sides of the narrow passage and waiters scurry across balancing full trays of hot food.

We took the Fiat up the winding way to Piazza Garibaldi atop the Janiculum Hill, passing the Aqua Paola Fountain, also illuminated by night. The view of Rome from the top is not one to forget.

Palestrina and Tivoli, Monday, August 7

Today was one of the hottest of this season, and I fled Rome to Palestrina, where I hoped to find it more comfortable, but it was just as hot. The bus driver used his horn more than his brakes, yet we fetched our destination intact.

The Temple of Fortune once occupied the bold rise behind the town—the ramps and terraces that surrounded the place suggest a structure that almost hung on the face of the hill. It was large and dramatic, as indicated by the existing substructures. The Barberini put up a palace on these foundations, which now preserves the antiquities found in the area, including articles from the Etruscan cemetery. As it was Monday, the museum was closed. A monument to Giovanni Palestrina, "Founder of Modern Music," occupies the center of the town square. He was born here.

The bus to Tivoli passed several characteristic hill towns which perch in the highest places. I wondered how the people carry all their needs to those astonishing heights. In Tivoli I had renewed hope of finding relief from the pervasive heat by virtue of the fountains and terraced water courses of the Villa d' Este, but this hope was dashed because it was too hot for fountains to have effect. Therefore I found the most comfortable spot possible and read the newspaper reporting the story of the Soviet astronaut Titov's long orbital flight.

Then I returned to Rome in time for community supper at the *pensione*.

Rome, Wednesday, August 9

Everything was parched save for Rome's flowing fountains, which continue to gush until evening crowds go home, when they are turned off. I have often seen the thirsty tourists—the young carrying backpacks—drinking and filling canteens from the spouting cannon of Bernini's *Barcaccia* fountain in Piazza di Spagna.

As much to find relief from the heat as to see the works of art, I gave several hours to the air-conditioned Vatican Museum today. It closes at two o'clock, when one is compelled to reenter the real climate outside. The museum is one of Rome's principal tourist attractions since it holds the Sistine Chapel and many other treasures. Therefore, masses of visitors collect there and swarm through the galleries. It could be likened to crowds at the Grand Canyon, though there is more foot room on the canyon rim. The tide breaks upon reaching the Michelangelo masterpiece. The bodies pile up because people cannot move and crane their necks upward simultaneously. You can also get caught in a counter current.

An Albanian arrived at the Pensione Ripetta today. He told us of his flight from Albania fifteen years before. He is a linguist and teacher who studies the dialect as it is spoken in eighty-four southern Italian villages settled by Albanians 500 years ago as they fled the Turks.

Tarquinia, Thursday, August 10

Today I went into Etruria as far as Tarquinia, site of an outstanding necropolis consisting, formerly, of some thousands of underground tombs once mounded over by earth tumuli. The logical beginning of a visit to the open tombs is the excellent collection in the National Museum of the Vitelleschi Palace, which is a handsome building all by itself. It contains the collection of objects recovered from the hypogea—the underground tombs that have revealed large numbers of sarcophagi, vases, bronze artifacts and wall paintings. This cemetery occupies an area three miles by about half a mile, despite the loss of the majority of graves in the nineteenth century—desecrated by wanton treasure hunters.

We were led from place to place by a guide who spoke Italian slowly and clearly, using his hands, which helped the foreigners among us. I walked with a French couple, interpreting for them. These much praised painted tombs show their occupants enjoying domestic life, feasting, dancing, loving, and relaxing in conversation and games. We were shown some eight examples dating from the sixth century B.C. to the late fifth century B.C. They are cut into the soft tufa below the soil, then finished off by a tumulus of stone and soil on top, but many have vanished as this terrain became cultivated. Our guide told us of a recent tomb-opening that took place on Italian television. A narrow opening was cut into the top and a TV camera was inserted in order to photograph the interior.

These are family tombs with at times several chambers. The walls are painted with domestic and other scenes that reveal how the Etrurians wished to live after death.

The French couple were *pieds noirs* (black feet) from Algeria, who had returned from that country when it became independent of France. We discussed a few political subjects en route to Civitavecchia, where I was invited to accompany them. They were inclined to conservative views.

I enjoyed swimming in the sea before boarding a train to Cerveteri and another look at the necropolis, a different type from that of Tarquinia. The more-developed family tombs are like Etruscan homes with the family gathered around on couches, offering food and gesturing to each other. The walls are decorated, as aforementioned, in relief.

In returning across the fields I observed several small holes in the surface, places where archaeologists located and pierced tombs seeking valuable objects or wall paintings. There were ripe grapes next to the path.

Rome, Friday, August 11

Wanting to get out of the city before the heat and crowds increased, I found the Church of S. Maria in Aracoeli, which occupies the crest of the Capitoline Hill. It is reached by a great towering stairway, which is best mounted slowly, especially on a hot day. Before entering the church, I turned around to admire the view from this high point, which is the most prominent in the heart of Rome. There is no place to equal it, though good views are found in other locations in Rome. Edward Gibbon in visiting this church was inspired to take up the project of Roman history that was his masterpiece.

The rear exit is more accessible and takes the visitor down to the edge of the Forum. There I walked again before ascending the Palatine. The heat remained intense. Yesterday Rome reached a maximum of 37 degrees centigrade, which the paper reported was the highest in Italy.

On the Palatine as I passed a group of American women, I heard one exclaim about the good colors in the frescoes of the House of Livia, an excavated residence nearby.

In the evening Roberto, Lina, and I attended an open-air concert in the Basilica of Maxentius. The temperature moderated in the course of the evening. We walked along the panoramic way to the Campidoglio and sat on the benches near City Hall, where for a long time we talked about the postwar years in our countries, present affairs, and other subjects until it grew late. It was 2 A.M. when I reached home, and the streets were nearly empty. It is marvelous to be here in Rome.

Rome, Saturday, August 12

August 15 brings the festival of the Assumption of the Virgin celebrated by all Italians in one way or another. People say that Rome will be left nearly empty except for the tourists, so great is the exodus. I shall wait until it is over before leaving for Trani, my next destination.

I visited the Church of the Gesù, mother church of the Jesuits. It is one of Rome's splendid baroque creations. The nave vaulting, apse, and other surfaces are painted in consummate perspective— the figures appear to soar or hang in space and angels inhabit the clouds.

Before 8:30 supper at the *pensione*, I accompanied one of the guests to a wine shop in Via della Croce, where we shared a glass in the company of others. After supper I attended *Aida* in the Baths of

Caracalla. A brilliant spectacle assured my wakefulness throughout. Most of the audience appeared to be tourists.

Rome, Sunday, August 13

I joined Roberto and Lina in viewing the Etruscan collection in the Villa Giulia Museum. This very complete grouping of Etruscan artifacts provides further confirmation of that mysterious people's artistic genius. Most of their inspiration came from the Greeks, though they supplied non-Greek motifs also. The articles on view are mostly from tombs where thousands of figured vases, copies of Attic Greek pottery, have been brought to light, most of them by treasure seekers, who destroyed those without immediate commercial value.

This afternoon I found only one church open, S. Pietro in Vincoli, which was overflowing with tourists and tour groups hoping to view the Michelangelo *Moses*. It appeared the church was open for their benefit. They were assembled around the famous figure to hear a guide describe it and try to get a full view, nearly an impossibility. I stood back to watch and got only a glimpse of Moses' head and horns.

[Government figures show that in 1960 more than 18 million foreigners visited Italy. In 1950, a Holy Year, only 5 million arrived, myself among them.]

Later that afternoon, churches opened again. Rome has about a thousand. I met Roberto next to the Arch of Constantine from where we walked to S. Pietro e Paulo, Santa Maria in Domnica, Santo Stefano Rotondo, and out to Porta S. Sebastiano to visit the Domine Quo Vadis? church. The last is named for a legend concerning St. Peter and Christ, which is said to have occurred here. Santo Stefano is the largest circular church in existence says the 1904 Baedeker. It is of early date and built on the foundation of a large Roman market—Macellum Magnum, a Roman supermarket. The existing church is diminished in diameter from the original ninety-two yards to seventy yards. The outer circle of walls was still traceable in places at the time the guide was published. In the church's early years it was "gorgeously decorated with marble and mosaics. Then it fell into utter decay."

At 9:30 we met Lina with Renato Bracale and his wife for supper in an open-air *ristorante* off the Corso, from where we migrated to our regular cafe in Piazza Navona for *gelato* (ice cream) and espresso. It was another late evening.

Rome, Tuesday, August 15

Renato offered to lend me his beautiful Lambretta motor scooter for the day. It's a small-wheeled model, very similar to the Vespa, which I had owned when I was in Europe eight years ago. With it I had the means to visit several more interesting churches such as S. Agnese, Santa Costanza, S. Lorenzo Fuori le Mura (outside the walls), S. Bibiana, and S. Prassede.

Constantia was Constantine's daughter and the church was originally her monument erected by the emperor. Later it was converted to the church of Santa Costanza. S. Prassede has a chapel in the form of a miniature Byzantine church (St. Zeno) with ninth-century mosaics. A niche inside on the right contains the columns at which Christ is said to have been scourged.

Following dinner at the *pensione* because zipping across half of Rome is a simple matter with a motor scooter, I set out to see more. The streets are much busier than they were in 1954; more cars and fewer two-wheeled vehicles occupy the very limited road area. I retraced the road up the Janiculum, this time pausing to see S. Onofrio where the poet Torquato Tasso is buried. I rolled up the hill and down again, then onward to the Appian Way. My vehicle carried me along the famous road as far as it was possible, ending at an unbridged watercourse barring further progress. I could see the outline of the ancient roadway ahead, bordered by still more tombs. It was a good place to park and relax before turning around. Ripe blackberries and grapes were there for the picking. No one was present except myself; nevertheless in the distance I could hear the rumble of traffic on the Via Appia Nuova.

I received an invitation to dinner at home this evening, a kindness offered by the Bracales and Prilis at the former's apartment in Sacre Monte. It was a most enjoyable evening and the table was full of home-cooked food and wine. I believe Roberto may be a Communist. He reads *L'Unità*, the party newspaper, and supports Russia. Afterward we moved to the Prili apartment to visit and sip Marsala and coffee. This was my warm farewell to Rome and the new friends made here.

Trani, Thursday, August 17

It was by an indirect route taking me through the mountains of Abruzzi that I reached Trani on the Adriatic coast. I had an invitation to visit Paolo d' Erarrio, whom I had known in 1953, when both of us were living at the Pensione Ripetta in Rome. The house was already full and Signora d' Erarrio, who recognized me, directed me to a hotel where a room was reserved for me in expectation of my arrival.

Trani, Friday, August 18

Paolo arrived on his bicycle wearing his bathing suit. Over espresso we spoke of recent events and sketched plans for my visit. Then he guided me on a walk through the center of Trani, pointing out various old buildings. This is a small and attractive city situated in the southern province of Apulia. After Rome and its congestion it is more peaceful and relaxing, with few vehicles, less noise, and apparently few foreign tourists. Conspicuous is the small cathedral in Apulian Romanesque style. It is in light-colored stone, which, in the strong sunlight, reflects almost painfully into my unshielded eyes. Several uncommon features that stand out, such as the original bronze doors, very old, made by a local craftsman. Also, the porch with columns supported on crouching lions. A slender *campanile* (bell tower) is constructed over a Gothic arch, while window and door surrounds are elaborately sculpted in Romanesque manner. On the north side are attractive exterior stairs leading into the church, necessary because the whole building is raised a few feet. The much later baroque interior was "*in restauro*" and off limits. Workmen had left a sarcophagus outside, the cover broken and dislocated, which left exposed the dry bones of a cleric dead for five hundred years.

We swam off the Braccia, the city mole, which extends into the clean Adriatic. Then we lunched, joined by Paolo's friend Vito. I discovered the local white wine, which is so good, and reordered the same wherever we took meals. The *giardino publico* lies next to the sea, which is glimpsed through the palms, live oaks, tamarisk, and pines. Nearby is the ruined abbey of Colonna. My companion pointed out more of the old city, port, and several baroque church facades.

Thence we found the patrician residence of Paolo's friend Franco Broquier, where I was made to feel welcome. We sat in the high-ceilinged parlor. Franco held a small electric fan in his hand, though I did not find it too hot when protected from the direct sun. Probably I was enjoying myself too much to be bothered by the heat. I was shown a cavity containing the entrance to a tunnel that communicates with the sea, but was not told its purpose.

Paolo and Franco belong to the lesser aristocracy; Paolo claims to be the cadet of a line of marquises, while Franco is a baron. Not being in the direct line of title holders, neither has the appanage attached to the elder line. Paolo owns some land near Bari and a small property in Rome. Franco has the wherewithal to purchase land and begin exploitation of a quarry for Trani stone, which is a cheap substitute for marble used in stairs, floors, and window moldings.

We were joined by Vito and Franco's friend Nino from Rome in the latter's Fiat, and the five of us traveled south along the coast to Bisceglie where we dined al fresco next to the Adriatic. Enroute home, we sang—grand opera. I requested an aria from *La Bohème* which was granted. Then we tarried near the derelict abbey of Colonna and sang more. It was pleasing.

Trani, Saturday, August 19

Today we ventured into the territory of Bari. The group consisted of four, including Paolo, me, Franco, and Nino in the Fiat. Getting started late in the morning—possibly because the others are aristocrats—we stopped several miles above Polignano, whose whitewashed houses are visible from a distance extending down to the water's edge. We planned to swim, but the sea was too agitated and rocky.

Then we traversed Bari's sizeable agglomeration, and came to Mola, where Paolo indicated the *palazzo* where his grandmother was born. We visited Castellane Grotte, which are recently discovered caverns. Already a tourist establishment has been installed for their exploitation. In the course of the day we took several coffee breaks, one of them at Alberobello. This is the so-called *trulli* capital of Apulia. *Trulli*, small round stone structures with pointed roofs, generally used for agricultural purposes, are widespread in the province. Here a group of them has become a tourist attraction equipped with hotel, restaurant, souvenir shop, and cafe. The *trulli* are constructed by laying down circular courses of small flat stones so each course projects over the one below, finally reaching a pointed or ridged summit. *Trulli* are another instance of the Mediterranean genius for masonry building—this one a more primitive example.

We stopped to dine in Turi, where fresh fish was served. At Giovinazzo we came upon a *festa* and paused long enough to observe the gaily decorated piazza: strings of colored lights outlined the church facade, the fountain, and tall wood arches, making the darkened piazza resemble a hall of light. The strains of opera could be heard over the commotion of the scene.

Trani, Sunday, August 20

This morning we swam at the Braccia before meeting Signora d' Erarrio for dinner in a seaside restaurant. We spoke of the social system and southern Italian customs. The d' Erarrios do not consider themselves to be of the people. My friend's mother explained that the origin of their rank lay in services that their ancestors performed for society and for which their elevated status was the recompense.

Here in Trani life may be better than in some southern towns. This is not the south of severe poverty. The quarries and the stone-cutting rooms provide employment and I observed no signs of distress.

Trani, Monday, August 21

Paolo and I boarded an early bus in order to visit Castel de Monte, one of southern Italy's outstanding buildings. The Holy Roman Emperor Frederick II constructed it in the thirteenth century as a residence. Crowning the summit of a moderate hill, it forms a regular octagon in two stories with octagonal turrets at the angles. Each level is divided into eight trapezoidal rooms, which originally were paneled in marble. The overall style is Gothic. An octagonal courtyard occupies the center of the building. The Castel possesses nothing pointing to a defensive or offensive purpose; neither does it show a ceremonial or administrative character. The best description for it may be "hunting lodge" of very high quality. Frederick wrote a treatise on falconry based on his own research; perhaps Castel de Monte's flat roof lent itself to this purpose. One can almost imagine the emperor and his birds up there, working. The building embodies outstanding workmanship in the execution of an aristocratic concept. It has beautiful windows on the second floor. The government is beginning restoration and landscaping around the Castel. Our bus was departing soon, so our visit, regrettably, had to be cut short.

Once returned to Trani we took a final dip off the Braccia and then played a game of quoits followed by dinner. I made preparations for my departure. We met again in the evening when Vito joined us for supper. These several days have been delightful; bidding adieu is sad, yet I must continue on my way.

Brindisi, Tuesday, August 22

I stopped first in Bari for several hours, hoping to see a little of the town including the cathedral and the Church of San Nicolá. Both were closed. San Nicolá is a pilgrimage church built especially to receive relics of the saint, which were brought from Myra in Asia Minor. Nicolá is the fourth-century bishop who was transformed into Santa Claus in the Middle Ages. A band of sailors from Bari removed the saint's remains from the Orthodox church in Myra, now a ruin. I had lunch in company with several local citizens in a small tavern of the old city. Their dialect was unintelligible to me, yet when speaking to me they used standard Italian and we had a good discussion. They wanted to know about America.

I fetched the port of Brindisi in late afternoon. Here ends the Appian Way from Rome. It is also the gateway to Greece and the East. Virgil had a house here where he died on his return from Greece in 19 B.C. He is buried in Naples.

Brindisi also saw Romans of all sorts—emperors, poets, and ordinary citizens—leave for Greece, where they studied in schools, carried on business, or saw the sights. Crusaders also departed from Brindisi and a few thousand hapless ones perished of hunger and pestilence here in 1227. I enjoyed a good dinner in the second floor restaurant of the *Stazione Maritime* while looking out over the nighttime port. A bookstall sold Nagel's guide to Greece for U.S. $7.00 and I began studying it. My ship, coming from Venice and going to Piraeus, would leave at midnight and so I settled down on a bench in the station to sleep, asking a policeman to awaken me betimes. Once aboard, I lay down on deck, saving the $8 cost of a berth. Despite some soot from the funnel settling on me, I slept well while starting this new phase of the journey.

Joanina and Meteora, Friday, August 25

I touched the Greek mainland at Igoumenitsa and accepted a ride from there as far as Joanina with some English travelers I met aboard the ship. We enjoyed our first Greek meal in the garden dining area of a restaurant in the town. Before leaving I walked in Joanina long enough to see the two mosques here—both deconsecrated and converted to museums. Turkish rule of Greece ended in 1829 when the country gained independence.

I found Meteora, a monastic settlement that I knew to be a favorite of tourists, very unusual—worth the visit beyond a doubt. The government has recently constructed an access road to a few of the strange monastic houses that formerly were reached only by rope and ladder. The community of monks here has mostly departed, although a few elderly brothers still hang on. They live and work in chambers hollowed out of lofty rock pinnacles rising from the town of Kalabaka. Monks settled here in the fourteenth century, when the territory was insecure. The number of monasteries grew to twenty-four before beginning to decline in the last century.

My visit encompassed brief visits to three of the partly viable establishments, namely Haghia Stefanos, Grand Meteora, and Varlaam. I found three cenobites in the first, but on the whole there were more tourists than monks observing the faded frescoes and pitiful accommodations within. Their condition recalled those I saw at Mt. Athos in 1953; if anything Meteora is even more run-down. As the new road indicates, the government is interested and perhaps more will soon be done to help Meteora survive. I hope so because it is an excellent example of what faith can accomplish in difficult circumstances.

This afternoon on the bus to Trikala I became acquainted with a young Greek army lieutenant, who spoke good English. We traveled together to Larissa, enjoying conversation and also glasses of *ouzo* with coffee at roadside cafes. He insisted on giving me money with which to send him postcards from Iran and India. I must remember to do it.

Volos, Saturday, August 26

The bus fetched Volos yesterday after nightfall. Volos is a good-sized port city sheltered at the top of the Gulf of Pagassitikos, where a destructive earthquake occurred in 1955. Reconstruction has been carried out, though the result is monotonous in appearance.

Between the gulf and the Aegean is the peninsula of Magnesia, which is probably an interesting and attractive area. I missed it, instead taking a boat down the west side of the gulf, where are found the ancient Greek city of Pagasai and the Macedonian Démétrias. The acropolis of Pagasai reveals traces of twenty-seven towers. This was the home port of Jason and the Argonauts.

Démétrias had its walls with seventy-six towers. In Volos the museum contains a room full of beautiful funerary stele, which were reused in the walls of Démétrias, preserving them including traces of original color. As the museum was not officially open, I was allowed but a quick view of these interesting relics before being ushered out the door, for which I was sorry.

Following the sightseeing I took a swim and had lunch in a beach-side restaurant before taking the boat back to Volos. It was hot, causing me to lose the desire for further exploration. I waited the rest of the day until midnight for the boat to Chalcis. It was comfortable sleeping on deck under the stars.

Chalcis and Athens, Sunday, August 27

As I awoke this morning we were sailing down the Gulf of Euboea. I was astonished to find the deck surrounding me filled with new passengers whom we had picked up during the night. I dressed under the blanket. The Euboean shoreline is beautiful. Then we fetched Chalcis, where passengers disembarked by lighter. After visiting the local archaeological museum containing some nice pieces of Greek sculpture, I traveled down the island of Euboea to Eretria. There are a series of ruins here to indicate its former importance. I was alone to wander around the place. There are scattered remains of a variety of civic structures and walls, all available to the ambitious visitor willing to walk the area, which is entirely pleasant in and of itself, not to mention sundry ruins. A tomb of the Macedonian period attracted my attention. It contained sarcophagi in couch form as well as other furniture carved from living marble. I remained within to rest and cool off.

I reached Athens the same day by ferry crossing the gulf to Oropas, from where the bus goes to the capital. Athens has increased in size since I was here in 1953—more people, congestion, tourists, and pollution. The city draws more and more people into its vortex from all of Greece. After trying my old pension under the Acropolis and finding it gone—it was a pleasant place operated by Mr. and Mrs. Pakis—I found a temporary haven in a student hostel, sharing a landing with three other travelers because all bunks were filled.

Athens, Monday, August 28

I returned to the Acropolis today. I remembered that in 1953 the environs had preserved a rural village character; chickens and goats could be seen at the foot of the mount, which might have been the last trace of the Athens of the last century when it was hardly more than a large village. Now the approaches are all tidied up, planted, and provided with new paths. Using my guidebook I went over everything carefully, trying to see it all. The Acropolis Museum is now open, and I saw the remarkable contents for the first time.

The Theater of Dionysius, the Theater of Herodus Atticus, newly equipped with marble seats over the old broken ones, and many other things I saw today. I visited the Agora (ancient market), which the American School of Classical Studies has recently excavated, and also the Stoa of Attalus, restored and now a museum containing finds from the Agora. But I saw nothing breathtaking there. Ten drachmas admission is charged and the Thesion is thrown in. Then I climbed the undisturbed Pnyx Hill, planted in pines through which you glimpse the Acropolis.

Athens, Tuesday, August 29

As I found it reasonably priced, I moved to the Hotel Rhodes, taking a sunny and quiet room leading off the roof terrace, reached by a spiral stair.

The great National Museum held my interest today. Since I was here in 1953 new galleries have opened. The gold, ivory, and ceramics from the royal tombs of Mycenae and elsewhere, including the Vaphio cups, gold masks, metalwork, and jewelry are on display, composing a brilliant collection of early Greek artisanship.

Perhaps I at first approached the sculpture galleries jadedly because I was not especially moved by them. Yet after I rested and observed anew with a fresher eye, my outlook improved, and I noticed the variety of expression, the freedom and naturalness, even the charm of the pieces before me. This experience seems to say that Greek art requires renewed attention, especially because the harried tourist's senses are likely to be gorged by having seen so much previously.

Athens, Wednesday, August 30

The Iranian consulate granted me a visa today. Enroute there I passed the ruins of the Olympeium, large Roman temple to Zeus with fifteen standing columns. It contrasts pompously with the more seemly Greek monuments.

After supper I walked up the Lycabettus, the prominent mount that stands apart like a slender beacon illuminated at night. The summit, reached by stairs, affords a wide view of Athens.

On the boat to Tinos, Friday, September 1

Today I began an island tour before leaving Europe for the East. Sailing from Piraeus at noon for Tinos in a course that passed close to Cape Sunion, I had a very good view of the Temple of Poseidon on the tip. Improved access by road has been followed by the expected cancer of development, namely villas and hotels bordering the highway. Such a site is too fragile to sustain very much of this, and Sunion, once isolated, belonging more to the sea than the land, is now exposed to assault by the road.

As we sailed on to the Cyclades, the wind blew and the Aegean became turbulent. Many passengers experienced mal-de-mer, and eventually I succumbed. I found that taking a head-down position helped, As waves broke over the bow the deck passengers were soaked.

We fetched the island of Tinos after nightfall. A woman on the quay spoke to me in Italian to offer a room in her house. Before retiring I had a small conversation with another guest, who spoke English.

Tinos, Saturday, September 2

My hostess served breakfast in the kitchen—warm milk and bread. The stove was a single kerosene burner only slightly larger than the one I carry with me. The parlor where I slept had two double beds and a cot—to accommodate the many pilgrims who frequent Tinos on March 25 and August 15. They are the sick who come to worship at the Panaghia Evanghelistria Church. I ascended the broad pilgrim way leading up to it; a mass was in progress, which limited my visit within the sanctuary. However, I observed many votive offerings affixed to the interior, some of which were testimonials to a miracle that preserved a fishing boat from disaster when it was pierced and the sea poured in. According to the belief a fish swam into the breach and saved the ship after the crew had prayed for divine intervention. The chalk white houses climb the flank of the modest hill to the church, itself whitewashed and illuminated at night, making it visible from a distance whether by day or night. It would be a moving experience to join the crowd of faithful on a feast day.

Then I set out on foot along the beach for several miles, hoping to come across the ruins of the antique Temple of Poseidon and Amphitrite. After a lengthy hike I met several people who indicated where I would find this ruin behind a wide crescent beach. Then I met a group of students in the charge of a priest who spoke French. He guided me to the site and we stayed there for a good hour during which he told me some things about the island, the church, and the country. He turned out to be a Syrian, from Damascus, who was in Greece to learn the language and work at the school.

After lunch the ship arrived, and before long I was on the quay at Mykonos.

Mykonos and Delos, Sunday, September 3

My host wrote his name on a card so I might find the house again, then led me through narrow, twisting passages, all a cluster of whitened walls and pavement, to the port where I found bread and café au lait and awaited the daily *caïque* which would carry those who wish to visit Delos across the water between the islands.

Delos is several miles in length; its small size and lack of water make it impossible for a large population to settle there, and therefore visitors have always outnumbered residents. I had been there in 1953 and so was aware of much that is to be seen on the magical island, hardly more than dry rock, and nearly barren of plant life. I wanted to become reacquainted with the place, for I felt the magnetism of its mythical past, its beauty, and its peace. At any point the sight or sound of the sea is present, and skies are usually clear, revealing the marble fragments of ancient shrines, porticos, and columns to advantage.

Pilgrims sought this place in antiquity, to touch the soil where Apollo was born of Leto. Delos was the cradle of the god, who presided over poetry, medicine, music, and prophecy. The god's power of prophecy was marked by the Temple of Apollo at Delphi.

A modern visitor also finds reasons to stop in Delos. The guidebook lists the many ruins to be admired—more than in any other location in Greece. This island is unquestionably beautiful when bathed in sunlight and sea breezes. Its smallness and difficulty of access, combined with minimal facilities for receiving visitors, make Delos complicated for large groups.

This morning two motorized caïques shuttled 100 odd, modern-day pilgrims to the island in one hour, and we disembarked at the same point as our ancient predecessors. In a few steps I was in direct proximity to the remains of those buildings that had served the public—agora, porticos, smaller temples, and the sand-choked merchant's port. Then, I walked to the Sacred Lake (now dried up) which is surrounded by more remains relating to the cult of Apollo and Artemis, twin sister of Apollo, who was born on Delos as well. Among the remains are the bases that once supported dedicatory sculptures, all now vanished.

There is not enough time to see all in one trip. The caïques return early, whereas in 1953 they remained all day. Then I had eaten lunch and dinner on the island at an open-air restaurant where the chef first presented the evening meal for approval before preparing it—live pigeons. It is now a souvenir shop.

Mykonos, to which I returned this afternoon, is a pleasure to visit. It has walks and views of the environs that are peaceful and relaxing. I dined at a plain restaurant offering good prices and help in choosing dishes. The typical menu consisted of lamb, rice, salad (tomato, olive, feta or other cheese), and bread. There is also retsina wine, which is cheap and good. Cold water is served without the guest asking. Frequently I visited the kitchen and chose dishes from among those ready for the table.

In the evening near sunset, I walked up the narrow road behind the houses, and there met a young girl who offered me a pungent herb, then waited for a tip. After receiving it she smiled and waved goodbye.

There are a few windmills on the island—also whitewashed. I watched the sun go down behind the island of Rhene next to Mykonos. A weaving industry exists here. People do the work at home, it seems, for there is nothing like a factory in sight. I purchased a colorful summer shirt for several dollars, a good-quality handwoven cotton, which endured.

Delos, Monday, September 4

This morning, not satisfied that I had seen enough, I returned to Delos. Mt. Kynthos, 368 feet, required climbing because the view is splendid. Also one finds more souvenirs of sacred Delos on its slopes, including rows of white marble blocks, the remains of small shrines to Apollo.

I wanted to revisit the considerable remains of private houses in the commercial quarter. These are Hellenistic, dating from a period when the island became a magnet for merchants and trade, as well as pilgrims, though I cannot perceive how many could find the area for business activities or residence on the tiny island. On either side of the road leading to the theater are very fine, well-appointed examples of domestic building. They are fully provided with marbled and frescoed rooms, peristyles with the column bases in place, rich mosaic pavements, stairs, and kitchens with cisterns and ovens. In effect, as I walked into these fascinating domestic locales, I could almost imagine being personally invited by their owners to enter.

Vathy and Pythagorion, Tuesday, September 5

It was soon after dawn that our ship fetched Vathy, the modern capital and largest town on the island of Samos. Samos is part of the Sporades group near the Turkish mainland. After reserving a room at the Hotel Parthenon near the port—it cost the modest sum of fifty cents—I stopped at the cafe facing the harbor for breakfast in the sun. The port is ringed by low hills whose lower slopes are occupied by houses. The plaza between cafe and port contains a fine white marble lion marking Greek independence. The archeological museum here proved moderately interesting. While looking at the collection I fell into conversation with a young Greek named Emmanuel. We continued to talk while consuming glasses of lemonade at the cafe, and in this way I was able to learn a few things about the island. He also helped me with a few Greek expressions. He located a tailor for me, who repaired a few clothing items because my small traveling wardrobe is receiving heavy wear. Vathy, though attractive, did not hold much of interest for me because it is modern.

Having previously heard favorable things concerning the village of Pythagorion, which occupies the site of the ancient capital, I felt the urge to visit the romantic-sounding place. I found a bus that followed the unpaved inland route to the village. Very soon after I arrived I was convinced that Pythagorion would justify a longer visit and began looking for a way to fit it in.

The site adjoins a calm green sea fringed by sandy beaches punctuated by rocky promontories, all basking under a warm sun. Modern intrusions were absent and I could see no other tourists, although later on several appeared.

Soon four boys about ten years old attached themselves to me and together we climbed the steep ascent to the ancient acropolis of Samos. The weather being hot, we did it slowly, enjoying the views and observing vestiges of old construction such as walls and towers. My companions knew what interested me and pointed to those features while plucking small offerings such as ripe almonds, figs, prickly pears, and grapes as well as a good-tasting pod containing inedible seeds, which they told me to avoid. My escorts perhaps reckoned that I would understand so they carried on a constant dialogue with me in Greek, but I could comprehend very little and confined my answers to brief acknowledgment of their speeches. Once atop this mount I was shown the Church of Panaghia Spiliani, which contains a pool of fresh water. Local people revere it as a pilgrimage place. The extended view of Samos and its surroundings includes the single standing column of the ancient Heraion at a distance of several miles. We descended the uneven terrain again to the village, where I thanked the friendly escort and added a few coins to their pockets.

Following lunch on a restaurant terrace facing the plaza, I enquired how I might reach my subsequent destination, Patmos, if I should decide to come to Pythagorion for a longer stay. My informers said that no regular service existed but I might stay for several days until a small boat decided to go to Patmos. One of the people I spoke to was Mr. Linaikis, who had learned his English while attached to a Greek unit in the British armed forces in the last war. He invited me to put up at his house until the day a boat would take me away to Patmos. The second man had spent many years in the United States, where he owned restaurants in Cleveland. Now he is back here living on U.S. Social Security.

Then I returned to Vathy via the paved coast road, which affords paradisiacal panoramas of fine sand beaches and rocky points of land washed by a gentle green sea. There was hardly an indication of human activity other than olive groves on this road.

My accommodations at the Hotel Parthenon were simple and clean: a horsehair mattress supported on boards—no springs—I slept soundly.

Pythagorion, Wednesday, September 6

Emmanuel, my companion of yesterday, came to bid me adieu and I gave him two paperbacks. He would like to emigrate, but that is more involved now because host countries, such as Australia and the United States, have imposed controls.

I returned to Pythagorion, where I awaited a boat to Patmos while enjoying the charming surroundings. It took five days, yet I was well satisfied and living was cheap. My bed at the Linaikis house was comfortable, and on some nights the spare beds in the room were also filled. Also, one of the cats climbed a tree outside the balcony and entered the room at night so I had plenty of company. Soon I was taking full board with the family, which included two young daughters, Maria and Catherine, nine and eleven.

In Greece it is possible to travel for less than it costs to live at home. Every evening before dinner I joined my host and his friends for a glass of ouzo served with small fried fish or other snacks in front of the house near the roadway, which held little traffic of any kind except bicycles and donkeys. A few steps away on the opposite side was the sea.

Pythagoras the philosopher was born in this place. The name was adopted a few years ago in his honor and, most likely, to attract attention as well.

The tyrant of Samos, Polycrates, also brought renown to this city. He was a builder of famous structures. Herodotus related that he checked on his good fortune by dropping his gold ring set with emeralds into the sea, recovering it later in the stomach of a fish served him for dinner.

Today I visited the antique Temple of Hera lying a few miles west of the village. I took a hired motorboat because the walk along the shore is strenuous. Hera was born, the legend says, where the stream Imbrasos flows to the sea. That description fits the site, a moist place on the edge of the sea. The remains are sparse and I was hindered by the boggy conditions. The guidebook mentions ruins of unidentified religious and domestic structures, which I could not see. The last temple to be erected here was never completed. The columns were not fluted. One of them has been raised again by the archaeologists.

The boatman hooked three good fish on the return trip and grilled and served them on shore near the Linaikis house. The outdoor dining arrangements were simple and effective, consisting of marble slabs supported on column drums and improvised seats. Several others joined the party. The fresh fish tasted perfect with a glass of retsina wine and bread.

The intense sun at midday necessitated a daily rest period. In the village all activity slowed or ceased after lunch and didn't revive for a couple of hours or longer. I slept or read in my room.

Pythagorion, Friday, September 8

Ancient Greek Samos was a principal protagonist in the Aegean region, and her wealth was reflected in her famous building projects beginning with the Hereon and including a monumental mole, which may have been terminated by a lighthouse. There was a famous aqueduct which tunneled through rocky hills to bring fresh water to the city. It was acclaimed a great engineering feat at the time and parts of it have survived until now, open for exploration by anyone with a good light.

My meals *en famille* were enjoyable occasions. Mrs. Linaikis prepared a simple and satisfying supper, which included small servings of meat or fish and was accompanied by retsina. This island also produces good muscatel wine made from muscat grapes. On one or two occasions I joined citizens at the cafe in the port where ouzo (an anise-flavored liqueur) was the typical before dinner choice, with little fish, freshly fried, or raw vegetables. Retsina and ouzo are acquired tastes.

The average daily wage in Greece is the equivalent of $1.50. Depending on family size and location, that is barely enough to live on. In Athens a family requires much more and unemployment is rife in this large and growing city. In the past Greeks have adopted emigration as the solution. One who works in the United States and saves $10,000 can return here a wealthy man; many Greek-Americans return to their homeland to live comfortably on their U.S. Social Security checks.

I met a young man at the cafe who invited me to see a mosaic pavement at his home on the edge of town below the acropolis. I welcomed the chance to walk with him and was rewarded not only by seeing the mosaic but also by meeting his personal donkey tethered in front of the house. After my guide, who knew English, gave me a pocketful of almonds and figs, I invited him for an ouzo at the port cafe. All around us the people were enjoying the stroll *en masse* which occurs every evening at this time.

A single English visitor arrived to take up a room at the Linaikis home today. He paints and told me he is happier abroad, like me.

I hired a small lateen-sailed boat and pilot for a short cruise along the coast to the east, which approaches the Asian mainland of Turkey. I would have preferred going alone: however, it appears the local boatmen do not let their craft out. The two-hour cruise gave me an opportunity to swim in the shallow green water of a cove with a fine sandy bottom.

Pythagorion, Saturday, September 9

Today I was offered an opportunity to visit Ephesus. The people who invited me arrived in a beautiful sailboat, which they chose not to risk in Turkish waters. Therefore they hired the *Katina*, the small local motorized caïque. I declined the offer because I had visited Ephesus in 1953, also because the visit could be expensive and brief, while Ephesus is an extensive ruin field requiring some time to explore. Upon their return this evening the couple came to the Linaikis house interested in the purchase of amphorae—"bombs" as they call them here. Fishermen can find them intact in their nets. The woman visitor was French and had lived in the United States. I offered them a glass of muscatel of Samos. Somewhere in the train of business concerning the amphorae the Greeks present grew excited; I could not understand the reason until it appeared that someone had informed the Port Police about the proceedings. There is a law prohibiting the transfer of antiquities and the "bombs" were returned to the seller.

A boat will go to Kos, I learned, tomorrow, and therefore I considered omitting Patmos to strike out for the other island instead. I had been waiting a few days for the accidental Patmos boat and was losing time. When I spoke to the captain he appeared to be planning to ask for an excessive amount because I was a foreigner. At the

Port Police, where passengers register, I asked about the standard fare for such a trip. The captain refused to tell the officer this and then asked for 200 drachmas, which appeared too high, so I decided to wait.

Pythagorion, Sunday, September 10

This morning some townspeople put on their best clothes and attended church. Others went to the beach; they might have attended mass the previous evening or early in the morning.

In the port I encountered an American family with two children who were staying in Pythagorion for two weeks. He was a journalist in Israel and told me they were tired of densely settled places.

This evening Mr. Linaikis and his daughters tried their luck fishing off the mole. When they had very little success, they said their disappointment was slight because it was merely sport. The waters around the island contain few fish because food for them is scarce. There are no major rivers to carry food down to the sea.

I enjoyed dinner with the English visitor at the local restaurant. Then, while sitting around the table, we entertained the two Linaikis children and a friend with lemonades.

Patmos, Tuesday, September 12

The entire Linaikis family bid me adieu early this morning as I embarked for Patmos. In a rough sea the caïque *Katina* fetched the barren little island of Agathonisi after pausing at the north side, where there were only five fishermen's cottages. It is a wonder how they live on such a barren spot—perhaps surviving on fish, potatoes, and bread. We delivered grapes and small items to the islanders.

I swam in the clear green water of the cove that serves as a tiny port. For lunch there were two fried eggs, bean soup, and hard bread. Following a six-hour holdover here the old caïque *Panormitis* picked up the approximately twenty passengers for Arki, the next stop, and Patmos. The boat was not particularly clean and needed paint. The sea, being still rough, tossed us around for the next three hours and many became ill, but not me. I thoroughly enjoyed the journey.

Aboard was a Frenchman, whom I asked to suggest a place to stay on Patmos because he was staying there. He took me to his guest house, where I had a comfortable double bed with springs. The proprietor was a kind woman who recommended a stay of a week on Patmos because it is "charming." She was talkative and, like the

Greek people who are curious about strangers, wanted to know where I was from, where I was going, and other things. I explained it all to her satisfaction.

Patmos, Wednesday September 13

Patmos was the place of exile of St. John the Evangelist. He was sent here from Ephesus in 94 A.D. during the persecution of Christians. Tradition relates how John lived in the small grotto situated midway on the Sacred Way leading from the port up the long incline to the monastery, a scrupulously whitewashed landmark visible for miles.

I undertook the climb this morning, first finding the small chapel which precedes the Grotto of St. John, then reaching the lofty Monastery of St. John. Here a monk speaking English gave me a tour of the church, treasury, library, and refectory. This house has not been plundered for centuries and possesses some notable works of art—icons, frescoes, and a rich treasury containing objects of gold, silver, and embroidery. My guide said that a thousand valuable manuscripts are preserved in the library. Diligently working there copying music was a young German student. Through the corridors the sound of workmen's chisels and hammers resounded. Recently uncovered in the refectory are old frescoes, overlaid years ago with plaster.

Then, ascending to the terrace atop the crenelated building, I could survey the far reaches of this corner of the Aegean, beginning with the three connected blocks of Patmos and extending to other islands of the Dodecanese, which stud the sea. The coast of Turkey is quite close. Samos and, faintly, Pythagorion are visible. All together it is a magnificent sight.

Returning, I found a monk at the Grotto who showed me various features of the saint's retreat. A desklike cutting in the rock is called the place where the disciple Procharos copied down the visions as dictated by John. A rock cutting near the floor is regarded as the saint's pillow.

Patmos and the Evangelist have drawn a number of people to settle in the vicinity, and also pilgrims or tourists, though hardly any were to be seen today. The atmosphere seemed even friendlier than usual, evidenced by smiles and greetings from people I passed in the street. I also had the impression they were more educated, perhaps because of the influence of the monks. This monastery is richer and more favored than others I have seen in Greece, and attracts more brothers.

Living near my guesthouse are a man and woman who once resided in England and this evening they invited me to visit. After supper I called, and we conversed while customers came and went in the small front-room bakery which the woman operates.

In my room hangs an old photograph in which I found the likeness of Ferdinand de Lesseps, the builder of the Suez Canal. It is inscribed, "To my old collaborator, Gauthier."

Patmos, Thursday, September 14

The ship for Kos arrives in the middle of the night, and therefore I had today to relax, read and, write, as well as take a walk to the bay on the south. There is a peculiar soft rock here that appears to turn hard in contact with water. I observed no industry exploiting it so it cannot be the substance used in concrete.

Kos, Friday, September 15

Aboard ship I retired on deck under a star-studded sky, caressed by cool Aegean breezes. Stopping briefly at Kalimnos, we then fetched Kos in the early morning. Our ship was too large to enter the small port; therefore a lighter met us outside the mole. Once on the quay I selected one of the offers of lodging and was led to the Hotel Actaion very close to the port. The grounds were planted in palms, tamarisk, bougainvillea, azalea, and hibiscus—all giving a floral introduction to this green island. The accommodations were comfortable and the people kind. I was offered a bath, the first in a week. Then I rented a bicycle with which I toured a portion of the island.

Kos, along with Patmos, is one of the Dodecanese Islands. Italy controlled them from 1912 up to the end of World War II. Under Italian tutelage improvements were made in the road system and other places including the excavation and landscaping of the several archaeological sites. The earliest dates from the eighth century B.C.

Mention of Kos requires reference to Hippocrates almost in the same breath. The Asclepeion, or sanctuary of Asclepius, the Greek god of medicine and healing, was the site I was most interested in visiting. I cycled down to it on a good tar road. The excavated area was empty of people, and I was able to amble over the foundations of the various buildings that composed the ancient hospital, undisturbed. The Italian workers had also planted the grounds. The site faces the strait between Kos and the place on the coast of Asia Minor where stood the ancient Mausoleum of Halicarnassus, a few miles distant. Those seeking cures usually slept in the sanctuary so that Asclepius might visit them by night. Tradition says that Hippocrates studied here. It is a special place and attractive as well.

The Italian archaeologists unearthed a large Roman residence of forty rooms near the port. Some parts have been restored to their original elevation and preserve wall paintings and carved ornament and paneling in marble and colored stone. Mosaic pavements are seen in a few places including three atriums. A small theater, or odeon, in marble has been planted with cypress trees and bougainvillea.

As the sun went down I swam near the hotel. There were few tourists and all was peaceful.

Kos, Saturday, September 16

While awaiting the ship to Rhodes, I had a conversation with a Greek-American from Clearwater, Florida. I also talked to a Greek who spoke Italian and had a brother in Boston. He piloted the caïque that carried passengers out to the roadstead for boarding ships.

The ship *Karaiskakis* put in at Leros, Tilos, and Symi before fetching Rhodes late at night. With the other passengers I debarked onto the quay. Floodlit walls rose beyond the port.

Rhodes, Sunday, September 17

I left my hotel in the modern quarter of Rhodes and soon found myself in a surprising tableau comprising the old city surrounded by large walls, towers, and bastions. I call it a tableau because everything harmonizes—buildings, walls, and streets. All I saw was well ordered and clean. The substantialness of the structures impressed me. You can almost forget that you are in a "museum" of restored history. Strolling through the narrow ways, hardly busy but still lived in, I watched the character of medieval Rhodes unfold before my eyes.

All of this city was originally the creation of the military order of the Knights of St. John of Jerusalem. The Italian trustees of the present century carried out the restoration and made the park that now occupies the strip between wall and town; and the visitor may enjoy the walkway which encircles the town. It is also practical to follow the summit of the wall.

The Knights were divided into "languages," nationality groups of which the largest component was French. Each group had an *auberge* (inn) of which there were eight. Each *auberge* was led by a bailiff who participated in the governing council presided over by the Grand Master elected by all the knights.

The Knights of St. John had been established for the protection of pilgrims in the Holy Land. Islamic armies drove them out and they came to Rhodes in 1309. In 1522 a Turkish assault obliged them to depart for Malta.

Now Rhodes is becoming a magnet for tourists, predominately Germans, and hotels are rising in the new city. I appreciate the willingness of the Greek people to adapt to all this change. The foreigners are usually graciously received, considering the baleful effect on popular, often fragile locations. Prices remain reasonable, perhaps in part because few Americans find their way to this island.

By renting a bicycle, I could try the gravel road leading to the interior, where I found a pleasing, undisturbed country. Coming to a small valley where some large pines were clustered, I spoke to a farmer who knew English because he had worked in Australia for five years and had earned the wherewithal to purchase his farm. He offered me figs from his own trees. Returning by the tarred road, I passed a luxurious hotel—totally out of keeping.

Rhodes, Monday, September 18

I found a comfortable youth hostel here and moved in. Among the few guests was a young Dutch traveler named Rolf.

Today I continued to look around in the old city, observing the Street of the Knights, the museum occupying the Knight's New Hospital, the facades of the various *auberges*, some with coats of arms, the Palace of the Grand Master, and other places. There is much to see in Rhodes.

A large cat contingent exists here, some of whom are tame. I provided scraps of fish to a few appreciative felines.

Lindos and Rhodes, Tuesday, September 19

Rolf and I rented a small motorbike for the excursion to ancient Lindos, thirty-six miles from the city on the east coast. (The island is about fifty miles long and twenty-three miles wide.) We had to leave early and ride three hours over a good, lightly traveled, tar road. We paused at attractive points along the coast. At a small open-air cafe we enjoyed fresh figs, washed down with cold water.

When the distant acropolis of Lindos appeared we knew we were coming closer to the goal. It is a prominent, steep-flanked mount revealing traces of buildings and fortifications from several epochs. A few columns stand, conspicuous from a distance and suggesting former glories. As we arrived, the city seemed very tranquil and unspoiled by commercialization, a situation that may not persist as tourist volume builds.

To refresh ourselves after the long ride, we swam in the sheltered basin north of the acropolis. The perfectly clear green water, quite shallow, has a satin-smooth sand bottom.

After lunch we ascended to the top of the acropolis from where the view is splendid. There are many traces of the old Lindos, which at one time before the founding of the present city of Rhodes, was the maritime center of the island. Under the south scarp of the acropolis is a miniature harbor where St. Paul is said to have landed, and so it is named.

We found Lindos to be a perfect pleasure and unforgettable.

Enroute home a driver stopped his car and offered to give one of us a ride back. Rolf accepted while I followed on the motor bike.

Pamukkale, Thursday, September 21

The ship *Panormitis* which brought me to Rhodes also took me to Turkey today. The distance that separates Europe and Asia is here only a few miles. The mainland port is Marmoris and here I met a returning British traveler, who sold me his *Blue Guide* to Turkey, a valuable asset for the traveler. Here I was in Asia again and anticipating a rewarding journey along the Mediterranean littoral of Turkey.

An unusual sight, not far from the port of Marmoris is Pamukkale (Cotten Castle). I arrived there by *dolmus* (shared taxi). The traveler who has seen Mammoth Hot Springs in Yellowstone National Park already knows a similar natural feature. A hot spring pouring from the top of a 300-foot cliff has deposited a frozen cascade of mineral calcite, forming white and cream-colored basins and shelves of hard stone. The water temperature 55 degrees Fahrenheit (35 degrees centigrade) is suitable for bathing, and a small hotel is close by. Several people were enjoying the water and so I waded forth in it to refresh my feet. These deposits continue to form while the abundant waters flow on.

Adjacent lie the jumbled ruins of Roman Hierapolis. I walked rapidly through the area, failing to enjoy them perhaps because the stone used is dark in color while classical buildings are more beautiful when constructed of light marble. There are myriads of ruined cities in this region—indeed in all of Turkey—and I lacked transportation or time to see many. In 1953 I had the privilege of seeing several significant excavations north of here, Ephesus, Priene, and Pergamum especially.

The government is planning a motorway which will provide better access to the many treasures, natural and manmade, of the Turkish coast; however little of it is ready and therefore my road journey to Antalya was slow and tiring, involving a couple of nights in small, scantily equipped hotels. Also, I have lost the diary-letter covering this segment.

Antalya, Monday, September 25

Once in Antalya everything improved temporarily and the sun emerged. Antalya is attractive and in future years will lure many visitors.

I found a pleasant room to myself in a hotel near the Mediterranean, and set out to see this city, its parks and its surroundings. I felt relaxed while enjoying the southern sun and sea breezes. The architectural relics are not to be compared with the cluster of ancient cities which dot the plain behind Antalya. The natural features and spectacular setting facing the large bay, the surrounding plain backed by high mountains, all distinguish Antalya.

Termessos, Tuesday, September 26

I visited the unusual ruined city of Termessos, reached by bus from Antalya, followed by a long walk up into the foothills; altogether a lengthy excursion for one day. I was forced to turn back sooner than I would have liked because of lack of time. These ruins leave the visitor wondering who the Termessans were and why they were different from the inhabitants of other Greco-Roman cities. There are remarkable architectural remains, however difficult of access and concealed by the forest—walls, cisterns, a theater, a temple, and more. All seems to have been very solidly and tastefully executed, though I saw only the small theater before turning back. It was half intact. I sat alone, in a middle row, contemplating the scene around me. I might have missed it. I only just happened to see masonry jutting from the foliage as I passed on the trail going up.

Alexander passed this way in the fourth century B.C. and attempted to take Termessos by siege, but he gave up to move on. Perched atop this large hill, strongly defended, the city must have had a firm economic base, but no one knows what it was. Perhaps it had suzerainty over the surrounding region.

I returned down the long trail where the only people I passed were occasional woodcarriers returning home with large bundles of fagots on their backs.

Perga, Wednesday, September 27

Perga is situated on the Mediterranean in a trade-oriented location, as was preferred by the Greek colonists in Ionia. In A.D. 45 St. Paul and St. Barnabus disembarked here after leaving Cyprus. A rapid purview of the ruins gives one an idea of the brilliance of ancient Perga, and the multiplicity of formerly grand buildings— now grand ruins—show the city's civic spirit. I saw Perga prior to complete excavation and partial restoration of some buildings. The theater seated 15,000 and the stadium 22,000 spectators. A Roman basilica, later converted into a Byzantine church, is notable. The Street of Columns, city walls, gates, and other civic amenities are likely to astonish the modern observer. The Department of Antiquities is building a new access road, and in the Antalya Museum I had noticed a freshly unearthed, richly sculptured sarcophagus with soil clinging to it which could have been found here.

One passes miles of empty, unlittered beaches on the coast road. West of Antalya lies Demre (ancient Myra) whose bishop was sanctified as St. Nicholas. A partially intact Byzantine church at the site is the locus of a special mass for him every December 6 and again in May. The saint's relics are in the Church of St. Nicholas in Bari, Italy. I did not see Myra.

Sidé, Thursday, September 28

I left Antalya today and reached the coastal city of Sidé forty-seven miles east. The road, traveled by bus, also passes within sight of ancient Aspendos, where the near perfectly preserved Roman theater is visible from the road. It is called the most complete of its type and the best preserved ancient building in Anatolia. There was no practical way for me to stop.

As Sidé lies two miles from the highway, I was offered a ride by the sheik of the village, who spoke English. He guided me also to the small cafe of Suleyman Subasi, next to the ruins and the sea. I had met a German family, the Browers, at a restaurant in Antalya, who invited me to look them up here when I arrived. I did so.

I went swimming in the delightful little bay, followed by a simple but tasty lunch of fried fish, sliced tomatoes, and flat bread, consumed on the shaky balcony above the water. Then the Browers returned from fishing to offer me more fish, which they had taken in the Manavgat River a few miles distant. Mr. Brower said that it abounds in trout and he took several dozen in two hours. Hooking them requires a three-pointed hook, which the Turks don't have, a lack that appears unfair to local fishermen.

A curious scene took place when I tossed my fish bones into the water—hundreds of small fish appeared suddenly to strip away every edible morsel.

Sidé occupies a rocky peninsula flanked on two sides by sand beaches; at the tip lies the ancient port. A new museum is being arranged, which will make use of parts of the ruined thermae (baths). The curator led me through the ruins, speaking French, showing the baths, agora, theater, several fountains, gateway, portico, houses, shops, and public toilets. Finally I walked to the place where the port stood. Now the scant remains of three temples and a Byzantine basilica can be seen. In the town is the Temple of Fortune. I savored all this in ideal weather and the absence of other tourists.

The Browers are leaving tomorrow to follow the coast eastward. I am doing the same, but their car is too small to take another passenger. This evening there was a going-away party in which I took part, assisting in the consumption of good Turkish beer and melon. Two of the Turkish women brought their small children, who at first cried at the sight of strangers. Then the couch on which I was to sleep collapsed. We had no electricity; kerosene lamps and a Coleman lantern furnished the light.

Alanya, Friday, September 29

The Browers left early today for Adana. We said goodbye after breakfasting at the cafe. The same sheik whom I had met yesterday picked me up and dropped me at Manavgat, where a small bus carried me to Alanya, thirty-eight miles east. The road is in good repair in places, not so in others.

Alanya is perched impressively on a lofty peninsula, the summit of which is occupied by a Seljuk fortress. This rock rises 985 feet. Before sightseeing I went swimming, the last time before leaving the coast. Refreshed, I undertook the climb to the town and found a hotel and restaurant. Shortly after, as I walked past a doctor's office, he spoke to me in English and invited me in for tea. While we conversed on several topics of interest, the doctor told me of a cave in Alanya where he treats asthma sufferers. The humidity is a steady 98 percent, the temperature at 72-74 degrees Fahrenheit. Every day he puts his patients in the cave for four hours.

He asked my opinion of Turkish politics and elections coming next month; however, I could not say anything. He plans to visit the United States in two years for study.

I enjoyed a very good supper in a garden restaurant, including Turkish wine. It was a full-bodied red wine, which I diluted.

My doctor acquaintance told me how I might find a way to Silifke, 120 miles east. Traffic is scarce on the road and the bus requires a minimum three days if one starts on the right day to make connections. By starting today it would require five days, for the bus from Gazipasa to Anamur does not travel until Monday. Or I could take the Sunday bus to Anamur, sleep there, and pick up the Tuesday bus to Silifke, where it is easy to reach Mersin and Adana.

I saw no foreigners in Alanya.

By bus to Mersin, Saturday, September 30

This morning before it became too hot I climbed to Alanya's Seljuk fortress. Two young girls escorted me and hoped to sell silk and lace sashes. Inside I was shown the empty *han*, or bazaar, the ruined Byzantine church, and other components of this collection of walls and rooms, also affording distant views of the surrounding country.

In Alanya again as I passed the doctor's office, he informed me that a *dolmus* would be arriving from Antalya and sought passengers for Mersin. When it arrived later, the doctor happened to be passing and he bargained with the driver until a price was agreed on. So here was a stroke of luck which enabled me to fetch Mersin, although I missed the experience of observing the spectacular stretch of coast along the way because most of the trip was by night. It is some 180 kilometers from Alanya to Mersin, a stretch of coast which offers fine scenery with pine forests, red cliffs falling into a turquoise sea, banana plantations, orange groves, and white sand beaches—all sprinkled with medieval castles (Byzantine, Armenian, Crusader, and Seljuk) and Hellenistic and Roman ruins.

We stopped in the darkness to observe the twin castles at Korykos. This is the same place I had visited on a Sunday in 1953 in company with Dr. Nute and his family. I remembered it as a romantic, subtropical paradise where the ruins of the ages lie about everywhere. One of the castles, that constructed by the Armenians, occupies a small island slightly off shore.

The constant motion of the bus left me feeling ill. At a restaurant, I was offered lemon juice, which perhaps helped me to recover because I finished the journey feeling alright, though exhausted. The road is winding and rough. There being only one other passenger during part of the trip, I had the full back seat to stretch out on. The only cars we passed were a couple of Jeeps and a party of Germans coming from Palestine, whom we met at a roadside spring. One of them spoke English and we exchanged road information.

In Mersin, in the early dawn light, the driver located a hotel, where we had to pound at the door until they let us in and gave me a bed.

Adana, Sunday, October 1

Leaving the commotion of busy Mersin on the Mediterranean, I said adieu to the south for a while and moved inland. The highway to Adana traverses the Cilician Plain, skirting Tarsus, birthplace of St. Paul and the first meeting place of Antony and Cleopatra. I found no mail waiting at the Adana post office and could not locate the American Clinic, which Dr. Nute had directed in 1953. Perhaps the area has become too prosperous to require such an adjunct to health facilities.

It was several hours wait for the Gaziantep bus. I walked across the Stone Bridge of twenty-one arches, fourteen of which are Roman. Justinian restored it in the sixth century and the Crusaders crossed it on the way to Antioch. The river is the Seyhan, and people were busy washing laundry, themselves, and their animals in its shallow waters.

Aboard the bus we crossed broken terrain before beginning to ascend the Central Anatolian Plateau, which is enclosed on the south by the formidable Taurus Mountains. The famous Cilician Gates are almost the only passage through them in this region.

We stopped for supper in an open-air *locanta*, where I met a customs employee who knew some English and was also going to "Antep." We fetched it later and he directed me to a hotel.

Urfa, Monday, October 2

Gaziantep possesses a Byzantine-Seljuk castle, glimpsed from the bus as we left by the Urfa road. Earth-toned walls encompass it. The region between here and Urfa is arid and thinly populated. At Birecek the road crosses the Firat (Euphrates). We paused for a time, allowing passengers to get off and look around. Children and men were selling fruit, *gazoza* (soda), and shish kabob cooked over coals contained in a bucket and served with flat bread. It looked appetizing.

Our arrival in Urfa at midday would have provided the chance to visit the place, which was the former Edessa. Gwyn Williams calls the town "friendly, gay and bustling;"* and I found it special. There is a pool containing sacred carp near a mosque; tradition says

*Eastern Turkey: A Guide and History, 1972.

they are associated with the prophet Abraham, whom Muslims also revere. The fish are not to be eaten.

Urfa has a long history, which includes a significant role in the Crusades. It was my eagerness to make progress on the road to India that dissuaded me from seeing more than the main street of Urfa.

A *dolmus* was about to leave for Diyarbakir and I took a place. One of the passengers spoke some Italian and had spent time in Milan studying telephones. Upon our arrival in Diyarbakir he directed me to the Sur Palas Hotel for lodging and the Turistik Palas for good meals. I noticed many well-dressed people in the dining room.

Diyarbakir, Tuesday, October 3

In Turkey the hotel holds a guest's passport for the duration of the stay. You must remember to pick it up on leaving, which I neglected to do at Gaziantep yesterday. Therefore I went to the police and explained the difficulty to them and requested their help. They secured the aid of an English-speaking official of the Vakiflar Bank, Mr. Ergüney, to interpret for me. He informed the government officials concerned about my missing travel document, for I was in a military district. Our talks were carried on in a friendly spirit, including tea drinking, at times in the bank, also in the police station and the government office. The first step was to telephone the Gaziantep police and ask them to find my passport.

Then I set out to see the city. The most defining features of Diyarbakir are its very large walls of black basalt, a most striking sight from any point of view. They were begun by the Romans and added to and restored by numerous later rulers. Towers and bastions punctuate their five-mile circumference. They may be followed within or without. My tour took me around half the exterior perimeter and then into the gate where the main street begins and so through the busy heart of the city, where diverse citizens—merchants, villagers, colorfully dressed Kurds, and townspeople—move and bargain for the wares displayed in the shops. Automobile traffic in the city is rare; most of the transport is by cart or light truck. Diyarbakir is the heart of Kurdish country. Kurdish women and children wear layers of bright-colored dresses with ornaments and embroidery. Kurdish men wear ordinary jackets and trousers; all of them appear poor. They are part of Diyarbakir's colorful panorama of life in eastern Turkey.

Diyarbakir, Wednesday, October 4

Hearing no word about my passport, I returned to Mr. Ergüney to inquire and there met a policeman who said the document had not been located and the police wanted me to return to Gaziantep to find it, a task that I gently resisted because it would involve two or three days of uncomfortable travel. All was not lost, however; Mr. Ergüney revealed himself to be familiar with the street plan of Gaziantep, for he had recently been posted from there to his present job. With his help a good map was drawn of the main street on which we located the hotel where I had put up. I recalled enough to enable him to identify it. Then he telephoned a colleague at the bank and even as we spoke my passport was found and redirected at last. All of this was accomplished while sitting in Mr. Ergüney's office sipping tea, making the police look somewhat ineffectual. I was told that upon receiving my document I would have to leave for Iran, Diyarbakir being a restricted area.

At my hotel I was introduced to Teoman Günnar, a university student from Istanbul, who, instead of military service, had chosen to teach in a village school for two years. Mr. Günnar knew English and together we visited the Ulu Cami (Great Mosque), which was founded by the Arab conquerors of the seventh century, restored by a Seljuk sultan of the eleventh century (according to an inscription), and incorporates Seljuk features in the courtyard. It presents an amazing mélange of arches interspersed with Corinthian columns, enhanced still more by entrance inscriptions in Kufic script and reliefs of lions attacking bulls, suggesting a long-lived Persian motif.

I have missed some of the best Seljuk remains on this journey, Konya for example. The Seljuks did some pleasing work in stone, notably mausoleums.

After seeing the interior of the Ulu Cami and repassing the charming agglomeration of stonework in the courtyard with its two ablution places sheltered under painted cupolas supported on stone pillars, we visited the museum housed in a Seljuk building of 1190, a theological school until converted to its present purpose in this century. The country has become more secularized since the rule of Kemal Atatürk in the early twentieth century. The collection on display was unfamiliar to me because my knowledge of the historic eastern Turkish cultures, with the exception of the Hittites, is almost nil.

Diyarbakir, Thursday, October 5

There being a U.S. radar station twenty miles from this city, I decided to expose myself to a taste of home today by visiting the installation. The service club had U.S. news magazines, which reported events I had not known about. I was fed army chow without cost; it did not agree with me, but I assumed that was because my system was accustomed to Turkish cooking. Later three of us—an American teacher in a local school, a Turkish military pilot, and I— were given a ride back to Diyarbakir in an army car. Everyone went to the Turistik Palas Hotel for conversation and arak. They showed me the longest word in the Turkish language—forty-two letters.

Diyarbakir, Friday, October 6

Teoman, my friend and guide, took us to visit the citadel, where the walls look down several hundred feet to the narrow stream which is the Tigris. It's an expansive view in the clear atmosphere. You see a poor village of mud huts next to the river, and above, a village of stone and painted wood houses. The season is late and the land all about the city appears nearly barren of plant life. This is the dry season and animals, trucks, and autos raise plumes of dust which can be seen at a distance, crisscrossing the country. However, the region contains gardens and orchards that are praised, and cereals are produced in the Diyarbakir basin to the north. I have already mentioned the good food in the restaurant.

Diyarbakir has had a long succession of masters, who would require much paper and ink to list. Since the early sixteenth century, when the Ottoman Sultan Selim I arrived, it has been mostly peaceful.

Teoman took us to visit a fortune teller who lives in a poor district. She dipped my finger in water and proceeded to speak but, after a few minutes, Teoman said, "Let's go." Then he told me what she saw—not very much. The fee was fifteen cents.

We followed the way down to the Atatürk House, which was not open but is surrounded by a flower garden. From there the path led to the ten-arched stone bridge over the Tigris, said to be of Roman origin and restored by a Byzantine emperor, a sign of far-reaching Greek dominion before the Islamic conquest.

That evening we visited a night club and drank beer. I tried to be polite and remained until midnight, seeing a Turkish belly dance as well as a dance performed by men holding hands and handkerchiefs. The music is strange to my ears. At the same place were several German petroleum prospectors, who told us that the region is beginning to yield some oil.

Bitlis, Saturday, October 7

Calling at the Vakiflar Bank this morning, I was pleased to find my passport had arrived. Everyone was glad to learn the news and I expressed my gratitude to those who helped. I owed the enjoyable interlude in Diyarbakir to the very contretemps that had separated me from my passport.

As a *dolmus* would leave for Bitlis soon, my friend Teoman hired an *araba* (two-wheeled carriage), which we took to the bus station. The *dolmus* was a small Czech sedan; my long legs have difficulty because the Turks are a shorter people. As usual the baggage was lashed to the roof. We traveled fast on the unpaved road. The wheels sounded almost as if they were falling off, but later I gained confidence. We paused in Silvan long enough to permit a brief view of the Ulu Cami—in very good condition. Gwyn Williams* mentions enjoying "an excellent meal in a spotless restaurant with a little fountain inside, on the north side of the road through town." Beyond Silvan the road traverses a tributary of the Tigris on a graceful hump-backed Seljuk bridge in perfect condition.

At nightfall we took supper in a poor village restaurant, but the meal did not unhinge me. I am becoming accustomed to local fare.

Confined by the narrow valley of the Bitlis River and well endowed by man and nature, Bitlis is an interesting town that would repay a visit. There are substantial houses and some noteworthy Seljuk building, which I did not see. Ancient Armenian terraces are still cultivated.

Bitlis, Lake Van, and Ercis, Sunday, October 8

By morning I was rested and prepared to push on again, but first I walked the main street to find something for breakfast— sweet hot milk and bread. A Jeep station wagon departing soon for nearby Tatvan on Van Golü (Lake Van). I took a place in it. On some days a ship connects this place with Van, which is on the east side of the large lake.

In Tatvan I discovered that a bus would soon leave on the road which follows the north shore to Ercis. Mechanical trouble delayed our departure. While waiting I met several university students enroute back to their village teaching posts. One of them, Hamami, who spoke English, was very pleasant and helpful. We remained together all day in Tatvan and on the bus, and he prevented me from

* Opus cit. p 56.

paying for anything myself, insisting that I was his guest. His hospitality extended to my hotel room at Ercis. We progressed slowly on the rough road and took the full afternoon and early evening to fetch Ercis in the northeast corner of Lake Van. The day was cloudy, but the lake was visible from the road. We passed Ahlat, and the little I saw made me regret that there was no way to stop, for the Seljuk cemetery is exceptional. Of it Gwyn Williams says, "This long abandoned graveyard is one of the strangest sites in Turkey and should not be missed. The forest of tall, scrolled and lichened stones seen against the background of the lake and far mountains seems no longer to have any reference to life or death, but a strange and absolute beauty."*

It was Ahlat, glimpsed from the passing bus, which won me over to Seljuk art and building. The mausoleums are small but eloquent in their purity of form. The color of the stone resembles chocolate, showing very little weathering beyond a smoothing out of the forms. The stone is as hard as iron. I could not stop as it was near dark.

At this point a policeman noticed me in the bus and asked to see my passport. He found that I did not have the special endorsement required to visit this region of the country. Yet, after discussion with the students and police, I was permitted to proceed and had no further difficulty in Turkey.

Lake Van is a large sheet of water, shallow, high in soda and minerals, having no visible outlet. Its surface area would accommodate six-and-a-half Lake Genevas. Mountains surround it, falling directly into the lake southwards and standing back on the north.

Only one species of fish tolerates the waters, a small member of the carp family, which is said to be tasty. Seagulls dwell along the shores of the soft blue waters, and there are a few sandy beaches. According to Gwyn Williams, "In summer the water is warm and soft to the skin, marvelous to swim in, buoyant. It's like gliding through silk and your skin feels silken when you come out of it." I observed no tourist accommodations on the north side, which is barren and rock strewn.

We reached Ercis after dark. After dining, I promptly retired while Hamami visited with his friends. Five of us slept in the same room—a record on this score, similar to a dormitory. Beds also occupied the corridor.

Agri, Monday, October 9

I was up early this morning as is my custom. There being no hot water, I heated it on my Burmos. An early bus was about to leave for

* Gywn Williams opus, cit. p 56.

Agri. I thanked my friends and got Hamami's address, for he requested a postcard from India. At the bus, waiting to leave, was still another teacher returning to his post for the opening of school. During our journey together he related, in good English, the difficulties and discomforts he had experienced in the job. It was very cold in winter, he said, and travel at times was impossible. The Kurds in the village did not like him. They refused to send their girls to school. He could not eat their food and so prepared his own. He washed his own clothes because the local women used only water and stones to clean garments.

The government has built a school and teacher's house which otherwise would be a mud brick shelter. The fuel is ox dung furnished by the oxen that the district utilizes nearly exclusively to draw the plow and solid-wheel carts. They cannot afford horses or their more expensive feed.

Early in the afternoon we reached Agri, where I found a single room in the Can Palas Hotel, a comfortable and well-lighted place to rest and read. Such relative luxury is delightful. I wanted nothing more than to crawl into bed, read the guide, listen to my transistor radio, and sleep.

Dogubayazit and the border, Tuesday, October 10

This was my final day in Turkey and was spent largely in border-crossing formalities. A bus converted from a truck body left Agri at nine for Dogubayazit, the last stop in Turkey. A young German photographer who was also going to India was aboard. When we arrived in Dogubayazit, we saw parked next to the Dogubeyazit post office an English tourist bus with several young people standing outside. These Europeans, of whom I had met none in my transit of southern Turkey, had taken the northern Black Sea route across the country. The two routes meet and join here.

The English group had started in London and was headed for Colombo, Ceylon; some of the passengers were going home to Australia and New Zealand. As I continued to talk to them, I was told of their many trials and delays along the way. They had experienced breakdowns, hardship, hunger, and even strife among themselves. They lacked enough money to purchase food. At the outset there had been three buses, but one had broken down and been abandoned. The present one had been stuck in Dogubeyazit for three days waiting for a document needed to enter Iran to arrive in the mail. I learned most of this from a Punjabi who had a round trip ticket on the infernal bus. He told me he would prefer to go through the invasions again than take such a trip.

The German traveler and I spent our last Turkish liras for lunch before leaving for Iran, a few miles east. The most exciting sight here is Mt. Ararat (*Ağri Dağı*), 16,946 feet high. It is a dormant volcano, partly obscured in cloud today. This district is scattered with irregular volcanic rock, which makes for very rough terrain.

Formalities required to enter Iran were lengthy and thorough. My visa was valid, but the German's had expired. Since it was printed in Farsi (which uses the Arabic alphabet), he probably could not have known unless someone had told him. After a long worrisome wait it was extended for a fee of several dollars. Also waiting was an Austrian couple in their own car, who had arrived without a visa and returned all the way to Trabzon to get it—a four day's journey. They were annoyed to realize that they probably could have paid to get it at the frontier. I had the impression that the Iranians didn't like us. Some Iranians do not like foreigners. It's a part of their past.

All documents being in order and the Austrians, the German, and I having taken a cup of tea, the four of us departed in the Austrians' car. It was pitch dark and travel was slow on the gravel road. We could see little sign of habitation in the empty countryside except one or two villages. Suddenly a front tire blew and we came to a stop in the solitude and darkness. There was no spare and nothing to do but make the best of it until morning. No traffic passed, for this was a no-man's land between two countries, where bandits might be waiting, as we were later informed. Less than a mile behind we had passed a small restaurant, so two of us walked back to purchase several eggs, bread, and orange drink, which served for dinner. Afterwards we settled down as well we might. The temperature dropped and I wrapped my blanket about me.

Tabrìz, Wednesday, October 11

The castaways were awake at first light. On emerging from the cramped space into empty surroundings, we seemed to be still more abandoned. Shortly after, the red disk of the sun surmounted the ridges and its beams burst upon the flanks of Ararat, still visible behind us, turning the mountain red.

We were able to assemble a satisfying breakfast from leftovers; last evening's bread, the Austrians' Nescafe, the German's water, and my small stove to heat it. The result tasted as good as anything of its kind.

To stand guard by car and baggage it was necessary to leave someone behind and the driver's wife accepted this unwelcome duty while we three males, carrying baggage and wheel, hailed a passing bus. As I did not meet the woman again, it is unknown how she fared in the hours that her husband was absent. The bus was already laden with passengers, baggage, market goods, one ewe, and one calf. Our destination was the town of Khöy at a distance of 36 miles. It was not expected to be a restful journey and it wasn't.

At Khöy the driver found a pair of tires and returned to the car alone, while the German and I proceeded to Tabrìz because we did not wish to accept any further favors from the Austrians. I could foresee additional contretemps because they needed three new tires plus spares in this region of long distances, poor roads, and few services. Before leaving Khöy the German and I enjoyed a good meal of braised lamb, rice pilaf, salad, and water, served with excellent flat bread. Then an English-speaking policeman helped us find seats on a bus for Tabrì z. It is awkward not speaking the language.

The 120-mile journey revealed an arid, sparsely vegetated country, alternately flat and hilly. We fetched Tabrìz after sunset. While my companion departed, a student spoke to me in English as I left the bus, offering to take me to a hotel. I invited him for dinner. In this way he found a way to practice English and I received an introduction to Tabrìz and Iran. He told me that a dialect of Turkish is spoken in this city. The national language is Farsi, written in Arabic characters. He provided several words and phrases in Farsi, which I transcribed phonetically in my notebook.

It was especially good to sleep in a bed tonight.

Tabrìz, Thursday, October 12

Tourists are required to register upon arrival; thereupon they are issued an identity card. This formality over, I sought out whatever might be of interest in this city of 250,000. First I went to the Blue Mosque. It was in a ruinous state, the majority of its blue tiles gone. Then I found the bazaar, which is a covered market having main passages and narrow side passages, crowded with men and donkeys carrying goods on their backs. The enchanting agglomeration of hundreds, even thousands, of individual stalls, displays every sort of finished goods, many handmade on the spot and before the patron's eyes. There are dealers, craftsmen, assistants, and buyers in profusion. They offer metalwork, kitchen utensils, furniture, boxes, clothing, objets d'art, embroidery, spices, and food items. The fast food is shish kabob and tea or sweets. Prices are not shown and bargaining the rule. People and animals flow without interruption—to and fro within the bazaar and to the city and surrounding villages.

Passing the rug dealers I paused before one of the displays where a bright young fellow sat on a pile of rugs. He answered my questions about the way the rugs are made, the origin of the designs, the regions in which they are made, and standards of quality. The stalls face each other across the narrow passage, and thus there is nowhere to display a large rug unless in the passage itself; pedestrians and donkeys continue to pass over it while the client decides. The boy said a nine-by-twelve-foot rug in a design of good quality could be had for $300 plus the cost of shipping and duty.

Later I boarded the train for Tehran, traveling in a third-class compartment. It was not crowded on the nineteen-hour journey. During much of it I had only a single railroad employee with me who kept others out of the compartment so I might sleep stretched out on the seats. The train crossed a semi-arid country interspersed with areas of cultivation. In a better season it would be greener.

Tehran, Friday, October 13

When an English-speaking teacher came into the compartment, I asked about the people who weave rugs in Iran. They are well paid, he said, but the labor is hard on the body and the eyesight. As a consequence, the weavers cease at age twenty and take up other work. Three boys can complete a rug in two to three months on average. A coded pattern is placed before each weaver, and as the weaving proceeds on the vertical warp, the finished part is rolled upwards. The train fetched Tehran at 9:00 a.m. Two university students, Mustafa and Ebadian, as well as a policeman, helped me find a hotel, the Gilanov, in Ferdowzi Street, a main avenue. Tehran is a large, partly westernized city. At the Gilanov life again became more comfortable and the food was entirely satisfying. I learned soon to be optimistic concerning Iranian food and looked forward to meals. Hot and pleasantly seasoned rice pilaf with butter or raw egg on top; good meat; fresh salad consisting of a grass-like green, mint, and radish; and freshly baked flat bread—always good—would be a typical menu.

Since it was Friday, the Muslim religious day, when nothing remains open, I walked to the American embassy, which was also closed. It is a large modern building with surrounding lawns and flower beds.

My hotel has a garden restaurant in the rear, which I tried with good results.

Tehran, Sunday, October 15

Today the Pakistani Embassy granted me a visa on the spot and without charge, which was gratifying. Then I hailed a taxi, the foreigner's preferred transportation, and showed the driver an envelope with the address of the Institut Pasteur on the face. This effort of communication caused a minor contretemps, for he took me instead to the post office. But it was rectified, and at the small clinic, which appeared very efficient, I was given two inoculations free of charge. I was told that after visiting India I shall require small pox, cholera, and typhoid-Para typhoid to re-enter the United States without delay. The series requires three weeks.

Tehran has city buses with a few English double-deckers. As they are marked in Farsi, the user must be able to read the language. Taxis are cheap and plentiful. The two students, Mustafa and Ebadian, invited me for a city walk including a visit to their campus, the scene of frequent student demonstrations. They showed me the library and student center of the Iran-American Society. There is a U.S. Information Service library in Tehran.

The vexation of money problems seems likely to follow me everywhere. When leaving the States I was owed money for work I had done, which I have not yet received. Then I have a habit of trying to get by on less money than is advisable. Here in Tehran the expected remittance from home has not caught up with me, or was never sent, and I cannot move until it or something else arrives.

Mustafa dined with me in the garden restaurant of the hotel. He described Iranian village life, which, he said, is greatly lacking in many conveniences and opportunities. He denounced Iranian politics, the waste of oil income, and autocratic rule of the Shah. He spoke of his medical studies, the teaching he had done before switching fields, and the Farsi language, especially words that are similar to the English. Here are a few: *barador* (brother), *dokhtar* (daughter), *pedar* (father), *pöf* (puff), *laugh* (leg), *behtar* (butler), *jangal* (jungle), *ferdows* (paradise), *adan* (Eden), and *garm* (warm).

The weather here is as agreeable as October is at home. The city is animated and vehicular traffic plentiful, including cars, trucks, buses, and carts pulled by men or horses. The pedestrian should be careful. Numerous small vendors chant a description of their goods, others say nothing. Some lay out their goods on the pavement. The nearer I approach India the more I see of varied street life.

The Archaeology Museum contains collections of ancient Persian pottery, and bronzes, and Islamic arts. It does not stand out especially.

The Gullistan Palace, former royal residence, appears not to be much visited. Initial enquiries suggested I would have difficulty in gaining access. However, I was given a pass at the Tourist Department. The rugs on the floor were interesting as was the garden. My guide spoke English, describing each individual piece. Among the sights is the Peacock Throne, a modern creation whose name comes from an old account that mentions such a throne on which the Moghul emperor of India sat in audience. A Persian Shah and conqueror stole the original from India. The resemblance to a four-poster bed is inescapable.

Mustafa and Ebadian showed me the Museum of the Iranian People, which appears to be a waxworks, though the figures are in other materials. Then we saw the modern Masjid-i-Shah (Shah's Mosque), a large building and courtyard in the center city. As darkness fell we strolled in the central bazaar where I bought a small teapot with Iranian tea to fill it. Compared to Turkish tea, Iranian tea is weak, so I beef it up with sugar. I have not observed cafes or tea houses, but tea is prepared in small stalls from where boys deliver glasses to nearby customers as in Turkey. Major brands of U.S. soft drinks are popular.

I sent a wire today requesting the money that I had been expecting. Then I read in the library of the Iran-American Society, which has U.S. books and periodicals. By boarding a city bus at random I ended up at the central bazaar, where I met my companion Mustafa. He took me to a U.S.-style hamburger place; then we both returned to the Gilanov. We had an abridged discussion of the religions originating in Iran. They include Zoroastrianism, Mithraism, Manicheism, Sufism, and Bahaism, the last two spin-offs of Islam. The ancient Persian Zoroastrians are represented in modern Iran by a few respected descendants of this ancient faith.

Tehran, Thursday, October 19

The money I sent for arrived today, although it is not sufficient to take me very far. I returned to the clinic for more immunizations in the series. Adjacent to my hotel are several rug shops where I have admired rugs costing from $700 dollars upward.

This evening Mustafa and Ebadian came for dinner on this, my last evening before departing on a tour of cities and sites of the southwest. These Iranian hosts have been most cordial and helpful while I've been here.

Isfahan, Friday, October 20

It was reassuring to find a modern bus with full-size seats going to Isfahan, which is a tidy distance south of Tehran. Somewhat into the morning we pulled into a desert wayside for refreshments. A second following bus also stopped and passengers from both mingled about the rude establishment. Then I observed a familiar face among the second bus's passengers. It was that of Charles Burney, an English archaeologist whom I had met in Egypt in 1953 when both of us were staying in a Cairo pension. Charles had given me advice concerning my Egyptian tour, as well as introducing me to other people in the field of Egyptian studies. Back in England I had visited him at his parents' place in Surrey. This was certainly a lucky coincidence. We spoke briefly before reembarking for Isfahan.

Iran is large and much of it is high desert or semiarid plateau containing widely scattered settlements. The partially improved road to the south serves a few villages and the holy city of Qom. The scenery is not interesting.

We fetched Isfahan in late afternoon, and after locating a small hotel I set out to explore. It is a well-built, prosperous-looking city, uncrowded and tranquil. The surrounding country is flat—traversed by the broad, shallow Zayandeh Rüd crossed by a stone bridge of twenty-three arches.

Isfahan is known to foreigners for its resplendently tiled buildings. It was the Iranian capital during the Safavid period under Shah Abbas the Great (1587-1629), who brought prosperity and artistic accomplishment to the country. The tile manufactory was sufficiently developed to produce tiles in large quantities and a great variety of patterns. An entire building, inside and out, might be encrusted with tiles specially designed with intricate floral decoration and inscriptions taken from the Muslim holy book, the Koran. The result is brilliant and characteristically Eastern.

The Maidan-i-Shah (central square) is one-third of a mile long. One end is dominated by tiled mosques and other noble structures, all of which have been extensively and tastefully restored in this century.

The Friday Mosque is the centerpiece of the narrow end of the Maidan, which it occupies. Two colorful minarets flank the brilliant tiled dome. I am not sure if it was still in use as a mosque, but I was able to walk through freely. Mosques are generally open to all whenever prayers are not taking place. The decoration of this one reminded me of a jewelry box.

On the adjacent side of the Maidan lies the Masjid-i-Sheykh Lotfollah Mosque, a tile-encrusted, domed funerary building, which is deconsecrated and accessible to all. The tiles are predominantly heavenly blue with patterns suggesting intertwining vines and plants giving way in places to ornamental script. It could be the Persian representation of heaven.

Then Charles appeared and we returned to the hotel where he and his wife were staying. It held many European visitors or employees of foreign companies, some of whom were in the dining room, where we enjoyed a good meal. We discussed subjects touching on his work and other developments since our last meeting. He had been lecturing on Near Eastern archaeology at Manchester University while devoting the fall season to excavating and study in Turkey near Van and Tabrìz. At the moment they were headed for Pasargade near Persepolis, where a new British dig has been started. He said that I could stop there and he would put in a word for me with the leader of the team.

Isfahan, Saturday, October 21

After preparing breakfast in my room, I descended into the Chaharbagh, the wide main street with little traffic and a pedestrian way in the center. Southward it meets the Zayandeh Rüd bridge already mentioned. In the time of Shah Abbas he and his notables were able to observe water pageants on the dammed river while comfortably seated in open rooms atop the bridge.

At this early hour, caretakers were at work sweeping buildings and walks, watering flower beds, and trimming trees in the Maidan. In the Chaharbagh Mosque a citizen washed clothes in the small canal flowing through the main court for ablutions. The scene was bathed in bright sunlight at that hour as I strolled through the gemlike tiled interior.

Shah Abbas liked to sit in high places where he might observe events taking place below. The Ali Qapu, like the rooms on the bridge, was another such perch. This building with covered deck was made for his use when attending festivities and games taking place in the Maidan. The royal box of the Ali Qapu is partly mutilated by time yet preserves a quantity of rich decoration, some of it in sculpted plaster designs surrounding wall paintings. Stairs lead up to the observation level, which is protected from sun and rain by a canopy supported by tall wood columns. From this you can see the immediate area and the city beyond; there are no taller structures in the way.

The Maidan contained a polo field in former times and preserves the goal posts. On the north the square meets the bazaar, and surrounding the great rectangle and unifying everything is an arcade. The description in the Encyclopedia Britannica sums it up as follows: "The Maidan-i-Shah united in a single composition all the concerns of Medieval Islamic architecture: prayer, commemoration, princely pleasure, trade and spatial effect."

In Isfahan women generally wear the *chadoor*, or large veil, black or printed, over the head and falling to the ground, which leaves only the face visible. The chin may also be shielded by the wearer's holding the edges of her veil in her teeth.

A wing of the royal palace survives—the Chehel Sotoon (Hall of Forty Columns). There is an inviting garden with a reflecting pool, which explains the name Forty Columns, made up of twenty true columns and their reflections. The building contains a small museum holding a group of unusual paintings—not done in a style I knew of previously.

The garden drew me into it; and I yearned to walk barefoot on the grass and began to do so. The gardeners disapproved, however, so I ceased. Some Iranians consider foreigners objects of annoyance, an attitude that may be a vestige of the old hostility to strangers noted by some travelers in this country. It might be that they were considered sources of pollution.

This afternoon I visited an old mosque, the Jum'a, situated away from the center. It is older than the Friday Mosque and others in that group, and the tiled surfaces are dissimilar. Attached are a series of rooms indicating that there may have been a religious school there. A caretaker showed me the richly carved pulpit and decorated *mihrab* (prayer niche) facing Mecca. There is also a Winter Prayer Hall.

I took a taxi across the city to the Armenian Vang Church because I had never visited an Armenian place of worship and wanted to see one. This one, I was told by the priest who met me, is the cathedral of their community. Everything within was very clean and orderly. Fresco decoration was divided into small panels depicting scriptural subjects, in an informal style. The priest told me that Soviet Armenia has 3 million Armenians and the United States 300,000.

Shiraz, Sunday, October 22

It is 300 miles to Shiraz, and so I was up early. One of my roommates in the hotel was kneeling in prayer in the darkened room. I was sharing the space with three others as a way to save money, and also to meet the people. The comfortable bus followed the arrow-straight, hard-surfaced road across an almost featureless landscape. Here and there I observed small "dust devils" racing over the land and kicking up little funnels of dry material. There was little traffic.

At one o'clock we passed the side road to Pasargade followed by Taqsh-i-Rustam (site of royal tombs) and Persepolis itself (a royal capital) to the left. Then we fetched Shiraz. Leaving the bus, I was addressed in English by a young man who offered his help. He led me to a hotel and restaurant, then remained as my guide all afternoon and evening. He was a teacher and besides wanting to render friendly service to a stranger, he probably also sought the opportunity to speak English.

My guide, whose name I neglected to preserve, took me to see the tiled kiosk of the museum. It is a former mausoleum in octagonal form, which is covered with fine tiles like Isfahan's creations. It dates from the mid-eighteenth century in the Zand period following the Safavids. Next we visited the principal mosque and bazaar. I began to see the advantages of this attractive small city, which is celebrated in literature. Poets praised its climate, wine, and rose gardens. The Iranians love their poetry. Two of the country's favorite poets, Hafiz and Saadi, were born here and lie in well-tended garden tombs, which my guide desired that I see. First the resting place of Hafiz. Some of the others present were reading his poems aloud, others were doing so in silence. My companion borrowed a volume and read a few lines, which were very graceful. It was nearly dark at Saadi's tomb, situated north of the city, in the place where he lived. A spring of fresh water issues from the earth and in it live large fish, perhaps carp. We fed them scraps of bread. Girls come here to splash in the waters of the spring because they believe it will enhance their chances of finding a husband.

So concluded my short the visit in Shiraz. It was greatly enhanced by the presence of my Iranian companion.

Persepolis and Pasargade, Monday, October 23

I made connection with the early bus that passes Persepolis. The air was cool at 7 a.m. when the driver stopped to let me off next to the ruins of the ancient royal palaces. No one else was there as I began to walk around and the sun rose above the ridge of the Mount of Mercy, which is a backdrop to the scene.

Before long a local guard appeared and informed me of the correct approach to the place on the west side of the terrace where the regal staircase is found. It is unusual to find something as old as these ancient Persian structures in such excellent state of preservation. The sculpted stairway has been protected by soil washed down from the Mount of Mercy behind. It rises approximately twenty feet at an easy pitch. This was the ceremonial approach to the Apadana Hall.

The reliefs along the stair walls on both sides represent subject peoples bringing offerings of many kinds to the king. The offerings include animals, cloth, vessels, skins, food, and other valuable articles for presentation in an annual ceremony. Each group of several gift bearers is led by a guard, who holds the hand of the lead figure. No women are present. The figures are approximately two-thirds natural size. Elsewhere a regular procession of guards mounts the steps on the east and west side, one on each tread.

After reaching the terrace, the procession passed under the Porch of Xerxes and entered the Apadana Hall, where the king sat to receive the tribute. This audience hall is the largest ruin on the extended terrace and preserves thirteen standing columns, tall and slender, without capitals. The hall was roofed in wood, making it very combustible. The capitals, fragments of which lie about the terrace, were in the form of bicephalic (two-headed) bulls. A damaged example is in the Louvre.

The second large building that once stood here is the Hall of a Hundred Columns. Less of this has remained. Reliefs flanking some doorways show the king followed by an attendant who shields his lord with a parasol. The summer climate here is very hot.

Cut into the face of the Mount of Mercy are three royal tombs with sculptured fronts. One of them held Darius III, whom Alexander defeated. It shows the king facing a deity—Ahura Mazda perhaps.

Persia was the first large empire in this region, and its administrative methods were later adopted by others. The Bible mentions the Persians, in the Book of Esther for example.

There are scarcely any tourist facilities in Persepolis, but I found lunch in a small place before picking up a ride to Naqsh-i-Rustam a few miles north.

The side road was devoid of cars and I walked in to the place where the seven rock-cut tombs of the Achaemenid rulers occupy the face of a cliff. At first sight they resemble the rock-cut tombs of

Egypt in which the tenant worships a god. On the level ground in front of the tombs is a low tower, nearly cube shaped, termed the Altar. It could have a connection with the Zoroastrian religion of the ancient Persians.

Relying on the assistance of another driver, I was given a ride along the main road to the junction for Pasargade, where I had another long walk to the site. Pasargade predates Persepolis and served as capital of the country before the newer city came forward along with Susa, Babylon, and Ecbatana as administrative centers of the empire founded by Cyrus the Great in the sixth century B.C.

It was an hour before sunset when I arrived before the simple rectangular tomb of Cyrus. An English woman was there waiting to take a picture. Charles Burney's account of his countrymen's dig at Pasagade explained her presence, and she told me where to go to find a place to sleep tonight. The excavation party used a small building nearby, where I was kindly received by Dr. David Stonach; he said Charles had left the same morning. I was given a cot to sleep on in the house while the staff stayed in tents. Then I proceeded on foot to the Throne of Solomon, as it is called by the Muslims, who revere this place as the location of the tomb of King Solomon's mother. I fetched it as the sun began to set and the diggers were leaving for the day. They have been at the job only four days. The excavation mound contains a masonry platform topped by earth showing that the structures on it were of sunbaked brick. Returning, I passed the Prison of Solomon, which resembles the Altar at Naqsh-i-Rustam. Nearby in the darkness was an excavated palace with a notable relief of Cyrus, but I could not see it.

Dr. Stonach has eight or nine university students who do the work here. We all had tea together followed by a very good dinner prepared by the Iranian cook. They made me feel that I was among friends. This team will remain here until mid-December before returning to their universities. I was also introduced to the expedition mascot, a young hawk who perched on my shoulder, entirely at ease.

Pasargade and Tehran, Tuesday, October 24

The diggers were up at daybreak and I joined them at breakfast before bidding them adieu and thanks. Along with two policemen who guard them at night, I was driven out to the main road in their Landrover. Shortly after, the Isfahan bus, on which I had reserved a place, stopped for me. After another long ride we reached Isfahan in time for me to take in the Maidan-i-Shah once again. Then I boarded the Tehran bus, where I was befriended by three youths, two of them Armenian. They gave me tea and candy in the holy city of Qom but spoke only a little English. It was 4 a.m. when I fell into bed at the Gilanov Hotel after a tiring journey.

Tehran, Wednesday, October 25

When I went to obtain the required Afghan visa, I found the consulate in confusion. It had moved recently and was not able to help me until Saturday—tomorrow being the Shah's birthday and Friday the Muslim holy day, so I waited to apply until I reached Mashad.

The season is becoming colder and the clothes I have less than adequate. This combination is an incentive to move on into warmer regions of India. Also urging me on is the shortage of money, because there should be some waiting for me in Delhi.

I was given my second cholera inoculation at the Institut Pasteur today. And I made one more visit to the Iranian American Society, where good reading is available.

Tehran, Thursday, October 26

Mustafa came to the hotel for tea this morning, and we walked to Shemran to the north, where the rich have homes in company with the Shah and government officials. Mustafa said the homes were paid for with money embezzled from the people. The shops contain luxuries.

A youthful German bicyclist is presently staying in the hotel as the guest of a newspaper; usually he sleeps along the road in his tent. This rugged traveler had left Germany in early September and his destination is the same as mine. His means of transport impressed me as being still more uncomfortable than my own, so I admired his endurance and determination, qualities that perhaps I can claim to share.

I prepared to leave Tehran and bid adieu to my friends Mustafa and Ebadian, who added so greatly to this visit. They are in Tehran University, where there is no tuition and a choice of faculties. The campus is new and situated near the city center. Students are politically active and from time to time stage anti-government rallies and demonstrations. At this time soldiers are standing guard at the Teachers Faculty after a recent confrontation with students.

The night express to Mashad was the better choice than the bus, and I settled down to sleep in the uncrowded train and passed a fair night. Iranian trains are good, although slow, and serve but little of the country.

Mashad, Friday, October 27

Six hundred miles and seventeen hours later the train fetched Mashad. It felt good to be approaching my goal, the subcontinent that is India. It always seems to me to be a land of rich possibilities, a friendly, welcoming land, and a land of mystery, variety, and magnificent art and architecture, as well as being holy ground.

However I was still in Iran. Our train touched at Nishapur, birthplace of Omar Khayyam, before reaching Mashad. Another famous Persian poet, Firdausi, was born near Mashad. Iran identifies itself through its great poets.

I was directed to the Firdousi Hotel, where, in a comfortable, warm room having a large Persian rug and good bed, I was at ease for two days.

Then I set out for the holy shrine of the Imam Reza, which, rather naively, I expected to visit without incident. I should offer a little information here. The revered Imam (leader), who was descended from the Prophet Muhammed according to the Shiah branch of Islam, died here in A.D. 818 after eating grapes. The tomb of the eighth-century caliph Harun al Rashid also occupies a place in the shrine; pilgrims sometimes kick it, thinking that he poisoned the Imam, who was traveling with Harun's son at the time. I did not observe either the tomb or any insult.

Over the years, as the Imam Reza's shrine drew more devotion from the Shiahs, it became richly endowed. Eventually a fifteenth-century shah and his remarkable wife, Gauhar Shad, built the present shrine and ancillary structures; they have acquired the reputation of being among the most sublime buildings in the Muslim world, which is saying a lot, because there are very many great ones.

The English traveler Robert Byron visited Mashad in the 1930s and left the following description of the Imam's shrine:

> The whole quadrangle was a garden of turquoise, pink, and dark blue, with touches of purple, green, and yellow, planted among paths of plain buff brick. Huge white arabesques whirled above the ivan arches. The ivans themselves hid other gardens, shadier, fritillary-coloured. The great minarets beside the sanctuary, rising from bases encircled with Kufic the size of a boy, were bedizened with a network of jewelled lozenges. The swollen sea-green dome adorned with yellow tendrils appeared between them.

But in all this variety, the principle of union, the life-spark of the whole blazing apparition, was kindled by two great texts: the one, a frieze of white *suls* writing powdered over a field of gentian blue along the skyline of the entire quadrangle; the other, a border of the same alphabet in daisy white and yellow on a sapphire field, interlaced with turquoise Kufic along its inner edge, and enclosing, in the form of a three-sided oblong, the arch of the main ivan between the minarets....*

By Byron's account it appears that the he gained access to the building; however the writer Wilfred Blunt in *Splendors of Islam* did not, and was obliged to observe the courtyard from outside. He says:

> Mashad already had a long history behind it (including an inevitable sacking by the Mongols) when Gauhar Shad began the erection of what many consider the most beautiful extant building in all Islam. The city owed its foundation to the burial there of Harun al-Rashid, who died at nearby Tus while on his way to suppress an insurrection in Transoxiana; it owes its sanctity to the bones of Reza, the eighth Imam, who also died at Tus; but its architectural glory it owes to the beneficence of Gauhar Shad and the genius of Qavam ad-Din. Non-Muslims will regret the sanctity of the golden-domed shrine of Imam Reza, which unfortunately extends to the whole complex, for the Unbeliever must generally rest content with a God's-eye view of Gauhar Shad's court from the museum roof or the top of a minaret.**

It seems that, on the whole, infidels are not admitted, although I somehow was able to penetrate the inner sanctum and blended with the numerous faithful, though I do not understand how my six-foot-four height could have escaped notice. It was Friday and the crowd may have been extra large. Though I was a tourist, it could be said I was masquerading as a pilgrim because I moved along with the others toward the tomb under the central dome. I don't believe I noticed the decoration around me and if I had paused to gape at the walls it would have given me away immediately.

Muslims entering a mosque remove their shoes and leave them in the courtyard, but instead of leaving mine I carried them in my hand. An attendant, seeing this, guided me out to a checkroom in the court where they were gathered in. Then I reentered the central area to follow the eager multitude. A steady sound of voices could be heard. There were side chambers, carpeted like the central hall,

* Robert Byron, *The Road to Oxiana*, New York: Oxford University Press, 1982.
** Wilfred Blunt, *Splendors of Islam*, New York: Viking Press, 1976.

where men sat reading the scriptures or reciting prayers, but the greater number flowed unevenly toward the large structure that protected the Imam's sepulcher. Heavy silver grilles surround it, and they are polished by the constant stroking of thousands of hands. The faithful press up to the grilles with arms outstretched, trying to reach over the heads of others to touch the enclosure; then they rub their hands over the face and head as if contacting a kind of holy electricity. It was only necessary to remain in the flow to be brought nearly in contact with the grilles myself, but I did not touch the holy place, thinking it might be profanation by an infidel. So fascinating was the entire experience that I went through a second time before emerging into the court to realize that I had witnessed something remarkable.

Mashad, Saturday, October 28

Today I was issued a transit visa at the Afghan Consulate. The vice-consul granted it promptly and then engaged me concerning several difficulties he had found in his study of English. Then I made arrangements for the journey tomorrow, including the early delivery of my heavy baggage to the bus station for loading on top. This was a mistake, however, because after my suitcase had left my custody, someone reached into it to take my camera; which probably should not have been there in any case.

Today when I tried to reenter the shrine again a guard prevented me. Somewhere I had read that fanatics have been known to mistreat non-believers found in Muslim holy places; however, I detected no sign of hostility.

Today I rested and wrote letters, preparing for the journey to Herat, Afghanistan, tomorrow. Yesterday the taxi driver who brought me to this hotel asked too much. When I resisted he went away without anything. These days I am conserving my money because I have so little with me. Later the driver returned with a box of tea I had forgotten, and the hotel keeper gave him his money without resort to me; I was obliged to reimburse the hotel. These are the contretemps that can happen to a traveler.

Evenings are cold now, and I carry only a sweater, tropical jacket, and blanket for warmth. In these garments I look perhaps akin to the Iranians.

By bus to Herat, Sunday, October 29

I arose at four to make one more try at entering the Imam's shrine; however, attendants turned me back. The bus going to Jusif-

Abad on the Afghan border was loaded to capacity with passengers, baggage, and mail, including my two suitcases on top, which held the binoculars and typewriter—both saved from the fate of my camera by good luck. The veteran bus rumbled over the uneven gravel road, and five hours later we bumped into the Iranian border station, where passport control and customs exacted much time. The agents try to enhance their importance by taking as long as possible to perform their duties.

Aboard was a Swiss student, who sat next to me. We were asked to get off the bus, leaving the remaining passengers and our baggage to vanish for two hours and we adrift at the post. Our lunch consisted of hard-boiled eggs, bread, and pomegranate. When the bus reappeared, we readied to leave for Islam-Kalah just over the border. There two cars from Germany appeared and the Swiss accepted a ride. I did not meet him again, though we were taking the same route.

The road between the two border stations was grim. The Afghans did not make a friendly impression, and unexpectedly asked for my vaccination paper. I had it with me—a contretemps avoided. After all was checked again, we switched buses and, after an hour's wait, departed for Herat. The trip from Mashad was but a taste of affairs on this leg of the trip, which will never be forgotten. There was nothing resembling a bridge across the occasional dry river bed, and the dust we kicked up came in the many broken windows, also the cold wind after sunset. The Afghans are inured to this discomfort and only wrap their turbans more tightly around their faces. I learned to substitute a towel, but nothing could keep the fine particles out of my eyes, which were soon aching. We stopped in the desert a bit before sunset and again after it for evening prayers. The devout Muslim prays five times a day. He performs ablutions with water, although earth may serve if water is absent, as I presume it was in this case.

These five hours of unmitigated discomfort were relieved when the lights of Herat came to view and we pulled up to Government Hotel. The food offered at that hour was soft boiled eggs, bread, and tea.

Another Swiss was at the hotel, a friend of the first. He said they had driven an old Plymouth to Tehran and sold it for $400, but subsequently they had a disagreement and separated.

By bus to Ferol, Monday, October 30

Herat is an ancient city that stood on the caravan routes across Asia. Alexander was here. The regular main street is bordered by cypress trees. Small water courses serve to wet down the area in summer and carry away householders' sweepings. The massive old walls, houses, and citadel are all the same clay color as the land, which is fertile when watered. In this season things appear more dead than otherwise.

I was given a guide to take me to the police station to register; then collected my baggage before connecting with the Kandahar bus. As it was late, I could secure only a third-class seat above the wheels in the last row. We were loaded with people and bulky parcels. A single woman passenger wearing the *chadoor* accompanied us. Space was cramped where I sat, resulting in little arguments with my neighbors. At first the Afghan next to me attempted to usurp my place, which had more leg room, being on the aisle. I achieved my purpose there but it left him aggrieved for a while. The men across the aisle looked like marauders who took signals from their apparent leader.

The route is unpaved at present, though the Soviets are providing road building aid. I was told that they are also doing road work in the north near Soviet Armenia. I met a customs official enroute home from Islam-Kalah. He sat in front and assisted me where language was an obstacle. I requested a seat up front when it became available. We stopped for lunch in a village cafe, where two passengers invited me to join them. In this country people eat with their fingers, a prediction of India. One of my table companions carried a pistol; he spoke some English.

The dismal trek continued until we fetched Ferol in the evening. I was given tea and bread in the poor little inn, where my bed felt like a pile of rocks.

By bus to Kandahar, Tuesday, October 31

Still feeling droopy this morning. The same bus continued on but left later in the morning. Today's trip brought more of the same, although a front seat became vacant and I moved up, where the ride improved. Still, every part of me ached and I could hardly keep my eyes open for the fine particles of dust blowing into them. Kandahar appeared in the evening, where Mr. Ardil, the customs officer, took me to Government Hotel in a tonga, the two-wheeled horse drawn cart common in India. I tumbled into the cot bed after nothing more than tea because I was suffering.

Kandahar, Wednesday, November 1

I decided to break the journey in Kandahar to recover from a stomach complaint that kept me in bed until noon. Then a bath and clean clothes made me feel better, but not entirely well. Mr. Ardil had gone on, leaving me without an interpreter. I spoke to a man in the hotel dining room, Mr. Bahary, who worked for the UN Special Fund and was going to Kabul. After I had told him a little about the bus trip, he suggested that I complete the trip to Kabul by plane. The fare is 560 afghanis, or $16, which had a certain allure in spite of my vow to travel overland. I told Mr. Bahary that my cash was very low and would remain so until I reached Delhi. Then the good man offered to pay 200 afghanis for me and I accepted. He went to Ariana Afghan Airlines to purchase my ticket. Then he hired a tonga and took me on a tour of the town; later we saw the Forty Stairs at sunset. The visitor may ascend the hill on these large steps cut into the rock. I did so and saw the view at sunset in spite of still feeling weak. Then we dined together at Government Hotel.

Kabul, Thursday, November 2

The facilities and new construction at Kandahar Airport impressed me. A hotel for 400 airplane passengers is going up, and they told me that in five years this will be a stopping place for international flights; passengers will deplane for Karachi here. I was puzzled because the region around Kandahar is so empty.

The DC-3 was piloted by a Filipino, and as I was speaking to a friend of his, we were introduced. There are a few Filipino workers in Afghanistan. The flight was easy, the terrain below clearly seen at our low altitude. We required an hour and forty minutes to cancel 300 miles of evil roads.

The Kabul may be the only good hotel here and it is expensive. Mr. Bahary brought me to the Maiwand Rest House, where I have been compelled to remain three nights. The room is cabinet size with a single bunk bed. One dirty sheet was provided, so I am using my own bedding. I have not seen a restaurant in the area near the Maiwand. For that reason and because I have very little Afghan money, I dined on grapes and tea in my room. There being no light, I cannot read or write after sundown. At such times the little German transistor is my companion. All-India radio is coming in clear now and they broadcast some English programs including news. This evening I listened to a commentary about family planning. The first time I listened to All-India radio was in Kandahar, when it all but brought tears to my tired eyes.

Kabul, Friday, November 3

Mr. Bahary returned to the rest house to give me a pittance of Pakistani money he had changed for me, then quickly left, causing me to wonder if I had done something to hurt his feelings. I longed to leave Kabul behind and reach Pakistan and India at last; however it was Friday and therefore everything was closed. No plans could be advanced and I could only walk about and wait for tomorrow. There were no good buildings to see within the city, so I trod the dusty streets thinking of Kipling and wild horsemen, of battle in the desert between the British and a host of Afghans protecting their land. The name *Maiwand* commemorates the battle lost by the British, which led to their withdrawal from Afghanistan.

I returned to my room to write letters by candlelight. At these times a cup of my own tea is the only comfort.

There are a number of Russians and Americans in Kabul. The International Cooperation Administration (ICA) runs cars back and forth. Not having talked to these people, I do not know what they do. The buses are Soviet built, as are the trucks.

The dogs of Kabul are a curiosity I shall not forget. There are perhaps thousands and they all bark together at night. The baying begins in one area, slowly at first, and the chorus builds gradually, spreading to other areas until the refrain is joined by all, *par tout*. Subsequently it dies away to a few scattered individuals until the baying stops entirely and all is quiet again. The performance repeats itself twice or thrice each night and sounds devilish, increasing the mystery of this unfamiliar place.

Kabul, Saturday, November 4

The Embassy of India here granted me a visa good for three months. It was agreeable to deal with Indians for the first time. Then I required an Afghani exit visa. After that I stopped at the Tourist Bureau, but it was too late to do any good.

I have questioned several officials about crossing the border into Pakistan while the present dispute between Kabul and Islamabad is going on. They are quarreling over the so-called Pashtoonistan, or Pathan state, which does not exist. This being so, I shall leave and see what transpires at the border. I desired to leave today if possible, but failed to locate a ride as far as Jalalabad. Dejectedly, I returned to the Maiwand Rest House with very little money in my pocket and supped in my room on bread, strawberry jam, two eggs, and tea, using my stove, good friend that it is.

Jalalabad, Sunday, November 5

The prime minister of India, Jawarharlal Nehru, has left on a visit to Britain, the United States, and Mexico, as I learned from Radio Kabul, which broadcasts the news in English. One hundred and forty-two miles separate Kabul from the Pakistani border. Today I fetched Jalalabad, two thirds of the route by shared station wagon taxi. The sinuous route follows the narrow canyon of the Kabul River. They say the stream is to be harnessed for power and irrigation. The volume of water is small at this time.

I secured a room at the Government Hotel, where two German students were staying.

Khyber Pass, Monday, November 6

A small bus picked us up early this morning; there were five of us since two Austrians arrived last evening. The road was new and we passed several camels. The Hindu Kush Mountains are visible to the north, while eastward lie the lesser mountains barring Pakistan and India. Both ranges have accumulated some snow by now.

Our group reached the border at mid-morning and we walked the short distance from Afghan Customs and Immigration over to the Pakistani side. We saw no sign of trouble and no more than the usual number of police and soldiers. The border has been officially closed for two or three weeks.

All of us were very pleased to be in Pakistan, which is to say, a place near and similar to India. We found the officials to be polite and generous with information. We paid a small head tax. Then a taxi carried us to the top of the famous Khyber Pass at Lundi Kotal, where we boarded a waiting train for Peshawar.

The renowned Khyber Pass is known less for its difficulty than for being the passage between Central Asia and the plains of the subcontinent. It is a thirty-mile-long, relatively wide gap in the Hindu Kush Mountains with an average elevation of 3,500 feet.

The rails, which begin at Lundi Kotal, carry passengers to Peshawar through thirty-four tunnels and over many bridges. It is a short train, which perhaps carries fewer travelers now because of the closed border. Nearing its destination, the line emerges suddenly into level country presenting a comparatively verdant face after my weeks of desert travel. Farms and gardens appear well watered in this season, a sight that rapidly improved my outlook. Besides, this was the beginning of the most anticipated phase of my journey. As the train rolled past, I observed signs of former British presence in many things: buildings, cantonments, names, and ways of doing things. Signs are often bilingual. We passed lines of barracks and the university before fetching Peshawar station.

We five travelers located Left Luggage—the same term as in England—then took a tonga to a restaurant, where I ordered an omelet (a reliable item) and toast with mild curry. The tea with milk and sugar was good and was my first experience with the manner of brewing it here. The tea, milk, and sugar are combined in the pot and boiled—perhaps as a health precaution but it also alters the flavor.

The two Austrians, who remained with me, and I were surprised by how well the country looked. People in the street appeared adequately cared for and many were well dressed. Many speak English and the educated know it well.

Deciding not to stay over in Peshawar, we bought tickets on the 7:55 train for Lahore. I was approaching another contretemps involving ready cash and it was important that I get to Delhi quickly.

We learned that trains in this country make use of five classes, namely air conditioned, first, second, interclass and third class. We were advised to travel interclass because it offered berths. Also, we were told how the seat reservation scheme operates because official booking is found solely in the upper classes. We made arrangements with an entrepreneur at the station to have three boys place themselves in three sleeping places—mere shelves without bedding—as soon as the train was open. Thus our places would be held for us. This valuable accommodation cost a modest amount for the organizer and his men, each of whom we paid directly just to avoid bookkeeping.

Now we were free to sightsee. The variety of humanity in the streets is entrancing. Here in the Northwest Frontier country several tribes and ethnic groups converge—Pakistanis, Pathans, Afghans, Sikhs, and others. The bazaar was also absorbing to observe as it contained a large variety of goods, merchants, and patrons as well as pack animals.

As train time approached we ate some kebabs before returning to the station and claiming our places. Passengers arriving late stretched out on the floor or squatted all night while we rolled east toward Lahore and India.

Lahore, Tuesday, November 7

We fetched Lahore's humming station in time for breakfast in the first-class restaurant. I enjoyed a full English table served by a waiter bedizened in white uniform, with red turban and sash. It felt somewhat as if I were dining with a maharajah. Then the two Austrians went their way while I took a tonga to the Hotel Lahore, a large guest house on McLeod Street. Bedding is not included in the basic tariff but can be rented. I used my own and will continue to do so throughout India. The ordinary traveler carries a bedroll like an extra suitcase and is prepared to stretch out not only at lodgings but on trains, on station platforms, or in waiting rooms. Trips can be very long and so can waits between trains.

I took a much needed shower bath in a stall with a cold-water faucet and a cup on a chain. I left my dust-laden clothes at the laundry, then set out. Lahore is Pakistan's second largest city and the most interesting. Congestion fills every street. Pedestrians, bicycles, tongas, cycle rickshaws, and small trucks occupy the roadways. I found myself on the Mall facing American Express and felt the urge to enter if only to see how it felt. I thought of a question to ask: How long would it take a letter to be forwarded from the Delhi office? This was my hoped-for remittance from home, and the reply was "long." I abandoned the idea and with it any hope of lingering in Pakistan. There is a notable group of Moghul buildings here that I missed entirely.

The afternoon passed in aimless wandering and gaping at the street scene. A mild odor permeated the air but I did not find it unpleasant. Many buildings appeared more or less decrepit. Small vendors abounded. There were few beggars.

At home I had known a student from Lahore, and with the help of a local citizen I attempted to call him, without success. Then the YMCA turned up in my path and I entered, finding tea and pastry set out. The surroundings were typical of Y's at home, which amused me. Tired out after the continuous walking, I returned to the Hotel Lahore.

Lahore, Wednesday, November 8

I was compelled by the state of my finances to seek out the U.S. consulate in Lahore and petition it for a small loan. After explaining my case to the man across the desk, he gave me fifty rupees (Rs)—approximately $10. This was my first experience of the kind and I was glad to find him sympathetic because otherwise I would have been forced to sell a piece of my equipment.

I visited the Central Museum quartered in a large Victorian building. The guidebook calls it the best collection of Indian sculpture, rugs, textiles, manuscripts, arms, and Islamic arts in the country. The Ghandaran period of Greek-influenced images of the Buddha is well represented. Rudyard Kipling's father was the first curator of this museum and is a character in the novel *Kim*.

After lunch I boarded the little train that took me to India. I felt relieved to be aboard though it was similar to riding in a cattle car—not because it was crowded, but because it was so bare. The two countries have very strained relations and I attributed the poor rail cars to that cause. We traveled thirty miles, crawling all the way. Although winter is approaching, cultivation continues and many people were at work in the fields we passed. They did not look up at the train but continued to stoop to their task. Then we stopped at the international border and Pakistani officials checked passports on board. The train restarted and we entered India.

Amritsar To
Adam's Bridge

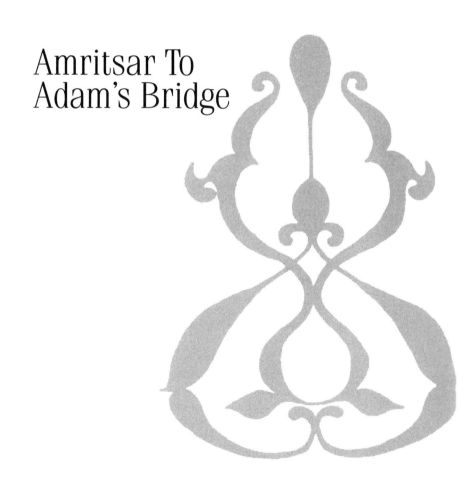

Amritsar and by train to Delhi, Wednesday, November 8

We quickly found ourselves in Amritsar station, where Indian customs and immigration took place. I was the sole European on the train. Then I realized that this was India at last; after all my reading and expectation, it almost felt familiar to be standing on Indian soil and speaking to the khaki-clad officials who used perfect English. I had expected the people to be friendly and was not let down. My visaed passport was stamped—good for three months in India before renewal time.

In the two hours to spare before the Delhi train would leave, I visited the Golden Temple. I had carried my baggage onto the waiting train and occupied a seat, not expecting it would be practical to see the temple as it was dark by now and I had no map or knowledge of how to find it. But then another passenger spoke to me in English and said that his party would take responsibility for my baggage if I wished to hire a cycle rickshaw to take me to the temple, and that is what I did.

The price of the vehicle was prearranged for me and we set off, the driver peddling through darkened streets and alleys. I gripped the sides of the pedicab and wondered at his adeptness in avoiding obstacles—such as a sacred cow we suddenly encountered in the narrow roadway.

Then we fetched the great Sikh shrine. In the darkness of the center city the temple is a brilliant sight, illuminated by numerous small lights and surrounded by a sacred pool, which reflects them. The pilgrim traverses a causeway to gain the temple. I was asked to remove my shoes and socks, dip my feet in water, and wear a hat. The visibility within was poor—the surroundings scarcely perceivable, so I returned outside to admire the overall view. The Golden Temple is exceptional.

This nocturnal probing was an introduction to India. Not wanting to delay, I rejoined my rickshaw *wallah* and we returned through streets still busy. [This ever present humanity is, I came to understand, a characteristic of this overpopulated land.] Back in my place on the waiting train, I was very tired, but I nevertheless saw that India would bring some highly charged experiences. The Frontier Mail departed promptly at 8:30 p.m.—a slice of the India of industry and progress. The two worlds exist in close affiliation.

I was able to find half a seat on which to attempt sleep. The train was uncomfortable and became crowded. There being no Interclass, I had purchased a second-class ticket. We continued to roll across northwest India (Punjab) all night long. Travelers without seats lay down in the aisles or crouched.

Delhi, Thursday, November 9

Just after sunrise we gained Delhi where, true to form, the degraded areas and poverty appeared first. Then we rolled to a stop in the main station. Immediately a great commotion began as the passengers alighted by the most convenient way, often a window. Baggage was passed through the windows to waiting hands. A great chattering accompanied this activity. I chose not to heed the calls of the coolies, all of whom were eager to serve a *sahib*. They gesticulated to me through the window, but I took my time and eventually exited by the normal way and carried my own bags, a great mistake in their view. This crowd of impatient servitors in Indian railway stations is unavoidable and must be coped with by being firm.

Delhi is the main railway junction of the country and India travels by rail. The International YMCA for which I was headed was several miles distant and I fetched it by motorcycle rickshaw. The driver was intent upon receiving the payment that he believed proper from a *sahib* like me. The clothes I wore could not be considered suitable for a rich European, but in his eyes I was still a *sahib* and therefore capable of paying. After a considerable discussion, which I tried my best to keep lighthearted as he spoke fair English, he failed to get his price. At present I am paying people on the same scale that I believe they use with local trade—or just slightly more to keep everyone happy.

The exchange rate is 4.75 rupees to a dollar and the rule of thumb for a foreigner is pay the amount in rupees that equals the dollar price. Therefore a trip that would cost $3 at home would be Rs 3 here, and that is probably more than an Indian would pay. This rate also explains why the drivers are poor and why a *sahib* should pay more.

The International Y is in the heart of New Delhi (a part of Delhi) not far from Connaught Place. I found it to be an ideal place for me and most congenial. The guests are of many nationalities. My suite of two rooms and separate bath contains five bunk beds with sheets. I am sharing it with a young Yugoslav, a French fellow, and two New Zealanders. When they left, some Filipinos and a German replaced them. Every morning the bearer brings a cup of tea for me to wake up by, then shines my shoes as I dress. The ground level room faces several tennis courts, where every morning office workers bat the ball before going to their job. They dress in white and the idea seems quite civilized.

The dining room is inviting and the long tables with white cloths suggest an earlier time when people congregated together and conversed with strangers. I take three meals a day here and pay slightly more than $2 per diem for everything. The dining area is open on the sides and small birds alight in front of the guests, picking up sugar and crumbs a few inches from the plates. It made me wonder if I had met with a kind of Eden.

As I departed to explore the city, I noticed the attractive gardens and landscaping. This part of the city, where the government is located, is open and pleasantly green—suggesting a campus more than the city.

At American Express there was again nothing for me, which meant a new contretemps. I wrote several letters to friends in India informing them of my arrival but not mentioning my plight. For a remedy I placed a classified ad in the *Hindustan Times*, one of the good English-language newspapers, offering to sell my binoculars, which I hoped someone would pay well for. I received only one reply, which came to nothing.

I visited the Tourist Department and found them supplied with free literature of high quality. Therefore I selected copies of nearly every title—a round dozen, which made it less important to purchase an all-India guide such as Murray's.

After the midday meal at the Y—they serve western style cuisine—I boarded a city bus for Old Delhi and the Red Fort. The Lal Qila is a Moghul complex begun by Shah Jehan. He wished to move his capital from Agra to Delhi, which he named Shahjehanabad. Construction began in 1639. Within the red sandstone walls the Shah established his sumptuous residence, halls of audience, a mosque, baths, and troops' quarters, as well as gardens of great beauty.

The Moghul rulers were cruel and bloodthirsty at times as well as being civilized creators of beautiful art and architecture. For example, one of the Shah Jehan's own works (Agra Fort) became his jail when his son Aurangzeb deposed him. The red walls face the Yamuna River for more than a mile. As visitors are permitted to wander freely through the complex, I could enjoy everything without being hurried along. The ambience here is different from that of a European palace, which displays a different luxury, one intended not so much to serve the owners as to display their power and wealth. In a European palace the owners withdraw into smaller apartments for living. In a Moghul palace, though luxurious, the spirit of the place is more amenable to daily enjoyment; the inscription on the wall of the Divan-i-Khas (Hall of Private Audience) is indicative of this spirit:

"If there is a paradise on earth it is this, it is this."

The Peacock Throne once stood here as well, and it lives on in descriptions. The imitation in Tehran is a shadow of the original, which was carried off to Iran by Nadir Shah in 1739. The Divan-i-Khas is in white marble enhanced by *pietra dura* (semiprecious stone inlay) as is the Taj Mahal.

The Divan-i-Am (Hall of Public Audience) is less rich; it possesses sixty red sandstone pillars, which support a lofty flat roof. The Moti Masjid (Pearl Mosque) is in marble. Nearby are the baths and the Khas Mahal—private palace of the emperor.

As I left the Red Fort, a bearded man wearing a white dhoti—a male garment related to the sari—approached and desired to reveal my fortune. To persuade me to accept he had framed letters from former subjects. I expressed a slight interest and from then on it was difficult to avoid him, although I felt like a sucker. He told me to write down the essence of his predictions and so I did. I thought it remarkable that a wandering fortune-teller spoke fair English. When he had finished I saw no resemblance to myself in his fortune tale. He said I would be a "government minister," recognizable as an Indian concept of good fortune.

There were very few beggars in front of the Red Fort. I expect the government clears them away from places tourists visit.

Delhi, Friday, November 10

Delhi's broad extension includes, it is said, eight different historical cores. The Muslim period begins with the Qutub Minar complex, which is found nine miles south of the present Delhi. The first Muslim rulers founded their capital here in the thirteenth century and built the Qutub Minar (Tower of Victory) which still stands. I thought it a beautiful object, overlaid with colorful tiles, breathing the spirit of Islamic architecture. It has five tiers with a balcony at each stage. It is 238 feet high and tapers from a broad base to a much narrower top. Three hundred and seventy-six steps lead to the summit, where the view is said to be grand. I did not have the strength to face the climb and regret it now. The decoration is fluting and inscribed quotations from the Koran. The Qutub Minar made a lasting impression on me.

The Iron Pillar, a few steps distant, is surprising in another way. The twenty-four-foot-high column has remained free of rust for a very long time since it dates from the fifth century. No one understands how the surface remains smooth and free of corrosion. A legend says that if, standing with your back to the pillar, you can reach around and touch your fingers, any wish you make will come true.

I observed workers in the area who have accomplished much in the way of cleaning up the ground and planting it to make the place an archaeological park with walks and flowers. Other ruins scatter the area, one of which is the Quwwat-ul-Islam Mosque—the first Muslim building in India, as it is claimed.

The weather now is agreeably warm during the day, becoming almost hot at midday. It is the postmonsoon season in Delhi, a period extending through October and November in which weather is comfortably fall-like and brings on winter. The cold season extends from the last week in November to mid-February. Average daily minimum temperature is 52 degrees F (maximum 70 degrees). Then follows a steady increase in temperature. By mid-March summer begins; it persists until the end of June bringing frequent squalls and thunderstorms, along with mounting temperatures (averaging 97 degrees F). The monsoon season of rain-bearing winds follows and humidity grows and becomes oppressive. The air currents are off the ocean and the average monsoon brings twenty-five inches of rain before ending in late September. Except in monsoon season, the air in Delhi remains mostly dry throughout the year. Very low humidity prevails from April to June.

Delhi, Saturday, November 11

I accompanied a young French traveler on a visit to the Raj Ghat, which marks the site of Ghandi's cremation in 1948. It is a simple masonry platform surmounted by a marker. An ornamental railing is being constructed around the memorial and there is also a Ghandi museum. With other pilgrims we removed our shoes before walking up to the marker, where people sit for a while if they wish.

After this we saw the nearby Jami Masjid (Friday Mosque), built by Shah Jehan. He intended it as the principal mosque of Shahjehanabad. It is a noble red sandstone building with two minarets and a large gateway. The whole is constructed atop a masonry platform 325 feet on a side. The unusual colonnaded cloister on three sides is for ablutions. This mosque is across from the Red Fort and there is not a larger one in the country. It can hold 25,000 people.

One side of the mosque is occupied by small dealers of every variety of old metal object—from nails to complete machines. Everything is rusty and arranged in rough order around the individual sellers. This market touches on the mosque platform. Everything has value for someone, and whatever the service or object, there is a market or supplier for each. One can purchase a rusty nail or a second-hand toothbrush.

A walk around to the opposite side of the Jami Masjid brings a complete change—to a well-arranged city park with green grass and a monument to King George V atop a pedestal. It was provided by the contributions of his Indian subjects, rich and poor, who erected it for his 1911 visit and Durbar in which he proclaimed Delhi the new capital of India, succeeding Calcutta.

This large and fast-growing city (with a population of 2,350,000 in 1961) covers a vast area. A greenbelt separates the city proper from the *nagars* (more recent settlements) and the villages that have always been there. Gardens, grazing space, wild vegetation, and jumbles of ruins occupy the areas between *nagars* and villages. A few Muslim tombs add picturesqueness. This great expanse is knit together by the erratic buses of the Delhi Transportation Undertaking (D.T.U.), which people nickname "Don't Trust Us," and by tongas, taxis, trucks, bicycles, bicycle rickshaws, and a few bullock carts. It adds up to much delay in moving about.

Delhi, Sunday, November 12

After many weeks' absence from church, I attended services at the nearby YWCA this morning. Sunday is a day of rest in Indian cities, although there is no religious significance in it for non-Christians.

The Jantar Mantar, which I also visited, is a strange group of salmon-colored masonry structures that have astronomical purposes. They begin with a large sundial, but include more. The complex makes a unique public park.

In the afternoon I visited or observed the exterior of several government buildings: Parliament, Central Secretariat, Rashtrapati Bhavan (President's House), and the Prime Minister's residence. Parliament is a modern circular building with an exterior colonnade. I joined a group of Indians who were being guided through it. We were shown both houses—the lower Lok Sabha and the upper Rajya Sabha—as well as the Central Hall. The streets in this section of the city radiate like a wheel and recall Washington, D.C. From Nehru's house I followed Wellington Crescent back to the Y and noticed that I was in the greenbelt demarcating the city from the countryside.

Delhi, Monday, November 13

Tomorrow a large-scale industrial exposition will open in Delhi. I stopped at the site this morning to look around and found only a few pavilions completed. The area was scattered with building materials and hundreds of leisurely working men and a few women. It did not seem that they would be ready to open before a week or longer; somehow they achieved a miracle and opened a part of the fair on time. The vice president, Mr. Radaskrishnan, inaugurated it. He is the same person who visited Cleveland several years ago and delivered a speech, which I heard. The last fair of this kind was in 1956, and this one is twice the size of the other, filling many acres. All the important Indian industries and government agencies are present. Many other nations are also bringing products for exposition.

I hired a motor scooter rickshaw, my accustomed transportation in Delhi, and buzzed down to the Purana Qila (Old Fort). It is on the site of the original city of Delhi. The fort, of massive construction, was later. Near here is the tomb of Humayun, the second Moghul ruler of India. His widow built his resting place, which is a proto-Taj Mahal dating 100 years earlier, 1565. The resemblance can be observed in the bulbous dome and the arched entrances. Both structures are surrounded by quiet Moghul gardens. Red and white sandstone, and black and yellow marble are the building materials. The emperor was in his library, which occupied the red sandstone tower nearby, when he slipped in hurrying down the stairs in response to the prayer call and fell to his death.

A gentle rain was falling, the first shower seen since it rained once in Italy.

Today my friend J.C. Desai telephoned me at the Y in response to my letter. He was in Delhi on business and came to the Y after lunch, when we made arrangements to meet again later. I visited American Express once more seeking my remittance and then wrote some urgent letters. A wire I sent was never answered. I don't know what is going on—a most vexing contretemps.

J.C. returned to the Y and we went to his office in Janpath Street. Then we visited a coffee house cum night club—I could not understand which—and talked under the dim lights as we drank tea and ate pastry. Partial prohibition exists in Delhi; therefore liquor is not served in public places. J.C. took me to the Handicrafts Emporium in Janpath Street. It is a department store for tourists and I found the quality and design to be excellent and the prices very reasonable when converted to dollars. The store offers products from many parts of the country and much beautiful and specialized hand-work in textiles, embroidery, hand-blocked fabrics, wood carving, metalwork, ivory, jewelry, leather, pottery, and marble—every variety of handicraft.

Delhi, Tuesday, November 14

The YMCA secretary asked me to find another place to stay because my bed was needed for a delegate to the World Council of Churches beginning on Sunday, five days off. Participants are already arriving and finding a hotel is tricky because of the several events taking place this month in Delhi. Also, I have been unable to pay my bill at the Y; however, the secretary said I might pay after leaving. This proposal I could only resist, and eventually I remained where I was until leaving Delhi.

The nearby Lakshmi Narayan Temple drew me as one Hindu temple that a non-non-Hindu may enter. Donated by a wealthy industrialist, Birla, it is of recent date (1938), and is architecturally undistinguished. Attached to it is a free hostel, where it was suggested I might stay.

One can see cattle and water buffalo roaming in the city. On most mornings I see a big black buffalo near the Y. Buffalo provide rich milk, transportation, and fuel for the cooking fire. Often the house crow is seen perching on the beast's back eating insect parasites.

Today I examined the collections of sculpture and miniature painting in the newly opened National Museum on Janpath Street. Other collections were not yet on display.

Distances are often given in furlongs here; a furlong equals 660 feet, or 220 yards. The unit of weight is the *seer*—about two pounds. New metric measures are being introduced and the old anna of sixteen pice is being replaced by nia pice—one hundred to the rupee.

The Indian Foreign Relations Council has a free public library in Sapru House, where I remained several hours this afternoon. The books on India are very helpful to a visitor. The same group also sponsors performances of Indian classical dance and music. On my leaving, a young man spoke to me and we walked together as far as Connaught Place.

I have been asked personal questions by the younger generation, and I believe they are repeating phrases they learned in school. They ask questions about religion as well that tend to put one on the spot.

This evening after dinner I saw an American movie with Hindi subtitles.

Delhi, Wednesday, November 15

The day was devoted to reading at Sapru House. It has periodicals and newspapers: the *Hindustan Times*, the *Statesman*, and the *Times of India* are very good English-language daily papers and serve an important need in this multi-language nation. I would say these newspapers are comparable with the best of their kind in Europe and the United States.

Later I visited K.S. Venkataraman, a meteorologist at Safdarjung Airport, and his wife. His brother, Dr. K.S. Visvanathan, a teacher of chemistry at Banaras Hindu University, was a friend whom I had met when he was at Case Institute in Cleveland. The Venkataramans, who are Tamils from Madras, served tea and good-tasting side dishes. They were carefully prepared and attractively served by Mrs. V. wearing a print sari. The government provides their bungalow situated near the airport. (The word *bungalow* is Bengali in origin and signifies a small house.) This was the first Indian home I visited. I found it to be plainly furnished in European style with very little wall decoration; on a large expanse of whitewashed plaster I could see interesting lizards moving about and eating insects. Everything was clean and uncluttered, while the hospitality was warm and genuine.

Delhi, Thursday, November 16

My French roommate and I visited the Industrial Fair this evening. The U.S. component had the theme: Industry in the Service of Man. The Soviet component included a measure of propaganda as well as industry and offered a stall selling publications in English, where I found several for travel reading. Among these were some short stories written by an Indian Communist, Mulk Rau Anand, which were good reading. Exhibits are present from East Germany, Viet Nam, and Rumania.

New Delhi, Friday, November 17

Cause for celebration! Today an insurance dividend check arrived. It caught up with me after having been sent to Athens. Now I can leave Delhi to begin my grand tour of the country feeling a good deal more confident.

At the government information center for press and radio, I purchased a set of government-produced postcards in color and had a talk with the manager. I depend on postcards in place of a camera. I was destined to find few for sale in India. Anyway, I no longer had a camera—it was lost in Mashad. However, this was a minor contretemps. The tourist information office also offered free postcards, illustrated pamphlets (many about handicrafts), and guides to noted places.

My friend Rama Rao met me in his old Anglia and we drove to his home in one of the outlying *nagars* for lunch. We had known each other for a long time in Cleveland when he was at Case Institute, and both of us were members and regular attendees of the International Students Group of the Cleveland Council on World Affairs. We were co-founders of the Inter-Cultural Forum, which met often for discussions led by foreign students.

Rao is an engineer from Hyderabad. The vegetarian repast was excellent. I was given eating utensils while the Rao family used fingers and *chapatti* (flat wheat bread). Mrs. Rao served the five people at the table including a son-in-law and two half-grown children. Everyone spoke good English, a proficiency that is characteristic of educated South Indians. Our meal was leisurely. After it we moved to the living room for coffee, conversation, and picture taking. The family is preparing to move to Ahmedabad next week, as Rao is changing his job. Their furniture will be sold before departing as shipping it 800 miles is out of the question.

Later, all of us attended the Industrial Exposition. The son-in-law, who lives in Hyderabad, has come to Delhi to tend to the exhibit by Andhra Pradesh, his state. This evening we looked at an endless number of exhibits of Indian industries. I was informed of the progress taking place in developing new industry. Many goods and services are being fabricated already, including autos, buses, typewriters, and railroad equipment. Consumer items, however, are scarce and expensive.

Suddenly, we encountered J.C. Desai standing under an oil rig from Rumania. Rao had also known J.C. in Cleveland and had not seen him since both of us bade him farewell at the Cleveland bus terminal as he left for home.

New Delhi, Saturday, November 18
J.C. and I, using his company car, attempted to find an Indian student whom we had known in Cleveland. In what we thought to be the right area, we not only looked for the address ourselves but asked others in the street to direct us. None could help us, not even the local post office, so we abandoned the search.

We had a Sikh driver. Traffic holds to the left. Three automobiles are being produced here—Fiat, Ambassador, and Standard. There are very few imported models on the road and nearly every car to be seen is one of the above or an ancient model. There is talk of manufacturing a "People's Car," the price of which has been rising steadily.

Following lunch, J.C. and I returned to the exposition, where we devoted more of the afternoon to the Indian exhibits. Again the handicrafts were of very good quality and attractive in design. India hopes to develop her cottage industries and maintain their present high quality while at the same time emphasizing modern industry. At the individual state exhibits, handicrafts occupy an important place. I was given a demonstration of the perfumes of India, which have an oil base and pleasing scent.

This evening at the Y the archbishop of Canterbury, Michael Ramsey, and the evangelist Billy Graham spoke from the same podium beneath a *shamiana* (colorful canvas shelter) erected on the lawn. Both notables are here for the World Council of Churches. The archbishop delivered his talk first, on the subject of the foot washing and humility. Then Mr. Graham spoke about the YMCA and its founding. The two men shook hands somewhat stiffly and the archbishop jumped down into the small assembly of possibly 200 listeners.

An Indian chap in my room, who had come here from the south expressly for the council, handed each speaker a manuscript which, he told me, God had inspired him to write on India's mission in the world. He also gave me a copy of one of his writings, although I could not comprehend it. His ideas seemed foggy.

Delhi, Sunday, November 19

The opening convocation of the World Council of Churches took place this morning behind the Vidya Bhavan (Hall of Wisdom) under the protection of a very large *shamiana* in colors. It was highlighted by a splendid procession of the delegates filing into their places at the front of the assembly. I was seated under the canvas in a good position for a view of the procession as it passed no more than a few feet away. The dignitaries made an impressive sight in their ecclesiastical robes carrying their banners and symbols of office. Following the worship service, they marched out again before the guests. I would not venture to guess the number, although by all appearances it was in the hundreds.

[The WCC was founded in 1948. Approximately 250 churches are members, including the Eastern Orthodox and the Anglican, representing many nations on every continent. Every five or six years they assemble somewhere in the world. The present gathering in Delhi marked the beginning of greater participation by Asian and African churches in the council. It was also the beginning of participation by churches in the Soviet orbit. Though the Roman Catholic Church is not a member, it cooperates with the council in some activities of which mutual help, education, international peace, social and interracial justice, and communication are important components.]

Later today I visited the Lodi Tombs and their gardens. Three mausoleums are included in the area; one is a proto-Taj Mahal of a type still earlier than Humayun's resting place. Subsequently the Safdarjung tomb attracted my attention. The Muslim tombs I have seen possess an articulate quality which I think is satisfying to an observer familiar with Western tomb architecture. I am reminded of Ahlat in eastern Turkey. Safdarjung's tomb is a large building standing on a high terrace surrounded by gardens. The roof affords a wide view of the environs including the small airport. The presence of gardens surrounding a tomb suggests continuity—and meaning beyond death.

Delhi, Monday, November 20

This is the final day of this visit to Delhi. I expect to return toward the end of my journey. Today I visited Delhi University and the Civil Lines, by the D.T.U. busline. An Indian student escorted me through the campus and invited me for coffee. The school faces the open country on the limits of the city. It seems a small place. On my return I stopped to see St. James Church, built by a man named Skinner on a vow when he was injured in battle. It is about 150 years old, very peaceful and encompassed by a park. Many of the wall plaques are dedicated to Englishmen who died in India.

Finally I walked through the systematized ruins of Feroz Shah Kotlah. It was the fifth of the eight historical cores of Delhi, named Ferozabad, and is situated between Old and New Delhi. One of Emperor Ashoka's pillars inscribed with his edicts stands here.

I talked with two German travelers staying at the Y who arrived in a VW bus camper equipped for sleeping and eating. One of them gave me the names of a few common birds of India. Some species live in close company with people and animals. Besides the small birds noticed at the Y, who like sugar, there is the Indian parakeet, a green bird with long tail. He is considerably larger than our domestic pet. As we spoke, a large bird called the pariah kite descended to pick something off the ground; his wingspan was more than two feet. Many Indian birds have bright plumage.

I stopped at the luxury Ashoka Hotel to see the handicraft shops it contains. Near here is the diplomatic enclave and new U.S. embassy. I saw it from the outside only.

This evening I was invited to dine with Mr. Venkataraman and his family. I learned some of the elementary principles of Indian cooking, as well as the names of dishes that Mrs. V. served to us. Then I returned to the Y, which I have grown to enjoy and shall probably miss. It's the only place where I was served a cup of tea in bed in the morning.

Agra, Tuesday, November 21

I have enjoyed my stay in Delhi and I am now ready to depart on a tour of the country and encounters with more of the people. Today I began my tour with a first visit to India's architectural *ne plus ultra*, the Taj Mahal. Rama Rao invited me to accompany him and his son Krishnan in their English Anglia because Agra is on the way to their new post in Ahmedabad. Our driver was a Sikh provided by the Automobile Association. Once the last *nagar* was out of sight we were in mainly rural country, although small industries appeared at intervals along the route. We passed villages off to the side and could see cattle, water buffalo, and people engaged in diverse agriculture. The road carried bullock carts, tongas, pedestrians, bicycles, and some motor traffic. Occasionally we passed between venerable banyan trees whose overarching branches drop aerial roots overhead. There were frequent watering places harboring water buffalo immersed up to the nose in their element.

We passed Mathura, birthplace of the Lord Krishna 3,500 years ago. It is a pilgrimage place with a museum of sculpture. A bit north is Brindavan where the boy god played games with the milk maids.

As we jolted over rough pavement, our car-top carrier lost its moorings and slid forward, but we came to a safe halt. Then the Sikh chauffeur took charge and everyone got busy looking for pieces and after reassembling humpty dumpty we were on our way none the worse for this contretemps. This experience with a Sikh [and others I met later] led me to respect them increasingly for their abilities and good will. They are frequently in mechanical, transport, and military as well as professional and business positions. I find them friendly, open people.

We saw many birds because the subcontinent is a brilliant home to more than 2,000 species and subspecies. Many are large and colorful, such as hornbills, serpent eagles, fishing owls, peacocks (the national bird), herons, ibises, storks, cranes, kites, hawks, vultures, geese, and pelicans. India also has many wildlife parks and sanctuaries.

A few miles before Agra we passed Sikandra, where the Moghul emperor Akbar's large mausoleum looms up. No one in our party mentioned it. Could it be that my friend did not know about it? I said nothing.

In Agra we dined at a small restaurant where we were served a vegetarian meal at a bare table; the walls were decorated with calendar art, mainly Hindu deities. Washing facilities were in the dining room and consisted of a sink without plumbing, a bucket of water, soap, and common towel. No printed menu appeared and everyone ate the same thing. The waiter served rice, *dahl* (similar to lentils), *chappatis*, curds (yogurt), and chutney into metal *thali* dishes. These are large trays with compartments or separate matching bowls for each portion. The seasoning was almost more than I could take—very hot.

Rao and Krishnan continued on to Gwalior tonight and I found the government tourist bungalow. While I was registering, three tourists from Thailand arrived—a man and two women. Only two rooms were available, so we two men shared a room. Each had a *charpoy*, the roped or taped cot common here. The room had a high ceiling and thick walls without decoration. A large fan hung from above, but the temperature did not require it.

My new *compagnon de voyage* was Mr. Kraikarnchana from Bangkok, who was accompanied by two younger women. While the latter said they would join us later, we two men set out to find the Taj, first by cycle rickshaw. When progress was slow we attempted to take the local bus, but the wait appeared interminable and we felt stymied. Thereupon two young men came along to wait also and assured us that patience would pay off and a conveyance was coming. They were teachers from Agra and spoke English well, providing information and company which alleviated the contretemps.

In time a loaded bus stopped for us, and a bit later it deposited us outside the gateway to the Taj where we followed the crowd to the gate. The grounds around are surrounded by a high red sandstone wall so that you cannot see the Taj until you have passed the portal. It was four o'clock as we entered, turned right, and stood before the unsurpassed emblem of love and of India. There I paused, endeavoring perhaps to remember this first impression. Here was the familiar postcard viewpoint of the Taj. Then the figures moved and I knew that it was real and that I had fetched my destination. I was grateful.

The four of us moved down the stairway to the garden plane and reflecting pool, to put ourselves into the scene. The person honored here is the wife of Shah Jehan, who reigned from 1627 to 1658. Her name was Arjunand Bānū Begam, better known as Mumtaz Mahal (Lady of the Palace). She died giving birth to their fourteenth child. A council of architects from India, Persia, Central Asia, and beyond formulated the design for her mausoleum, which required twenty-two years to build. Italian artisans and others contributed their skills in working the marble and *pietra dura*. The similarities with earlier buildings in India and elsewhere are clear. The Safavid Persian influence can be seen in the bulbous dome, lofty gateways, and overall decoration.

As the afternoon grew shorter and the light changed we walked in the garden among palms, poinsettia, canna flowers, and bougain-villea, always glimpsing the noble Taj through the greenery. The changing daylight caused the marble to change chromaticity and translucence. The image in the reflecting pool also changed.

Then the two Thai women found us, and our Indian acquaintances departed. Together we visitors ascended the platform on which the Taj rests, then mounted the marble plinth of the building itself and entered the dome chamber. Directly beneath the center is the marble cenotaph of the queen and next to it that of the Shah, both surrounded by a richly worked marble screen. The walls of this octagonal chamber consist of incised marble screens, which admit a most heavenly light. The surfaces are embellished with *pietra dura*, semiprecious stones inlaid in floral designs so accurately cut that the fit is perfect. As we continued studying the ensemble and the way it conforms to an integrated plan, we could better appreciate the architect's intentions. He wanted a complete concept that does not allow anything to be added or taken away. Therefore, beginning with the marble centerpiece and moving outward, the Taj is oriented to the cardinal points of the compass. North is the Yamuna River. South is the monumental gateway by which we entered. East is the mosque facing the paramount building, and west is the *jawab* (answer), which duplicates the mosque opposite. These two identical-appearing structures are therefore joined visually while the broad sandstone terrace that supports all these structures joins them physically. The lateral components are in red sandstone with white marble embellishments. The long axis of the reflecting pool extends the visual connection between the north and south. The compound is

surrounded by a high, red sandstone wall with corner turrets surmounted by cupolas.

We remained until darkness. After visiting the tomb chamber,
where the two personages lie directly beneath the dome chamber,
we returned to the garden for more Taj gazing prior to leaving to
find something to eat.

Fatehpur Sikri, Wednesday, November 22

Agra and vicinity contain full many remarkable sights because
this was the Moghul capital before Delhi. This morning the three
Thais and I visited another notable place by bus, the ghost town of
Fatehpur Sikri, now a great attraction for tourists. The rural life to
be seen in passing was pleasing. Here and there the new crop of red
peppers covered the ground, carpet-like, to dry in the sun.

We got down at our destination to find we faced the Buland
Darwaza (Gate of Victory). Akbar the Great, who built Fatehpur, intended to make the monumental gate to commemorate a military
victory. It is part of the Jami Masjid and also symbolizes the climb
up and out of this world into the realm of religion. The worshiper
mounts a broad, and steep stairway before passing through the fifty-
four-foot-high gateway and entering the harmonious courtyard of
the mosque. Here you see a *mélange* of Muslim and Hindu forms
because Akbar advocated eclecticism in art and religion. It could be
said that he was an earlier, Indian version of Martin Luther King
because he had a dream that Hindu and Muslim India could live in
harmony. He had a Hindu wife and studied other religions. His studies led him to formulate a new "world religion." It did not go far; you
never hear about it. The courtyard contains the tomb of the Muslim
saint who predicted the birth of the emperor's first son and heir, the
future Jahangir. It is protected by white marble latticework and a
cupola. Many women pray here for a son, but I do not know if they
are of both faiths.

Before visiting the other buildings connected with the administration and court, we took a guide. There was so much to see that
we might have omitted much if we had been on our own. We were
introduced to the important halls, chambers, residences and harem,
as well as places serving the administration of Akbar: audience
chambers, treasury, mint, and records office. The Palace of the
Winds amused us because it served the court ladies as a place
where they could be protected behind pierced stone screens while
watching happenings in the streets below.

Fatehpur Sikri is uncommon if it is anything and made me re-call the Alhambra in Spain. The important difference is the absence of water here; there are no fountains or rivulets of fresh water in the pavement as at Grenada. This lack is said to have caused the city's abandonment after only sixteen years.

Everything is stone in this unusual place. The extensive use of columns and piers to support roof and cupola, and the use of open lattice screens in stone lend a lightness to the buildings. Sandstone is once again the raw material with marble for decoration. The level ridgetop is covered in marble. The result is charming and livable. The Archaeology Survey of India maintains these numerous structures.

Our guide was capable and could have been government trained. Guides everywhere are known to insert odd yarns in their talks, apparent fabrications that are nevertheless entertaining. Ours was one of these.

We returned to the Buland Darwaza and there watched a local daredevil jump from the summit of the gate into a well far below. The sight caused some trepidation.

Upon our return to Agra, the ladies left us and Mr. Kraikarnchana and I went on to visit the fort. Peacock feather fans were sold at the entrance and I purchased one, which served the purposes of comfort and beauty for some time to come.

Agra's fort was the prototype for Delhi's when the Moghul capital was transferred there by Shah Jehan. Both are in red sandstone, facing the Yamuna River, and both enclose fine interiors. Two miles separate the Taj from the fort; they are visible from each other when the observer is facing the Yamuna. Standing on the walls of the fort, I found the scene of the Taj partly veiled by river mist and, while the *dhobis* (laundrymen) worked at their trade below, to be an evocative one.

The Moti-Masjid (Pearl Mosque) in pink marble is situated within the fort. They say the proportions are perfect. A small building, it possesses an enchanting arcaded marble courtyard and decorated marble prayer hall. The mosque and other Moghul structures, large or small, are just like those illustrated in miniature paintings of that period. We explored all—visitors are free to move about unaccompanied.

Inhabiting the fort are many monkeys. A strange scene they make scampering over the walls in the main court. They scale the verticals with the ease of squirrels, as the young cling to mother's underside. You should not stare at them because they do not like it and dart at anyone who does. We had to leave at the closing signal, with some reluctance.

In the tourist bungalow we rejoined the ladies and dined at the Ashoka Hotel before departing again to visit the Taj in the light of the full moon. By two cycle rickshaws the trip needed three-quarters of an hour to do four and a half miles. We enjoyed a bonus: enroute we passed two wedding parties. The bridegroom was dressed in white and mounted on a horse. Musicians and torchbearers led the way to the bride's house, which was illuminated and decorated.

Even by night streets were full of life and activity—pedestrians, dogs, rickshaws, carts. In places there was an unpleasant odor; it was useful to carry a clean handkerchief for breathing.

We remained at the Taj long enough to see it bathed in subtle radiance. The full moon lent the building an insubstantial character, a sense of mystery that was enhanced by wispy mist rising from the river. The evening air grew cool and we wrapped ourselves in our blankets to return to our lodgings. It had been an extraordinary day.

Sikandra and Agra, Thursday, November 23

To honor the preeminent Moghul, Akbar (1542-1605) we all traveled to Sikandra by tonga this morning. He is buried here in his splendid red sandstone and marble mausoleum. You might be asked how such a structure, completed in 1613, has survived so long. One reason could be its situation in a walled garden; another could be the attractiveness of the building itself, which is an inviting stack of cloister-like open areas that overlook the spacious garden in every direction, affording the visitor the opportunity to catch every stirring air current in the hot season. The smallest earth tremor might appear sufficient to bring it all down in a heap; however, it is in excellent preservation and its gardens well tended. Each of the four lateral walls is provided with a large gateway in one of the four architectural styles: Hindu, Muslim, Christian, and Akbar's own new style.

Our tonga *wallah* stopped unbidden at a souvenir seller's, where my companions found one of the miniature marble Taj Mahals to take home with them as a remembrance.

Then we saw the small and delicate mausoleum of Itmad-ud-Daula. The perfection of decoration is gemlike and even more notable perhaps than that of the Taj Mahal because the *pietra dura* is extremely fine and on a smaller scale.

Our last meal together consisted of fried cakes of chick-pea flour (gram), *pukauri* onions, and bananas.

Our last visit to the Taj took place at midday. The bright sun, I thought, deprived it of mystery. We walked in the garden, automatically keeping one eye on the centerpiece. The poinsettias grow to eight feet tall and are now in bloom.

It is said that had Shah Jehan not been deposed by his son Aurangzeb, he planned to erect a second mausoleum in black marble for himself directly opposite the Taj with the Yamuna flowing between. In my opinion it would have taken away from the Taj as it stands, alone, a tribute to love and womankind.

It was time for the Thais to leave while I waited until evening and the train to Banaras. The station platform was soon filled with waiting passengers. At this time I began to use third class as an economy; the cost was half that of second class and afforded a close look at the people. Among those on the platform were prisoners in chains led by a guard.

After a late-night change of trains at Tundela, I was fortunate to get an empty bench on which I placed my air mattress and there went to sleep.

Banaras, Friday, November 24

From Agra to Banaras was a long journey aboard a jammed rail car, stopping often, never briefly, enabling only fitful rest. I was willing to endure all of this. Somewhere I had been told that third class is the better way to travel and see the people of this great subcontinent.

Uttar Pradesh Province occupies the western Gangetic plain and a part of the Himalayan foothills, where the sacred river Ganga (Ganges) emerges. Most of the area is flat and low lying and the train passes a constant succession of mud-built villages, which appeared as the sun rose. Then I could see the first morning activities of the people and animals, some heeding the call of nature—no bathrooms here. There were cattle, water buffalo, bullocks, but no horses. People, young and old, and animals were operating water-raising equipment and drawing loads; women gracefully carried large water jars on their heads.

At stations before the train came to a stop the activity was underway. The inevitable *Chai wallahs* (tea sellers) raced along under the windows of the slowing train crying, "*Chai, chai, do anna.*" They serve a brew of black tea, milk, and sugar in cups which they rinsed in pails of water after use. Then come the vendors of such food as peanuts, offering newspaper cones of unshelled nuts for pennies, to passengers who lean from the windows, accompanied by steady chatter. I saw the ever present *sadhus* (holy men), who are nearly naked, their bodies covered with streaks of dye and wood ashes. They carry the long staff of a pilgrim and travel regularly to the many pilgrimage places which dot the country.

The rail line passes the city of Allahabad where the Yamuna River joins the Ganga at the *sangam* (confluence), famous for its annual *mela* (festival). Every twelve years the Kumbh Mela is celebrated in this place. It is likely the largest religious festival anywhere, when a million faithful gather for a holy dip in the Ganga. The river is wide and shallow here.

We fetched Banaras, where more windows on India were opened. Varanasi is the new (actually old—now restored) name of the city and I shall so refer to it hereafter. The stationmaster permitted me to call my friend Dr. Visvanathan from his phone. Then a taxi delivered me to the campus of Hindu University where, wearing a pith helmet, he was waiting with his bicycle. We had first met several years ago in Cleveland when he had a grant for study at the university. As he had given me a standing invitation to visit India, I chose Varanasi early on. At his home, I met Mrs. Visvanathan and their son Krishnan for coffee. Then we took a short tour of the house, which the school provides. The interior courtyard and flat roof area, for summer sleeping, relaxing, and the drying of food, are attractive features. Like the other homes I had seen, this one had little wood in its construction; walls were stucco and plaster.

Dr. Visvanathan and I walked to International House, a student building with dining room, for an Indian lunch. Hereafter I would take supper there and had lunch with my hosts; I slept at their house in one of the second-floor rooms on a *charpoy.* This afternoon we watched a cricket game between Hindu University and Allahabad University; then we visited the Sanskrit College to hear a lecture and discussion on Hindu philosophy, witness a yoga demonstration by an Australian, and listen to a disciple of the Divine Light sect, which did not do anything for me. On the way home we also visited the College of Indology.

The university was established around a school founded in the nineteenth century by the theosophist Annie Besant. The benefactor of the present university was Pandit Malaviya, whose wish was to establish an institution teaching Hindu culture and the Sanskrit language. The campus covers a large area—1,100 acres enclosed by a wall. A subcampus with its own wall encloses the Women's College.

Coeducation does not exist and classes are not shared. Parents
therefore feel confident in sending their daughters here to study.
The numerous campus buildings of stucco are painted in the colors
of "temple and monk"—yellow and saffron.

Varanasi, Saturday, November 25

My host took me to his own college this morning, the School of
Technology, where I met several colleagues. It includes the School of
Pharmacy, which teaches Ayurvedic medicine as well as modern
medicine. The pharmacopoeia makes use of plant remedies that
have been handed down through families for generations. Studies
are sponsored by the government, which intends to develop this ancient medical lore for modern use. I was told of an Ayurvedic drug
named *Rauwolfia serpentina* (snake root), which is effective in
treating high blood pressure; it is also prescribed by allopathic phy-
sicians.

We went home to lunch, the meal prepared from basic ingredients by Mrs. Visvanathan in her modest kitchen. Then Krishnan and
his cousin Murthi took me to the ghats which distinguish Varanasi.
We fetched the holy river Ganga at Harishchanandra Ghat, my first
view. Here we arranged with a boatman to take us up river along
the western shore three miles to Dufferin Bridge at Raj Ghat. After
the heavy monsoon, the river level was as yet higher than usual, the
water color brown as earth. Lower parts of some ghats were inun-
dated. At all points the faithful were at prayer, meditating, listening
to and reading the scriptures, or bathing in the holy flood. All ghats
are situated on the left (west) bank and the ensemble of structures
and people dramatically illustrates the importance of water in
Hindu devotions. The visitor cannot do other than wonder at the
scene he faces.

The following is taken from an old leaflet, put out by Indian
State Railways:

It is [at] the bathing ghats that the visitor to Benares will
see for himself something of the religious side of Indian life and
the morning is undoubtedly the best time to make the trip by
boat. Leaving his hotel at the earliest possible moment after
daybreak, the visitor may proceed by motor-car or by tonga direct to the Dasashwamedh Ghat, which lies south-west about
three miles by road, from the Cantonment railway station. The
route passes through a picturesque and more open section of the
town. Gaudy paintings of religious themes on the walls of white-

washed houses are the first promise of greater tableaux to come. Several palaces belonging to Hindu Maharajahs and Ruling Chiefs will also be observed. As the Ghat is approached, the roadway becomes narrow and it is then that the visitor obtains his first view of the hordes of mendicants and ascetics which infest the temples and the landing stages of Benares. Gaunt emaciated frames, ash smeared and dust-sprinkled, with knotted locks of hair and often voluntarily mutilated limbs, pose at every corner or carry out weird penances in the presence of all men; and from their lips arise perpetual invocations for alms.

A flight of stone steps now leads down to a primitive landing stage by whose side hover several quaint country boats, with tiny cabins, on whose roof the visitor takes his seat. The oarsmen slowly push their unwieldy craft out towards midstream and the traveller is not long in realising how favourable a vantage point he is afforded to view a riverine panorama such as no other town in the world affords. To left and right, for fully three miles along that wide curve of the Ganges north bank, he beholds a wonderful array of temples and palaces soaring to a hundred feet above him, while giant stairs ever descend to the water's edge. Spires, buttresses, domes, shrines and balconies, with every hue of the rainbow showing from arch, terrace and window, combine to form a spectacle which is surely as unique as it is impressive. Well informed guides will pour out their array of facts and will point out the temples and palaces, and recite the histories, but for the first few moments the visitor will find a less resistible appeal in the spectacle which he beholds of massed humanity surging at the feet of the causeway, where, obedient to age-old precepts, tens of thousands of devotees carry out the daily rite of purifying themselves in the sacred stream. Solemnly, yet with animated movement, they recite their prayers, assuming prescribed mystic postures, immerse themselves in the swirling green waters and scoop the liquid up in their hands allowing it to flow back to the river through their fingers. Here and there are groups of women, attired in brilliant *saries*, carrying out the same rituals; the bathing ended, they change into fresh raiments, slipping off their wet *saries* fold by fold with wonderful grace and dexterity as they stand knee-deep in the stream.

Many in that great assemblage carry a shining vessel filled with Ganges water to be taken to home or temple to purify the hearth or be an offering to the deities; and thousands of vessels of every kind, sealed and guaranteed by the priests, are daily taken away by pilgrims from Benares to the furthermost parts of India to ensure the peace and blessing of Ganga Mai to distant households. Each bather, as he or she emerges from the river, toils straightway up the steps to where, under great straw umbrellas or canvas parasols, the priestly Brahmins sit to dispense blessing and issue certificates of purification.*

Murthi had a very good knowledge of the characteristics of each ghat and I do not believe a more westernized Indian would know as much of these as did he. Through reading (and photos) of Varanasi, I had gained a mental picture of it, but when I actually saw it, it did not correspond to the way I had imagined it. I had pictured hordes of pilgrims who make the journey from near and far to be certain of expiring within the city and thus fetching paradise, yet the majority of pilgrims are healthy people of all ages and both sexes. I had foreseen crowds of beggars because the pilgrims would be moved, I suspected, to give alms for the benefit of their *karma*. Nevertheless, I found no more destitution in these streets or before these temples than elsewhere. Murthi told us that each temple has days on which it is auspicious to give alms and beggars gather there on those special days. At the Temple of Hanuman, I think, it is most propitious to give on Tuesday and Saturday. On other days, mendicants migrate elsewhere.

The ghats have been here for untold ages. There are approximately one hundred, creating an unparalleled sight. In 500 B.C., when the Lord Buddha stopped near the Deer Park in Sarnath, Varanasi was already established; and he wished by proximity to share in its religious significance.

We debarked and Murthi led us through the alleyways of the old city as evening came. We passed many small shops dealing in Banaras silks, brass, figurines, ivory carving and religious objects. Then we fetched the Gold Temple of Lord Viswanath, whose towers are covered with three quarters of a ton of gold. As a non-Hindu I could not enter; but we did ascend to the roof of a building across the street from where we could see the towers.

Then we took tea in the Kania Visram Mandar Restaurant-Hotel at Godaulia, which, at the time, I described as "the only clean eating place in the entire city." [Now, much later, I do not remember how I drew the conclusion, albeit perhaps it followed from the intermittent hopeless feeling I was subject to in India.] Later my host arrived and we all had dinner in that congested eating place, which was

* *Banaras*, India State Railways (pamphlet) n.d.

most likely wholly vegetarian, for I could not think otherwise, given his strong feelings on the subject. For instance, as we were having lunch at home one day, I inadvertently called one of the dishes, *masal dosa*, "stuffed chicken," because it was a piece of flat bread enclosing a potato and vegetable combination. This caused some alarm and the Visvanathans jokingly said their reputation would be ruined if I told people I had eaten chicken in their house.

Varanasi, Sunday, November 26

Today, Sunday, is the day of rest in India. Krishnan and I visited the unfinished temple on campus, donated by the Birla family. The interior was decorated with passages from the Hindu scriptures—excerpts from the Ramayana and the Mahabharata, and the full Bhagavad Gita. That they were in English translation was unexpected. There was a man who played a harmonium as we read.

Dr. Visvanathan and I visited a friend, Prakash, whom I had heard of when we were in Cleveland. He is an exporter of Banaras silks, such as scarves, and he showed me samples. They are in great variety and range of colors, and containing gold thread interwoven with the ground color. He proposed that I represent the business when I get home. They might fetch a ready market.

Prakash has his own weavers whom he supplies with silk yarn; then pays them for the completed piece. His enterprise is a cottage industry of the kind Ghandi and the government of India encourage. Prakash spoke of trips to Paris and New York, as well as dealing with the famous, and so forth. He is a good talker and probably a surefire salesman. I like Indian handloomed textiles of every kind and in the course of my travels could not resist purchasing many examples, for each region has it typical weaves and patterns.

We ended our visit with tea and sweets: *burfi, rasa gulla, malai chop,* and *chum chum.* They are milk based and very good.

Sarnath, Monday, November 27

Mr. Agrawal, a friend of my host, invited us to his house in Sarnath today. We were picked up in his Ambassador automobile and soon found ourselves within the great Buddhist center and object of pilgrimage, which lies due north of Varanasi. After a pause at the residence which was within sight of the excavations, I set out alone to examine the archaeological zone. It was here on the edge of the Deer Park of Sarnath that Gautama Buddha preached his first sermon and made the first five converts sometime around 500 B.C. The presence of two such prominent religious sites as Varanasi and

Sarnath makes the area potent spiritual ground. India has a small number of Buddhists—less than 1 percent of the total population. The number in other countries is far greater, and as I began to walk the paths past the ruins of several *stupas* (sacred mounds), temples, and *viharas* (monasteries), I was moved to remember the overseas Buddhists, for I saw few visitors.

The guide leaflet contained the following:

> Sarnath is a holy spot of Buddhism, as Buddha preached here his First Sermon. In Buddhist literature the place was known as Rishipatana and Mrigadā or Mrigadāya....The place was called Rishipatana, as it was here that the bodies of five hundred Pratyeka Buddhas or Rishis fell after their attainment of *nirvāna*; the name Mrigadāva owes its origin to the fact that herds of deer roamed here freely as they had been granted immunity by the king of Banaras moved to compassion by the spirit of self-sacrifice of [the] Bodhisattva born as Nyagrodhamriga. In medieval inscriptions the place is referred to as the Dharmachakra- or Saddharma-chakra-pravartana-vihāra. The modern name seems to be a contraction of Sāranganātha (lord of deer), still borne by the Mahādeva enshrined in a temple near by.
>
> After attaining Enlightenment at Bodh-Gayā, Buddha took the decision that he should preach his *dharma* for the welfare of all beings. He came to know that his five erstwhile companions were then staying at Sarnath. So he proceeded to this place and explained to them for the first time his teaching, which event in the Buddhist texts is known as the *dharma-chakra—pravartana*, 'Turning of the Wheel of Law'.
>
> An inscription of the late Kushan period found at Sarnath gives a partial record of this sermon. Buddha expounded here the Four Noble Truths (*ārya-satya-chatushtaya*). The first Truth is that there is sorrow (*duhka*) in this world; the second relates to the origin and cause of sorrow; the third explains the cessation of sorrow; and the fourth expounds the Eightfold Noble Path (*ārya-ashtāngika-mārga*), which leads to the end of sorrow and to the attainment of peace, enlightenment and *nirvāna*. The Noble Path consists of Right Views, Right Aspirations, Right Speech, Right Conduct, Right Living, Right Effort, Right Mindfulness and Right Meditation. Buddha told his disciples that there are two ways of life: the way of pleasures of the senses and of worldly enjoyments, which brings sorrow, and the way of the mortification of the flesh and the denial of pleasures. He held

that both these extremes are to be avoided and he preached the Middle Way, the golden mean of leading a sensible life.

This First Sermon comprises a unique and frank intellectual statement of the basic problem of life as well as its solution. It is universally regarded as the cream of Buddha's teachings. Sarnath naturally became the symbol and radiating centre of light throughout the Buddhist world.

At Sarnath, Buddha also laid the foundation of his *sangha* or the order of monks. Yaśa, the son of a rich householder of Vārānasā, together with his fifty-four friends, was attracted by his teachings and became his disciple. With them and the first five monks (*pañcha-vargāya bhikshus*) the Master founded the first *sangha* of sixty monks and sent them to various directions to preach his *dharma*.

After about two hundred years of the *nirvana* of Buddha, came Aśoka, the Mauryan emperor, who is rightly famous in the history of Buddhism. He waged a war against the people of Kalinga, but the suffering caused by it filled his heart with intense remorse and he decided to abstain from war for ever. This brought about a great change in his outlook and activities. He espoused the cause of Buddhism and employed all his resources and pious zeal to spread the message of Buddha. The charming life of Buddha exercised such a fascination on his mind that he decided to go on a pilgrimage to the holy places associated with the Master. At Lumbini (modern Rummindei in Nepalese Tarai), he caused a pillar to be erected on the spot where Buddha was born. At Sarnath he raised several monuments, one of which as a *stūpa* about 100 ft. high, called the Dharmarājikā Stūpa, which was crowned at its top by a monolithic railing. This *stūpa* was pulled down in 1794 by one Jagat Singh of Banaras. The other monument of Aśoka's is the monolithic pillar which was once surmounted by the magnificent lion-capital, now adopted by India as her State emblem, and placed in the local Museum. The capital was crowned by a large *dharmachakra*, of which several fragments were recovered. The high *stūpa* known as Dhamekh also seems to have had its origin in Aśoka's time.*

Sarnath and Buddhism were at their apogee during the rule of Emperor Ashoka, who himself was Buddhist and ruled benevolently over a large part of the subcontinent in the third century B.C. In his day there were numerous—hundreds of—monks in residence, and pilgrims in large numbers come from near and far. Two Chinese pil-

* *Sarnath*, V.S. Agrawala, 2d ed., Department of Archeology, New Delhi: 1957.

grims in the seventh century wrote about what they saw, mentioning the figure 1500 as the population of monks residing in Sarnath, and a *stupa* about three hundred feet high. An extraordinary place!

Only one active temple is presently found at Sarnath. Erected by the Mahabodhi Society in 1931, it is decorated with scenes of Lord Buddha's life.

There is a small museum holding objects uncovered in local excavations, among them the great Sarnath Buddha—absent on exposition—and the remarkable Lion Capital in polished stone. Since Independence this Ashokan masterpiece has been India's national symbol and appears on banknotes.

I returned to Mr. Agrawal's bungalow, whose veranda affords a view of the Chaukhandi *Stupa*, in ruins; at one time it could have held relics of Buddha. We were served tea, sweets, cashews, papaya, custard apple—and toast. Mr. Agrawal is part owner of a sugar refinery and seeks to enter another business. He enquired if I knew anyone in my country interested in collaborating with him to start an enterprise in India.

We were home for lunch. Mrs. Visvanathan's equipment is simple, consisting of mostly metal cookware and pottery dishes of good quality. The dried food items and spices are neatly arranged on shelves. A single male servant is dishwasher, laundryman, general housekeeper, and responsible for water and baths. Direct family care is performed by the woman of the house.

After lunch, Krishnan, Murthi, and I turned to the Ganga again for another trip by small boat. We departed from Asi Ghat, an easy walk from campus. The bargaining with the boatman was interesting to watch. Whenever boatmen see a foreigner coming, the price increases four to eight times. The first price this one asked was Rs 8, which he reduced sparingly, and we began to walk away while still bargaining over the shoulder. Finally, when we were nearly out of hearing, he came down to Rs .50, the correct amount, and he brought his boat up. I hope the hardworking boatmen are paid more by other tourists, yet their greater generosity makes it harder for those on a budget.

The twice-a-day bathers were already taking their second dip in the Ganga. The belief is that the water is so pure that germs cannot live in it. Now mud colored, the water will clear up later in the season—I do not know if that is sufficient to appear clean in a glass; however, I doubt it. It is said dead animals are consigned to the waters and, sometimes, dead children under five years of age because at that age purification by fire is thought to be unnecessary.

Along the western bastians were priests and scholars, and perhaps ordinary people with an urge to hold forth, to preach, relating tales from the scriptures to rapt, though small, audiences. Holy men and ordinary people perform *puja* (devotions) while facing the holy river. Some are protected from the sun by umbrellas, which can be canvas or concrete.

We debarked at Raj Ghat, next to the railroad bridge, and walked part way across the span, observing the scene from above. By now we were ready for tea and sweets. Enroute home on foot we came to a theatrical performance consisting of tableaux of religious themes, such as Vishnu slaughtering the Ogress, and also of scenes showing the domestic life of real people. The courtyard of a maharajah's palace had been loaned for the show. Varanasi attracts the seasonal residence of various nobles and wealthy persons from all parts of India. Some large palaces are on the Ganga, just behind the ghats, making them both more awe-inspiring.

Varanasi, Tuesday, November 28

The university has a collection of miniature paintings. They begin with the palm-leaf variety, and go right through the Mogul period and into the present. Today a man from Lucknow, whom I met at the International House, escorted me through the collection. We also saw a treasury containing jewelry, inlaid jade objects, jeweled arms, and sculpture.

Varanasi, Wednesday, November 29

Krishnan attends classes in the morning; Murthi is through university and seeking a job. Therefore this morning Murthi and I walked to the ghats together to observe the two burning places at Harishchandra Ghat and Manikarnika Ghat. You do not take pictures here, or carry a camera, if you are prudent. In any case I do not have a camera now. Fires burn all the time, even by night, on the two ghats. Priests and family sit near the pyre to await the dying away of the flames before consigning the ashes to the waters. I noticed only a few cremations in progress, which caused me think that fewer take place than I expected, despite the large reward for those who die and are burned here. The following is also taken from the travel pamphlet:

> To die in Benares is to ensure salvation; and salvation is doubly certain when the funeral ceremonies are carried out on the banks of the Ganges within the sacred limits of Varanasi it-

self. For this reason thousands of aged or ailing pilgrims throng to Benares to die there and be happy in the knowledge that their sins will be swept away in that last act of purification by fire. And so, as the visitor gazes upon the Ghat, he will invariably find there a still figure, shrouded in red or in white, upon high piles of faggots. Around stand a small group of mourners, and, after the reciting of mantras and the performance of due rites, the next of kin of the dead man or woman plunges a blazing torch into the foundations of the pyre. When all has been consumed, the ashes are strewn upon the waters of the Ganges, and the mourners bathe in the stream as an act of self-purification before they can break the fast imposed upon them during these obsequies.

The two ghats are not exclusively for cremations, for all usual ritual activities proceed here as well, even to the washing of clothes by the *dhobis*. *

[Later, after returning to my own country, I realized that I could have bathed in the Ganga, and felt regret that the occasion for this had passed me by. There are many places along the river where one can accomplish this and I think I would have chosen to go elsewhere than Varanasi for my holy dip.]

We saw the Durga Temple, vulgarly called the Monkey Temple because a flock of them live in the precincts. It is a dirty place, having no architectural importance, and is closed to non-Hindus. We were able to look down on the courtyard from above. You are warned not to approach the simians.

We ferried over to the opposite shore at Ram Nagar Fort, residence of the Maharajah of Banaras, which is open to visitors. We saw the collection of court furniture, elephant *howdahs*, old brocades, and arms. The richness of some objects recalls the pomp and circumstance of princely India. The maharajah also has a collection of tiger skins on display.

Varanasi, Thursday, November 30

The Temple of Bharat Matas (Mother India), is a modern structure opened by Ghandi and visitable by non-Hindus. The notable feature is a marble relief map of India on the floor, replacing the images of Hindu deities. Murthi and I saw this temple, situated well away from the congestion near the Ganga. Then we walked in the botanical garden, where the plants and trees have no labels.

* Op. cit.

Varanasi, Friday, December 1

These are my last two days in Varanasi. As I was reading in the university library, the other readers stood for prayer at mid-morning and invited me to join. I visited one of the university hostels, dormitories for students. A student who was my guide told me that the residents eat in groups, paying Rs 60 a month for all meals including afternoon tea. That is $12.00, using official exchange rates.

Some of the people whom I have met here returned to bid me adieu—Mr. Agrawal and two students. With Murthi we visited the Sankatamachan Temple, dedicated to Hanuman, and I was permitted to see the interior because my host knows the priest.

Because I am down to the end of my cash, the expected sum not having arrived, Dr. Visvanathan loaned me Rs 200. It will take me as far as Madras. Meanwhile I have applied for a loan on my life insurance.

By train and bus to Gaya, Sunday, December 3

We arose at 4 a.m. for my departure. The two rickshaws we requested yesterday were late; however we fetched the station in sufficient time. There I said goodbye to my kind hosts, who invited me to return in the spring to accompany them on a trip to the hills. The Visvanathans are very warm and welcoming people, and I could not adequately thank them for my most enjoyable visit.

The train left Uttar Pradesh behind and entered Bihar State, which derives its name from *vihara* (monastery). It is comparatively undeveloped. The several-hour journey to Gaya allowed some exchanges with passengers sitting nearby, for you find people who speak English in third class also. Those who cannot speak English sometimes find satisfaction in staring at foreigners. Others ask questions, possibly picked up in school, such as What is your name? Where are you coming from? What are you doing here? Why are you traveling third class? Where are you going? What are you doing in your country? Are you married? Women rarely speak; my interlocutors were young men or boys. They often ask about religion, but the discussion tends to be brief unless the person is fluent in English. If he is, there is no difficulty in pursuing regular conversation because Indians are poised, curious, self-confident, courteous, and friendly. A little later, as I was taking the bus to Gaya, a Bihari farmer spoke to me and extended a spontaneous invitation to visit his home, saying that his son studies at the University of Michigan. Unfortunately, my scrawny pocketbook did not permit me to take advantage of his generous offer.

On board this train were traveling mendicants, who use the occasion to collar a captive group of passengers. One of several favorite stratagems as they progress through the train is to give a concert, consisting of shrill notes, which I could scarcely appreciate as music. Then the cup is passed.

An alternative stratagem, one requiring more initiative, is to present a framed and mounted letter or statement portraying the seeker in a favorable light. These documents may be genuine or forgeries. The format can be a letter from a former employer or a master if the person is a servant. Occasionally the employer is British. The caste is often stated first, followed by a list of particulars on the position held and for how long. [Thus it becomes a fully annotated résumé, ready to fax?] I usually compensated, meagerly, the bearers of these informative, carefully prepared documents.

Here is a genuine specimen of this kind of appeal, inclusive of spelling errors:

JAI HIND!

Sir,
    This poor man is a Malayali The Bearer and his brothers are dumb and carnot sreak He lost his parent. His elder is blind and mad. His pounger sister is also blird and foolish. These three and depending on this man. His father was serving in South Indian-Railway Company Limited. Railwap Officers have excused the bearers so please kindly pay him charity and god healp you.
A. R. Shoranor Malayala, Krishnan Nayar M. S.
M. Madras, Drosani Christian.
(Please return his notice after persnal)
(1) Dr. U. Rama Rao (3) S. P. Abdul Karim.
(2) Dr. Cook.
Mrs. Padmabai B.A., (Principal) Theosophic Women's College, Banaras.

A darling, nevertheless heart-wrenching device of women and girls is the babe-in-arms, intended to emphasize her entreaty. I heard it said that babies can be rented by anyone who wants the argument of another mouth to feed.

The train fetched Gaya at midday and I lost no time in locating the bus to Bodhgaya, nine miles south. It was here that Siddartha Gautama dwelled for a time, meditated, and attained enlightenment. This is the sacred place, and here stood the Bodhi Tree, a clipping of which is said to be the origin of the existing one. I focused on the confined area which holds these marvelous things, such as the tree, a *stupa* next to it, the Lotus Pond where it is said the Buddha bathed, and the *Chankramana* (Jewel Walk) where he strolled in meditation and deliberation on whether he should reveal his knowledge to the world. The Mahabodhi Temple nearby is regarded as connected to a third-century Ashokan temple and to be itself nearly the same as one which stood here in the seventh century. A Chinese pilgrim, Hiuen Tsang, described it in 635 A.D. Finally I sat on the edge of the rectangular Lotus Pond, which held the blooming plant that is often seen in Buddhist art. A great deal of meaning is concentrated around these objects—awesome!

Then I turned my attention to a group of Tibetan refugees, who appeared to be encamped near the Bodhi Tree, on the platform, or next to it. They looked poor and needy, yet they preserved their self-respect and seemed happy. Their clothing was handmade of homespun wool—colorful and characteristic of Tibet, the homeland from which I assumed they had fled as the Chinese occupied it. Their small children were impishly appealing and unafraid. I did not learn how they live or if they are provided for by the government or the UN. They carry on a small business with visitors and pilgrims to whom they offer to sell coins and paper money of Tibet. The children begged—not as persistently as those often met here. They knew no English.

After lingering as long as possible, I had to return to Gaya, which itself is a significant Hindu place of pilgrimage and shares with Varanasi the same sacred traditions. As Gaya offered little in the vicinity of the train station, I dined there, where the food generally is dependable though basic. The train came much later in the evening and was already full to capacity; so it looked doubtful that I might squeeze aboard. Nevertheless, I was fortunate; one car carried students whose teacher called out to invite me to get aboard their reserved rail car. It was occupied by boys from Sherwood College in Nainital. Then we were underway, rolling eastward again,

toward Calcutta. My hosts gave me a fresh cup of coffee before I
retired in an upper birth.

Calcutta, Monday, December 4

While I was still aboard the student car this morning, their
teacher, Oliver C. Hakeem, invited me to visit Nainital as his guest.
It sounded like a charming location in the Himalayan foothills of
northern Uttar Pradesh, but I never got there.

Breakfast, which I took in Howrah Station, consisted of *chai*,
bananas, and fried bread—not a bad way to greet this city and
Howrah Station, a large terminus which is filled at every hour with
people and life—including, at various times, many refugees. Then I
found a bus to take me across well known Howrah Bridge to the
YMCA on Chowringhee Road. The Y was full, so instead I got a shave
and haircut in the Y barbershop. The barber was Italian and had
lived here many years and liked it.

Then I telephoned Raj Kapoor, whom I knew back in Cleveland.
He was not in town, so his brother offered to help me find a place to
stay. Then he sent a boy to the Y who escorted me to the elegant
Grand Hotel, quite out of my range. Mr. Kapoor arrived and I explained to him what I needed. He took me by car to his modern
apartment, where a servant made tea. Two additional friends arrived and we enjoyed a pleasant time together. Then Chinese food
was delivered for lunch. One of the friends worked for Lufthansa
Airlines, the other for the Indo-American Society. Mr. Kapoor himself was an exporter of Indian handicrafts and traveled in Europe
and the United States. The apartment was furnished in European
manner, so I gained the impression that these were Indians of a
Western stamp. In fact, perhaps I saw myself as more Indian, in
some ways, than they were. My khaki shorts with a white shirt are
like those often worn by Indians.

One of Calcutta's distinctive features is the Maidan—this city's
Central Park. It is a green belt two miles in length and a mile broad,
situated in the heart of the metropolis between the Hooghly River
and Chowringhee Road.

Since I still had no place to lay my head, I stopped to see the
Salvation Army Hostel, but it was also full. In Calcutta it does not
serve the destitute—the guests were a group of missionaries taking
language examinations. I was told to return if I found nothing else
and they would make room, and that was how it turned out after Mr.
Kapoor showed me two additional hotels. The hostel provided three
good European-style meals and a place to put down on the ve-

randa—all for Rs 6 per diem, about $1.20. I had the company of the other guests and met Dr. and Mrs. Gullison who run the Rural Mission Hospital in Sompeta. They invited me to visit them.

Now I began to take in the sights in systematic fashion, using my books and maps, but ready to alter my route if anything interesting turned up. Calcutta's terrible problems are impossible to overlook; in prior years the city harbored large numbers of refugees from East Pakistan, who camped everywhere. Now the situation has improved. To be sure the streets are still peopled by thousands of the homeless, called pavement dwellers in India. I learned that the term does not correspond to "homeless." Thousands of pavement dwellers make their homes there, remain in one place, prepare their food, live, and die there. Some of them have a home—a real home in the village, but they sojourn in the city to be near a job, to beg, or because they prefer it.

Calcutta, Tuesday, December 5

I visited the Indian Museum today, but saw only a portion of the large collection, which comprises both the art and natural history of the subcontinent. There are fine Buddhist objects from many sites, including the Gandhara region. I liked the sculptured railings found at Buddhist locations such as Bodhgaya, though it would be preferable to allow them to stay where they were. The Victoria and Albert Museum in London also holds a Bodhgayan railing in its collection of sculpture from India. It was restful to spend several hours here, though the galleries are noticeably run down, and crowded with objects. One room is full of meteorites, and elsewhere I saw a selection of metal jewelry, weighing sixteen pounds, that came from the stomach of a crocodile. No further details were given so I had to fill these in with the aid of my imagination.

This city is endowed with a special quality that I am trying to understand. It is very eastern, unlike Bombay, although it is also a major port. Calcutta attracts resident Europeans who find they can live well here on a limited income. If India had a "Places Rated Almanac," the city might get a high score. I was told that the European segment has grown since Independence in 1947, when displaced British colonials augmented the western settlers.

This afternoon I rode the dependable tram car to Kalighat to visit the Temple of Kali. The city was named for it; one of the original villages purchased by the Englishman Job Charnok was Kali Kata, made Calcutta by the English. Here are conducted rites for the black complexioned goddess Kali; she is a manifestation of Parvati, wife of the god Shiva. I was shown around by an elderly man who was familiar with the place, a good guide who knew English.

The temple has a stone platform on which sacrifices are made—goats. A sacrifice had recently taken place, as shown by blood spatters. The place did not appeal to my sensibilities. Close by is a fertility tree where childless women pray and, should a birth result, return to tie a votary stone to the tree. This is an example of the simplest forms of Hindu faith and worship, which can rise to lofty spiritual planes.

Upon leaving Kalighat and crossing the Adiganga canal, I was overflown by a group of vultures who dropped something on me. It appeared to be more than one at the time. Odd contretemps! In the same area I found the zoo, of average quality, holding a large collection of animals of India. There are 500 species found on the subcontinent. In historical India, as well as today, there is a tradition of reverence for life, although in modern times turbulent social change resulting from population pressure, economic development, hunting, and the presence of guns have left some species threatened—to the extent that a growing number are listed as endangered. In 1972 a Wildlife Act was passed, which led to the founding of more than 100 new preserves, parks, and sanctuaries, which may be visited.

Hinduism teaches respect for nature and all life; various deities are associated with specific animals; for example, Ganesh is half elephant and half man. The Emperor Ashoka prohibited the killing of certain animals and the burning of forests. The Jains are at the very center of this life-preserving philosophy, for their religion expressly states the principle.

Mr. Kapoor extended an invitation to afternoon tea with his friends. The Bengalis are a cultured people who are among the intellectual leaders in India. They furnished several leaders of the Independence movement, including the poet Rabindranath Tagore and the guru of Pondicherry, Sri Aurobindo. The best Indian films are made in Bengal, and poets, artists, and authors are established here.

Calcutta, Wednesday, December 6

Calcutta's transportation system appears to be better than Delhi's. It rests on a combination of services that cooperate instead of competing. Among them are thousands of man-powered rickshaws, which have a monopoly on small vehicle transport; there are no bicycle or motor-driven rickshaws. Some people criticize the continued use of man-powered transport, considering it degrading and undemocratic; nevertheless the operators hang on and earn a meager living. They are greatly exploited by the rickshaw owners, as Dominique LaPierre described in his *City of Joy,** a book about Calcutta that is well worth reading. [In more recent years Calcutta has completed the first short subway line in India under Chowringhee Road.] I preferred to take the crowded tram car, and lost my fountain pen to a pickpocket on one trip.

The city center is Dalhousie Square, and this morning I looked into American Express, where they had no mail for me and no money. From there I walked through the Maidan to the Victoria Memorial, passing a surprising polo game in progress. The Memorial is placed conspicuously on the Maidan, a large white marble building resembling a pavilion in a former world exposition. Before it is a statue of a mature Queen Victoria that is an unmistakable likeness. The structure looks something like the Taj Mahal in a muddled way. Perhaps the British could do no better for a memorial to their Raj. I suppose it isn't that bad because the Indians like Queen Victoria and this reminds them of her and may make them feel better amid the difficulties of nationhood.

I saw pictures of gala assemblies and watercolors of local scenery. There is a piano on which Victoria played as a young girl. It has found a permanent home here in India. Cameras are not allowed and the attendant would not permit my transistor radio into the building, which surprised me.

Next I visited St. Paul's Cathedral, a significant British addition to the city. I noticed that a Christmas performance of Handel's *Messiah* was planned. The body of the church was equipped with several dozen ceiling fans for the hot season. A new planetarium is under construction—a contribution of the Birla family, the generous philanthropists whose good works I have met with in other places.

Today's hostel lunch, at my request, included rice and curry.

This evening I went to the movies, where they showed a short film titled *How to Vote* because elections are approaching and a new voting system is being introduced. I thought it appeared complex.

Calcutta, Tuesday, December 6

I embarked on a day trip beyond city limits to the Ramakrishna Mission, called Belur Math. It lies on the shore of the Hooghly River several miles north of Howrah. The bus crawled up through the

*(Doubleday, 1985, New York)

crowded, poverty-stricken city to reach the prized destination. Ramakrishna was a nineteenth-century Hindu mystic and Brahmin priest in the Temple of Kali at Dakshineshwar, directly across the river. He preached the fundamental unity of all religions, saying that they shared the same goal and brought men to the same God. He himself had also practiced each major religion in sequence— Hinduism, Christianity, Buddhism, and Islam, an experience that led him to find their essential agreement. He also mastered each of the systems of yoga—and they number several. The saint's follower, Vivekananda, came to the United States in 1893, where he represented Hinduism at the World Parliament of Religions in Chicago. After four years of lecturing and teaching in the West, he returned to India and founded the Ramakrishna Mission, a monastic order that seeks to serve social needs. Although its head-quarters are Belur Math, it has branches all over India and other countries. There is a Ramakrishna Mission in La Crescenta, California. The main building of Bedur Math is intended, depending on your viewpoint, to resemble a temple, a church, or a mosque.

Upon opening I met a guide at the gate who escorted me through the grounds. His English was limited, but he helped. I had read an interesting book by the German scholar Max Müller, *Ramakrishna, His Life and Sayings.**

The pilgrim can take a small ferry across the river to the temple; however, bargaining with the boatman occupied so much time that I returned to Calcutta without seeing it. A picture of the temple shows it to be unusual for a Hindu place of worship—a cross between Byzantine and Art Nouveau styles.

Once back in the city, I was addressed by a student who volun-teered to take me to the area of the Chinese shops selling handmade shoes. I purchased a pair for Rs 24—$5. They are said to be good for ten years' wear. Then we looked at suitcases because mine is failing after the strenuous trip out to India. A large, well-made case costs $10 or less. I ended up buying a small all-metal case, which was securely padlocked and strong enough to sit on, upended. It cost about $2.

This evening I saw an Elvis Presley movie; the theater was three-quarters empty.

* Ramakrishna-Vivekanada Center, New York, 1942.

Calcutta, Friday, December 7

Today's excursion to the botanical garden was entirely pleasing. Crossing the Maidan past Fort William on foot, I came to the river and shoreline rails on which passengers may ride in small open cars propelled by two coolies who walk, barefoot, on the rails behind— one of he oddest arrangements I have ever seen. Then I took a small ferry across the river and walked through a poor district of very small, identical concrete homes facing an unpaved roadway. This led to the main road, where soon a driver picked me up and delivered me to the garden gate.

The large banyan (fig) tree here is famous. The garden was founded in 1786 by the British, so the tree is 200 years old, unless it stood here before that time. The plantings extend along the river for about half a mile. I was undisturbed as I wandered about on this peaceful day. Identification of trees or plants is often prevented by an absence of markers; however, I wanted merely to stroll alone, away from the crowded city. Lotus ponds filled with flowers encourage quiet meditation, or the visitor may hire a small boat for next to nothing and paddle among them in the warm sunshine, which is what I did. At a small stall in the palms, I drank fresh coconut milk directly from the shell.

After leaving the garden I was attracted by a group of Jain temples. These may have been the Sitambara temples, yet I am not certain. They are a group of small buildings surrounding a central garden. Their architecture was unremarkable. The exteriors were adorned in glass and tile. There were a few beggars ready to intercept me, but I got away free.

Then I walked through the neighborhood of Calcutta University. Presidency College is significant in history because it was here that English was first taught. The streets here are alive, with a preponderance of young students and many bookstores. Calcutta is the hub of book publishing in India, as you would expect, because this is where many are written.

Calcutta, and by train to Bhubaneswar, Saturday, December 9

The Russian cosmonaut visited Calcutta this week; I missed him. This ends my first month in India. It has been a most busy time. Today I had to visit the Security Office. No delay was involved. At exactly 4:15 the Madras Mail left from Howrah Station for South India. I fetched the station a full hour early yet did not secure a seat because the train was full. I upended my new case for a seat and braced myself for the long journey to Bhubaneshwar, 272 miles and nine hours from Howrah. This is extracted from the official time table: (BBS signifies Bhubaneshwar)

Timings

UP			DOWN		
Howrah Madras Mail					
Howrah	Dep.	16:15	BBS	Arr.	1:39
BBS	Arr.	1:15	BBS	Dep.	1:44
BBS	Dep.	1:20	Howrah	Arr.	11:35

Fares
Calcutta to Bhubaneshwar (Rs 4.75 = $1.00)

A.C.*	Rs 56.58 nP.
1st class	Rs 28.98 nP.
2nd Class	Rs 18.03 nP.
3rd Class	Rs 10.23 nP

* Air Conditioned

This gives the itinerary by road:

From	To	Distance
Calcutta	Bhubaneswar	533 miles

Route
Via Burdwan—Asansol—Dhanbad—Ranchi—Purulia Road Jn.—Jamshedpur—Chaibassa—Jajpur Road (impassable from June to December)—Ferry crossing of river Brahmanee at Jenapur—Chowdwar—Ferry Crossing of river Mahanadi—Cuttack—Bhubaneswar.

The train arrived in Bhubaneshwar an hour late, when I was done in. I was immediately told of the available retiring room in the station and collapsed into bed. It felt like heaven.

Bhubaneswar, Sunday, December 10
The rumble of passing trains could not keep me awake last night and this morning. It was like music lulling me back to sleep. The bearer who met the train late last evening and led me to this retiring room also stayed on hand this morning. He sleeps on the veranda floor, it appears, without benefit of a pad. My room had two good beds hung with mosquito nets. The sparse furniture included a peculiar chair whose one arm was a large, leaflike attachment, evidently a table, but larger than a student's armchair.

A pedicab was already in attendance outside the station, and the driver knew a little English. For breakfast he took me to the state tourist bungalow, where eggs, toast, and coffee were served. The bill for Rs 4.50 was plainly excessive and I gently declined to pay more than Rs 2.50, which was accepted. I was in the area of the new city, for Orissa State is progressively building a new capital here to replace swampy Cuttack. Several large new government buildings exist and a shopping centre with adjacent parking plaza, but there are no cars. Later I purchased a silver filigree pin in the Government Handicrafts Emporium. Cuttack is known for this work.

Orissa has a rich history; but every place in India has that in abundance. Here the legacy is recorded in remarkable architec-ture—in Bhubaneswar and not distant Konarak, which contain Hindu buildings of purity and majesty. It is said that 7,000 temples stood in the area of Bubaneswar, which is now a rather minor city. That was between 750 and 1250 A.D. There are now 100 in differ-ent states of preservation. These are the first Hindu temples of such distinction that I have seen. There will be others in South India.

My pedicab driver knew the way to go; first on his list was the Rajarani Temple, standing by itself in the fields where stooping cul-tivators were at work. Since it was deconsecrated and not in use, I could walk into the sanctuary. It is a small place and every exterior surface is carved in meticulous detail, without obscuring the form beneath. Ornament combined with mass expresses the character of Orissan art. Red sandstone is the material.

Hence my driver took me to the Mukteswar Temple. This one is thirty-four feet high, the exterior also entirely enveloped in sculpted shapes and figures. The decoration includes a procession of horses and elephants. A small detached *torana* (gateway) consists of a doughnut arch supported by thick columns. It suggests similar Bud-dhist additions seen in places such as Sanchi, of which I had seen pictures. Orissa had a Buddhist period in Ashoka's time.

Then I visited the Parasurameswar Temple, which has an un-decorated interior. This temple and others are to be found in an area of one to two square miles, not mingled with modern struc-tures, but standing apart, enhanced by their natural surroundings. We paused next at the Bindu Sarobar, a large, idyllic tank with a small island on which the whitewashed Water Pavilion stands. There were numerous bathers here because it is said to contain drops of water from every holy lake, tank, and pool in India. I talked to a man who told me he had brought his family from Calcutta for curative purposes. No details were offered.

In the old part of Bhubaneswar stands the great Lingaraj Temple with its large, 120-foot carved tower visible for miles. It is out of bounds to non-Hindus, so the visitor must ascend a platform outside the enclosure wall to obtain a partial view of the courtyard. The shrine is dedicated to the Lord of the Three Worlds—Shiva.

I took my evening meal in a Sikh-run restaurant in the new city. The owners spoke English and were hospitable. Sikh men mark their identity with the five *kakkari* signs, of which uncut hair wrapped in a long turban is the most conspicuous. The founder and first guru was Nanak, born in 1469. Sikhism became established in the sixteenth century. It combines Hindu with Islamic principles—trying to take the best of each. It rejects caste and once advocated pacifism, though the Sikhs later became a military community. [In recent times Sikh separatists have adopted violence to accomplish their ends.] There are approximately 15 million in the community and all bear the surname Singh—lion.

Puri and Konarak, Monday, December 11

My loyal bearer roused me for the timely boarding of the early train, which stopped at Kurda Road. From there a short spur runs down to Puri on the Bay of Bengal. The train moves slowly over pleasing farmlands where the people work near the line but pay no attention to the Iron Horse trailing cars behind it.

When I left the train, someone suggested I stay in a nearby sleeping car parked in the station for the use of visitors. Soon I was settled in my own first class compartment.

Puri is one of India's paramount holy places and sites of pilgrimage. The annual *Rath Yatra* (Car Festival) gave the word *juggernaut* to English. It derives from Jaganath, Lord of the Universe, whose image rides in the *rath* (temple chariot or car).

Puri is blessed with a broad, sandy strand extending for miles along the coast. I found the tourist bungalow facing it and had my breakfast while watching a group of men and boys hauling in fish nets. Their bodies are dark and nearly naked—a salon-quality photograph in the offing, if I had a camera. But before seeing Puri I wanted to attempt Konarak, because the full day was available for the lengthy side trip.

I learned through enquiry that a party had arranged for automobiles to take them to Konarak today, and I was invited to travel with them without cost. I was beginning to believe in my luck. The two cars were already nearly full, but I was squeezed into a back seat.

Before leaving there was an unexplained delay while we waited in the cars near the *Rath Yatra* field of action. It is a wide esplanade connecting the large Temple of Lord Jaganath to the Gundicha Mandir (Garden House). A few components of the *rath*—wheels, axles—lie about the uneven ground to remind us of the festival, but apparently the great body of the *rath* is constructed anew every year. The *rath* is forty-two feet high and thirty feet square. It rolls on sixteen wheels, each two meters in diameter. It would be a pilgrim's, or tourist's, dream to witness the festival when 4,000 pullers draw it about half a mile from the large temple to the Garden House and, two weeks later, back again.

Travelers who choose to may as well fetch Konarak by bullock cart along the coast; this ancient means of travel follows the roadless sands by night while the rider sleeps, perhaps on hay. The airline distance is twenty miles. These days some bullock carts have rubber tires; however I would reject them for the traditional wood wheels.

As we waited, a small group of curious folk stood around our automobiles watching—who could say what they were thinking? Then our small cavalcade set forth on the fifty-mile trek on unsurfaced roads. At the outset the land supported palms and grasses. We observed scrawny black cattle, which could have been a miniature breed. As the way turned seaward again, vegetation grew sparser, the terrain sandy, and people fewer. We saw pinnacles of mud—termite colonies, I was told. There were birds of several species, some large and others brightly plumed. India's feathered tribe is abounding.

The way ended in near emptiness, coconut palms and sand surrounded us. But we had fetched our goal—the Suryamandir (Temple of the Sun), also called the Black Pagoda. Approaching on foot we saw more of it, standing in the center of a large, sandy basin, surrounded by an eight-foot stone wall. Other visitors were present—all Indians, the men dressed in white, the women in printed saris. They were few and they made no noise. It was midday. I descended the stairs to the sandy floor of the basin. What at first appeared to be but a ruin, a pile of dark stones, began to take on more order as I looked. First wheels, some broken, stood out from the pile. After them the surviving horses, also shattered, came into the ensemble, and as the overall perspective became clear, the Suryamandir took on a distinct form. I was seeing the chariot of the god Surya, the sun god, as it is pulled along on twenty-four immense stone *chakaras* (wheels) by seven powerful horses. They strain, overcoming the resistance of the sand surrounding them, threatening to hold all in its grasp. The concept is inspired and its execution supreme. There is a non-Indian spirit in this—a dynamic of movement and overcoming.

The Suryamandir, like other temples, is literally covered with figures and detail. These cycles of images and forms occupy horizontal ranks, beginning near the ground. One of these ranks is filled with lovers—embracing figures, kissing cousins, and some caught in the act of making love. All this sculpture has survived since the thirteenth century. The temple formerly had a tower, which has collapsed and disappeared, but the main temple has been saved by filling it with masonry and concrete. The visitor, if he wishes, can climb upon the several ranks of sculpture and examine the many figures more closely—dancers, musicians, war scenes, trade, scenes of daily life, and animals literally blanket all surfaces and appear to demonstrate a veritable abhorrence of empty space on the part of the builders. The red sandstone has survived well; the lowest parts are the best preserved because they were covered with sand before excavation. I do not know if a city existed here in ancient times. The history of Konarak is sketchy—it is not known if the temple was finished. The Suryamandir may have been isolated as it is now. Puri's Car Festival and Konarak appear related to each other. The Suryamandir will be remembered as one of the memorable peaks of my travel times.

No food was available here—nothing that I would trust except hot tea and fresh coconut milk. There were no permanent buildings—only a small cluster of huts with thatched roofs. The scene suggested the South Seas; the Bay of Bengal is only two miles distant.

I encountered Jean Calmard and another French traveler whom I first met in the Salvation Army hostel, and we separated again.

I returned to Puri by bus, because my Indian hosts were going elsewhere. The trip back was protracted, and involved a roadside delay—not knowing if transport would ever arrive. If any cars had come by, I might have thumbed a ride, but there were none. The parts of Orissa I have seen are less populous than many other regions I visited. Nature is also less altered here, and fresher.

In Puri late, I took a rest in the sleeping car before dinner in the station restaurant. I was joined by an Indian fellow and we agreed to meet on the beach in the morning for swimming.

Puri and Sompeta, Tuesday, December 12

I took Nehru's *Discovery of India* down to the beach this morning, reading and waiting for two hours; but my dinner companion did not show up. The sea was too rough to go in. The beach is wide and beautiful. Besides two hotels there are several small villas facing the sea but otherwise nothing that could be called development of the resources of sun and sand. Fishermen carry their coconut fiber nets out to sea in small clumsy boats of leaky construction. After dropping the nets they return to shore and line up to haul them in with their catch. I walked barefoot along the strand and observed hundreds of darting sand crabs.

The Temple of Lord Jaganath is, of course, not visitable, although the tourist may observe a little by ascending a several-storied *math* (monastery) nearby, where a guide explained a few things. He told me of a great kitchen which feeds the thousands of celebrants during the *Rath Yatra*. No one said anything about sacrificial acts by the devotees of Lord Jaganath. In earlier times, I read, they threw themselves under the wheels of the *rath*, dying in the sight of the god.

Puri is a deplorably ramshackle place, dirty as well, and the beach above high water is one large outdoor bathroom. It will surely remain in my memory as the worst, dirtiest, most broken-down place I visited in all the trip. The one street is that wide swath of bare ground given to the festival of Jaganath. The town has no other streets passing through the center.

My train, the Puri-Hyderabad Passenger, was the slow one because it had to stop at Kurda Road and also Sompeta, my next destination, both small places. It left at 2 p.m. and required eight hours to reach Sompeta. It was late on arrival and the Sompeta station without electricity. Thus I was in near darkness, but a cycle rickshaw was waiting and I gave him the name of my hosts—the Gullisons—whom I met at the hostel in Calcutta.

Soon the driver stopped before the darkened bungalow that was the Gullison residence. Not wishing to disturb the family, I unpacked my equipment on the open veranda and bedded down while bats fluttered about and jackals screeched. I was in rural surroundings.

Sompeta, Wednesday, December 13

This morning, I was awakened by the manservant David, who gave me a cup of hot tea with milk before anything else. Breakfast was served by Mrs. Gullison in the family dining room, where I could see more likable lizards on the white wall. We discussed what

I would do while visiting the Rural Mission Hospital. It had been founded by Dr. and Mrs. Gullison twenty-five years earlier and was supported by the Canadian Baptist Church. None of the hospital buildings had existed at the beginning—the Gullisons gradually gathered together the resources to build them, section by section. I looked forward to seeing how the institution functions.

First, I was given a house tour. My hosts lived in a modestly furnished Indian-style residence, a bungalow. I enquired about David and learned that he has been with the family for fifteen years and is married with five or six children. The Gullisons furnish his cottage, an ordinary mud-brick dwelling behind the main house.

The Gullison's house has no window glass or insect-proof screens; openings are covered with wire mesh and beds are provided with mosquito netting. There is no plumbing; David carries the wash water and fills the pails. I have no difficulty taking a bath the Indian way by pouring water over myself.

Approximately 10,000 people live in Sompeta, which is in the northern tip of Andhra Pradesh State and two miles from the Bay of Bengal at Baruva. They speak Telegu, a language appreciated all over the country for its musical cadences. I thought its sound similar to Italian. If the figure of 10,000 population includes the surrounding villages, I would not be surprised because Sompeta does not impress me as a densely peopled place. Rather, it is penetrated by rural character and open space.

My hostess took me on a tour of the hospital buildings, all of them small, one story, Indian-style structures with unglazed windows. Then we arrived at the out-patient department and found Dr. Gullison providing care, accompanied by nurses and the *compounder*, or pharmacist. In the maternity section I attended the christening of a newborn. She was given the name Rose in Telegu by the pastor of the local church, John Ranga Rao. Improvements continue in the form of a new water tank and a small building for sick missionaries. The pastor is also getting a new house of concrete block. I was told that there are many delays in construction, since the funds come from abroad.

The hospital is also home to an eye clinic where "eye camps" are scheduled to attract large numbers of adults and children so they may be screened for eye diseases or vitamin deficiencies. An Indian doctor is in charge. The clinic has recently been given a Dodge van by American friends; a team use it to go into the surrounding villages on Sundays, broadcasting the appeal to villagers to present themselves at the next eye camp. The farmers and others, their eyes restored to health, are capable of increased output. The outstanding work consists of the large number of cataract surgeries performed here—up to fifty a day—by a team led by the eye clinic's director. For those who cannot pay for their operation a provision for free care exists.

[In 1963, following an address by Dr. Gullison to a group in Calgary, Alberta, a new support organization was established calling itself Operation Eyesight Universal. This has grown until, in 1992 alone, 23,862 men, women, and children were treated for a variety of eye diseases, including 2,333 people whose sight was restored through cataract surgery in the twelve developing countries where O.E.U. has programs.]

Leprosy is treated in the hospital, and Dr. Gullison is the only non-Indian on the state Leprosy Control Board. The disease (which is painless) is related to TB, affecting the skin and extremities instead of the lungs, and is spread where people live in crowded, unsanitary conditions. The malady is presently increasing in India.

I joined Pastor John on the first of several walking and bicycle tours of the area around Sompeta. It was fascinating to observe the life and work of the local people and ask questions. They work in cottage industries, which require small, if any, capital investment and provide the people with many everyday necessities. Such industries strengthen the national economy by satisfying the appetites that would otherwise turn to manufactured goods imported from industrial countries. The hard currency that would have been spent for these imports can then be utilized to import goods not produced locally. For all these reasons the government does a lot to foster cottage manufactures. Before Independence, handspun, handwoven cloth was rapidly disappearing from the market, driven out by cheaper machine-made cloth from British mills, which most Indians considered to be more desirable than homespun.

The assistance offered by the government consists of marketing services and price controls, and every city has its handicraft emporium where arts and crafts of the region are displayed for sale. I found them to be excellent in quality and reasonably priced. The products include coconut fiber mats and fishnets, pottery water jars, and plain cloth for apparel.

In the neighboring village of Jinkibudra we saw men tying the warp threads for plain cloth, the long threads extending many yards. The simple looms are in the cottages. The weavers sit on the ground with their feet in a trench under the loom, and throw the flying shuttle. Family members take turns at the work, completing a sari length in a day. The finished piece, seven yards in length, brings Rs 7 in the market, but the weavers do not receive the full amount.

Pottery is another Jinkibudra industry. I was absorbed watching the potter, who works out of doors on a balanced wheel with a heavy rim turned by hand or stick. The lump of clay is placed on the wheel as it revolves and in less than a minute takes the basic form of a large jar, leaping up under the skilled hands of the potter. Then he cuts the clay off at the base and places the bottomless jar on the ground to dry a little. Later, with a heavy wooden mallet, he beats the sides out to form the bottom. Then the pot is worked over several times with a mallet to temper and compact the clay. When round and finished it is set aside until firing. Then hundreds of pots are stacked in a mound, with combustible material between. The mound is covered with straw, then sand, and ignited at the bottom. The nearly airtight pile burns slowly several days until the pots are finished. A water vessel of three gallon capacity sells in the market for eight annas, Rs .50.

Pastor John took us to the neighborhood where people weave baskets or other articles out of bamboo wood—head carriers, rice strainers, mats, rugs, and bedding. As I watched a large head carrier in process, it appeared to be easy to do. The finished article brings eight annas. One man's output is eight per day.

Then we stopped to watch several men busy rolling and tying *beedis* (miniature cigars) which I tasted and found too strong. Regular cigarettes are also strong and cheap.

In Jinkibudra cooking oil is processed by grinding gingili seeds. A cow or water buffalo walks continually in a circle, connected by a pole to the grinder in the center; the oil flows into a large vessel. The animal needs a child or elderly person to keep it moving with voice and stick.

On a visit to the sea-front village of Baruva, Pastor John and I saw the government school which teaches the manufacture of coir (coconut) fiber products. The course lasts two years, as students learn to clean and process the material and then weave the coir into rope, fishnets, rugs, and mats. They adhere to standards required by the mass market. The students, who are poor, receive a small stipend and their keep.

Sompeta, Thursday, December 14
Pastor John and I used bicycles to reach the hill district to the west, where begin the Eastern Ghats. This is the range that culminates locally in Mahendra Giri, at nearly 5,000 feet. At the summit

are some small temples (visited once a year during a festival) and a British-built tourist bungalow, which was formerly popular but since Independence has been neglected. Our destination, however, was limited to the area inhabited by the Savara people, a primitive hill tribe with their own, semi-Hindu culture. We took paths that border the cultivated areas and attractive ponds full of bird life and, perhaps, fish.

My guide pointed out that in the short distance we traveled three language areas are included: Telegu, Savara, and, as we are very near Orissa, Oryia. Each of these is a distinct language; Telegu belongs to the Dravidian group of South India, Oryia to the Indo-Aryan group of the North, and Savara is unlike either—and only given written form by a missionary-linguist in the nineteenth century.

Pastor John told me the Savara are timid people who run when approached by strangers. We saw very few of them in the settlement. We could visit it because the pastor was known to them and could take me along without disturbing them. The Savara settlement consisted of about two dozen houses situated on both sides of an open area wider than a roadway. The small dwellings were connected to each other by single separating mud walls. Each had a slightly elevated platform in front; women and children sat in perfect quiet in several of the doorways. No men were visible. They were either hunting or working in gardens somewhere beyond our sight. To enter the area between the two rows of houses one had to pass a barrier. Nothing else attracted my notice—no water, stock, trees, or other furniture of living. The zone nearby was under cultivation. The hills began several hundred feet distant.

Along our way, Pastor John indicated some land which was available to anyone wishing to cultivate it. To my eye it appeared poor but usable, and there were signs that someone had tackled the job of putting it under the plow.

We fetched another village, where several residents invited us to hear a musical performance given by several men and boys in the village hall. The group made interesting noises on several instruments. The sound could be sweeter and softer, but I was not looking for pleasurable listening as much as knowledge of what the people do for entertainment. One of the group, a teacher, accompanied us a short distance and asked me to send a postcard from my country.

Next we came to a Brahmin village, which was built along a short street of some width. At one end stood a temple. The houses were decorated schematically by painted designs, equally applied to walls, door frames and a small veranda. The paint seemed to be some non-permanent substance—perhaps in connection with a festival.

As we left the village, a man came forward and spoke to Pastor John, requesting the help of Dr. Gullison. It could have been serious so we cycled back to the village to see the sick woman. Her husband explained the symptoms to the pastor, while I waited inside the door. It was one square room, poorly lit, with a thatch roof, very little or no furniture, and a storage place, perhaps for clothing or cooking equipment. Chairs and table were absent. There was a fireplace where the wife, squatting, prepared the family meals. There were probably some coir, cane, or grass mats somewhere. We would call such a home poor, primitive, or worse. However, Western rules and values do not apply here in village India. The household of the Brahmin couple satisfies its occupants. The woman's extra time is sometimes given to spinning yarn and weaving cloth. Ceremony also fills a part of the day, including pursuits such as decorating the house and also drawing religious patterns on the clean-swept, packed-clay in front—new ones every morning! Lime is used for this purpose.

Along our route—not a road but a path—we came to a recent small dam project, located where a water course issues from the hills. It was not very practical. It could not hold much water and the reservoir was already filling with soil washed down from the hills beyond. Pastor John told me that politics were behind the project. Today we noticed a few workers in the vicinity, busy in adding height to the earthen dam.

Next we fetched the cottage of a village couple, Christians, who invited us to be seated on their veranda. The wife served our lunch: boiled rice, vegetable curry, *puris* (fried dough), mango chutney, *rasam* (lentil soup), and *dosay*. Some dishes were too spiced for my taste; however, I endured them for fear of appearing impolite, and I wanted to try everything. As we bid adieu Pastor John gave them a little money.

We were approaching Sompeta again when the pastor stopped and pointed across the fields to a knoll covered with thick vegetation. Snake Mound, as he called it, was inhabited by reptiles. No one will approach it. The idea he conveyed was that of a dreadful and mysterious spot, respected in the fancy of the people, which could not be touched; I had no wish to approach it any closer or investigate the claim that it is home to numerous reptiles of all types. In fact, Dr. Gullison gave me a list of the snake species that he himself has seen in his twenty-five years in Sompeta: boa constrictor, cobra (found in their residence), puff adder (makes a sound like a bicycle tire losing air), common adder, viper, garter snake, water snake. Other reptiles in residence around this place included iguana (one to three feet), chameleon (fifteen inches and changing color), common lizard (wall variety), and toad (lives in house at peace with Dr. Gullison's dog).

Sompeta, Friday, December 15

It was bicycles again today and we fetched up the Bay of Bengal at Baruva, on the road this time, passing bullock carts and rice harvesting. Our first stop in Baruva was the government hostel for boys, whose warden, C.S. Prakasa Rao, told us how untouchable lads from poor families of the district live here, absorbing a healthy, prejudice-free life. He is a Christian and Pastor John's friend. I was astonished to hear they eat for only Rs 15 monthly—$3. Lunch is the one main meal and is always the same: boiled rice, vegetable curry, *dal* (purée of lentils), *rasam* (lentil consommé), and curds (yogurt). The milk powder for curds is a much appreciated gift from the United States. Dr. Gullison is a contact person for such aid.

At Baruva we took the opportunity to see the school that makes coir products and talk to the director. He told us something of two more industries: betel nut and cashew nut processing. The latter is a lucrative export, or re-export, because the unprocessed nuts are imported from Africa to supplement the local crop.

The seashore here in Baruva is close to a tropical paradise. The sand is pure, clean, and empty of people other than a few fishermen, while the sun bathes sea and shore in warmth and light.

There is a tourist bungalow, just a house behind a dune. It appeared empty. A ruined lighthouse stands nearby. The surf echoed in our ears; I never saw the Bay of Bengal either calm or stormy—always betwixt and between. The Gullisons say they have the best beach on the east coast, and in fact I cannot imagine a better. I hope it stays that way. We swam and paddled.

Mr. Prakasa gave us lunch at the boys' hostel. Each item of the meal was wrapped in a large leaf, which served to carry it in as well as to eat from. This is how "carry-out" is done here.

Wild life is plentiful in the district, perhaps due to the proximity of the Ghats and uncultivated areas. These animals include the leopard (also found in the villages on occasion), sloth bear (dangerous to meet up with—the hospital has treated their bites), jackal (very common, heard nightly), hyena, wolf, tiger (in mountains), several species of monkeys, baboon, flying fox, deer, mongoose, chipmunk (grey). The variety is astonishing and reflects the people's great tolerance of life, as well as their lack of weapons suitable to its elimination.

Later we revisited Jinkibudra, an interesting village for various reasons. Today we called upon a Christian family who live in a group of very long, narrow houses, a style common in this district. The corridor in a typical European house is only slightly less roomy than these dwellings. The entrance is carved and painted. When you face the doorway it is the wall on the right which belongs to the house on the right, while the wall on the left belongs to the house in front of you. Fire is a concern because all are covered by a thatch roof. The narrow cot beds are turned up on the side during the day to enable people to walk past. The family cow is the last to be brought into the house at night and remains in front, since it is also the first to leave in the morning. The chickens live in the rear because they never go out.

The mistress of the house we visited is a teacher. Many Christians are teachers, being often better educated than other Indians. She showed us the "suitcase post office" she manages, containing everything required to run the village post office—out of a suitcase. The government is experimenting with these and it seems like a good starter and a way to teach others. She served us sweets.

One citizen of Jinkibudra, who is president-elect of the village, has a garden that won first prize for Andhra Pradesh in the Agricultural Fair in Delhi in 1960. I met him and saw the photograph of Nehru handing him the prize. It was too dark to visit the garden itself.

Sompeta, Saturday, December 16

Following lunch at home Pastor John, Mrs. Gullison, and I took ourselves to a small country market about ten miles distant, driving the Willys station wagon, which also serves as ambulance. The pastor and I were considering cycling, but we were glad to accept the offer of a ride, and Mrs. Gullison carried a stack of twenty-five tracts with her, which she would sell at the fair for very little each. The fair is larger in other seasons than in harvest time, which it was now. It was still an interesting show. While Mrs. Gullison sold tracts, I accompanied Pastor John among the people and vendors. He is a kind and patient man who explained everything. The market is situated in the countryside, not near a village. The government would like to improve the facilities and has already made cement platforms for individual stalls—a series of these with open space between. Later it plans to construct a framed shelter on each, but the people are already refusing to occupy the concrete slabs and set up on the bare ground between the slabs. This preference demonstrates the Indian desire for contact with the earth—most Indians do not wear sandals and shoes are rare. Each vendor had a place on the ground where he displayed his wares along with those of his fellow dealers in the same kinds of goods: textiles, cooking utensils, cosmetics, dried food such as grains, and herbs and spices. Very few items were factory made. Pastor John could identify many of the plants and seeds, one of which contained the dye used by the *dhobis* (laundrymen) for marking garments. The cosmetics are powders, largely in shades of red or blue, stored in jars or bowls for sale. Women use the red powder to mark their foreheads, and devotees of Shiva or Vishnu mark their foreheads with the corresponding dye.

Before we left we bought betel nut to chew. The crushed nut is smeared with several savory pastes and wrapped in *pan* leaves. Each of us took a piece—my companions with relish and I with some timidity. It was not my first experience, for it had been offered to me in Varanasi. It's bitter to the taste. People here love it. We chewed our way back to the bungalow. The coconut palm is the source of betel and the government operates plantations.

Sompeta, Sunday, December 17

I prepared to leave tonight. Mrs. Gullison drove to a nearby village to pick up and return to their homes several "Bible women." They stay in the village several days to visit Hindu homes and preach the Gospel. This is the only way to proselytize women in India, for it is unseemly for men to go house to house, and women cannot be reached elsewhere than at home.

I rested in the bungalow, reading and writing letters. Something I ate disagreed with me and the doctor gave me a pill that cured it, for by evening I felt well again. After bidding my generous hosts adieu, I was driven to Palasa in the hospital station wagon, going to pick up some missionaries arriving by the Madras Mail, which does not stop in Sompeta. I was carrying a note to a Christian at the station, who gave me a place to sleep in the refreshment room, atop a table, instead of in the waiting room.

Madras, Monday, December 18

The Madras Mail halted before dawn and I began the longest, most difficult rail trip thus far. All seats were full and passengers were stretched out in the aisles, squatting or standing in every available space. Where were they all going? In India people do a great deal of moving about. The metal suitcase-stool did excellent service, as I was forced to sit on the upended box for about twenty-four hours. As I was nearly out of money, the only food I could afford was small vegetable *masala dosas*, ground nuts, and tea—the sustainer. These items were available from vendors who serve the train in every station, passing their wares through the windows and receiving payment. Second class was nearly as crowded as third, but I had no choice in any case, because it costs double third class.

Madras, Tuesday, September 19

We came to a stop in Madras Central at 6:45 a.m., and I breathed a sigh of relief. A rickshaw carried me to the YMCA, where I secured a cot bed in a room with three others. After several hours' rest, I telephoned K.N. George at the Madras School of Social Work, of which he is director. We had met in Cleveland,when he was studying there on a grant. He invited me for lunch, and then showed me his school, which occupies the bungalow of the former English Inspector General. A letter waiting for me said money was on the way.

In my list of addresses was that of Bertram Werwie, a university instructor from Germany whom I had met at the International Students Group, the people who effectively made this trip possible. I telephoned him today at Madras University only to learn that he was departing for Ceylon on vacation and would return in two weeks. I caught him as the taxi to the airport arrived at their door; however I had their invitation to visit later. Still, my affairs were in disarray due to lack of cash, and I returned to the Y feeling somewhat weary.

Madras, Wednesday, December 20

India disposed of Portuguese Goa today. A cartoon in the paper showed Nehru dropping a dead rat marked GOA in the trash while several Western leaders stood around, aghast. The event seemed to draw only moderate notice.

Madras is India's third largest city. It can claim some attractive qualities. It is the capital of Madras State [now Tamil Nadu]. Its location directly on the Bay of Bengal is outstanding and is enhanced by the long Marina Drive facing the sea, and lined with several imposing buildings. The area is planted and maintained. I set forth on foot to see what I could without money. This was the first English *entrepôt* in India, founded in 1653 by the East India Company before

Calcutta. I saw the Church of St. Mary, the first Anglican place of worship in Asia. It holds memorials of interest to an American traveler. The side walls of the church are covered with plaques dedicated to the Englishmen who died here where mortality among them was high. Elihu Yale, founder of Yale University, lies here. John Burgoyne is here, and Lord Cornwallis, British generals in the Revolutionary War. I passed along both sides, seeking markers of special interest. Judging by the inscriptions, there were many who ended their days far from home. India was their second home, the scene of lucrative and interesting careers. The church resembles a parish church in England.

An easy distance from the Y is Fort St. George, which served the Company. The museum in the fort holds souvenirs of the Company—arms, uniforms, pictures, letters, flags, and other memorabilia.

Leaving the fort, it is a short walk across the sand to the edge of the bay, from where the view of the marina is good. I observed workers in the planted areas next to the roadway, among them women performing the same heavy work as men, such as carrying loads on their heads.

I visited the tourist department for more free literature: its guides are well done. I walked north to the end of the marina and the university. Fishermen on shore were working the nets. Otherwise there seems to be no public use of the beach in this season.

I asked the Y secretary about pawning my binoculars to raise some cash; he said it was not safe to trust them to a money lender. He let me have Rs 10 as a loan on them. He had difficulty in finding even that amount; however, I am finding people helpful.

Madras, Thursday, December 21

Today I wrote letters and read in Nehru's *Discovery of India* and other books acquired in Calcutta: Ghandi's *Experiments in Truth*, and short stories by Mulk Raj Anand. I am now sharing my room with two German travelers waiting for a ship to Penang, Malaya. The fare seems cheap. One of them left me a good map of India.

I read in the newspaper of a severe cold wave in the north. In Bihar 105 deaths were reported, while the weather office in Gaya recorded 33 degrees F, "lowest in living memory." A district magistrate ordered fires built at major intersections to keep the pavement dwellers from freezing. They have so little.

As I had Rs 10 burning a hole in my pocket, I mailed nine letters and purchased several air letters, inland letters, and writing paper—all of which left me nearly broke again. It is a long time since I felt a little prosperity—and I have been guarding my expenses ever since leaving Turkey.

I admired the Victoria Memorial, a building in red sandstone surrounded by a garden. It held a small collection of contemporary Indian painting, which showed the influence of French, Japanese, and earlier Indian and Persian styles. It also had an archaeological section, and a bronze gallery. South Indian bronzes of all periods and high quality were on display.

The proprietor of the Y restaurant is permitting me to take my meals on faith that I will pay. The same good man invited me and another American for a drive on the marina under the full moon, in his auto. We continued as far as San Thome Cathedral (Roman Catholic), near the sea, where the Apostle Thomas is said to be buried. We walked on the beach watching the moonlight reflected off the surf.

Madras, Friday, December 22

At the U.S. Consulate an American employee loaned me Rs 50 with my transistor radio as security. With this money I recovered my binoculars and began to expand my range of sightseeing. San Thome and its neighborhood attracted me. Legend says the saint came to India as a missionary and found martyrdom at St. Thomas Mount in A.D. 72. The knoll so named is near the airport. They say he was praying before a stone inscribed with a cross when he was struck down, the same stone that may be seen behind the high altar in the sixteenth-century church of Our Lady of Expectation, which occupies the site of an earlier church supposedly established by the apostle. In this way Christianity could have been introduced to India, long before the Portuguese arrived in 1499.

A few steps from San Thome the Kapaleshwara Temple had already attracted my notice by its high *gopuram*, a truncated pyramid rising over the principal entrance. This is the first Dravidian temple I have seen. It also catches attention because it is covered with a profusion of carved figures of gods, demons, and animals, all brightly colored. It reminded me of a large store counter displaying every kind of costumed doll or animal figure. The *Kapaleshwara* means "Abode of Peacocks." I was allowed into the courtyard with the help of a guide; from there I glimpsed the inner sanctum, where the image of the god was being bathed in oil and flower petals. As Hindu worship is a private act, the chamber is relatively small. Peacocks are carved into the face of the tower and I was shown a single live bird confined in a cage.

A snake charmer in front of the temple had two cobras in a small round basket with a cover. He succeeded in charming one but not the second. Then both struck at him harmlessly—the fangs are removed. I think snake charmers can find a place in modern India, for their art provides entertainment and education.

I reached the suburb of Adyar by walking across a bridge over the Adyar River. There I found the international headquarters of the Theosophical Society, as well as the Kalakshetra School, and the great banyan tree which ranks among the four largest in the country. The branches were full of crows gorging on red berries. Pleasant gardens and spacious grounds are connected to the Theosophical Society. I walked through them to the sea, where, just at sunset, I enjoyed a sea bath, as it is called here. It was calm for once.

Madras, Saturday, December 23

Madras is the capital of Madras State and Tamil the language, though all educated people speak English, generally well. In the South, where Hindi is not native, they resist it and prefer English as the lingua franca. This makes it easy for a foreigner; so much so that it is unnecessary to learn any local language. In speaking to a pedicab driver, for example, I use English and suspect that should I use a Hindi phrase he would probably reply in English. In speaking to people who appear educated, one need not inquire if they know English but can assume that they do.

In front of the YMCA on the pavement dwell several families who appear to be permanent residents. They have numerous, nearly naked children who beg. Mothers prepare meals on a small fire contained in a circle of stones, using anything they can find for fuel. By night everyone lies down next to the foundations of the Y with no more than a gray, tattered sheet for cover. The nights are cool in the South, but not uncomfortable. When one mentions the pavement dwellers, other Indians may say it is unnecessary to live as they do, and a palm leaf hut on the city's edge or in an empty place is easy and cheap to build. But the pavement people continue their ways. I heard it said the government will not now prohibit the habit because an election is coming.

I found the marina pool delightful, clean, and warm. Furthermore I read somewhere that the offshore waters are alive with sharks. The pool seems to be too cold for the local people in the present season.

This evening I attended the opening performance of the Kalakshetra Silver Jubilee Art Festival in Adyar. Ever since I saw a movie at home showing *Bharat Natyam*, the classical Indian dance, I have wanted to see it in real life and this was the occasion. A temporary theater has been erected of poles and woven coconut leaves for this week's musical festival. The dancers, of both sexes, wear ornate, brightly colored costumes and are accompanied by instrumental music and song. The story was entitled *Andar*.

Tirukkalikundrum and Mahabalipuram, Sunday, December 24

Madras State Transport offered a day-long bus tour to this pair of places for Rs 5 and, though I had only Rs 10, I booked a ticket, securing a place on the one luxury coach having reclining seats and a toilet. Returning, it broke down and all passengers had to travel in the second, conventional coach, which was already near to full, so many of us had to stand.

First came Tirukkalikundrum, where we mounted a long stairway to the temple, comparable to a fortress. The country is green and irregular. The people were waiting to see a pair of sacred kites (hawk-like birds) arrive and be fed from the hands of a priest. At about noon the priest emerged and the birds swooped down to him. They are reputed to come from Varanasi, but I noticed both perched across a divide on the facing rocks before the feeding event. Both were nearly or wholly white plumaged.

Then came Mahabalipuram, which was more exciting and worthy of more time than remained. It is on the Bay of Bengal south of Madras where the beach continues along the east coast. Ports are scarce, but fortune smiled on the enterprise of the Pallava kings of the seventh century A.D. They were established at Kanchipuram to the northwest and launched far-reaching trade and cultural expeditions from the port which is now the quiet village of Mahabalipuram. Many relics of that vigorous dynasty of traders remain here, including some of the oldest Dravidian art and architecture. There are five outstanding examples.

The first is a large bas relief consisting of hundreds of figures—people, gods, and animals—covering the face of a granite ledge 80 feet long by an average 20 feet high. This result of Pallava artisanship has endured extremely well and is greatly admired by the many who come to this place, looking for inspiration and insight into India's once triumphant culture. Indian religious and aesthetic ideas blended with those of Southeast Asia, resulting in new national styles in such places as Java, Cambodia, and Thailand. The temples of Angkor in Cambodia, portraying both Hindu and Buddhist divinities, and the

Buddhist temple of Borobudur in Java serve as examples. Thailand and Burma emerged as Buddhist nations. In later centuries some of the Hindu influence waned with the arrival of Islam.

The Shore Temple is the second example of the architecture of Mahabalipuram. The Pallavas pioneered the Dravidian temple style and this is one of the oldest examples. At one time other temples existed here. They have been washed away, leaving the present one standing on a stubby peninsula protected by a sea wall. The Pallava builders seemed to set forth on the sea, so to speak, when choosing the site.

The third example in the area are rock-cut caves carved with lively representations of the goddess Durga in combat with evil, as represented by a buffalo-headed demon.

Fourth are the Five Rathas, small, richly decorated "temple-chariots" on the pattern of Puri's giant *ratha*, each carved from a block of living rock. Standing separately are life-size figures of an elephant, a lion and a bull. Each *ratha* reveals the form of a Dravidian temple in one of several variations.

The last of these five examples of Pallava art are the *mandapams*, which are porches consisting of carved pillars and columns, usually set before temples. Here they do not lead to temples because they are sculpted out of the living rock face.

The collection of these sculptural and architectural wonders provides convincing proof of the vitality of the Pallava age, though it was not long chronologically. It is sad that its history is not well known. Scholars are still searching for more information to cast light on the Pallava period, as well as those that preceded and followed it.

As I was examining Mahabalipuram I encountered a group of performers. I admit that their tricks sometimes amazed me. One of them seemed to disgorge stones larger than an egg, several in succession. A sword swallower actually put the sword some distance down his throat. A battle between a snake and a mongoose turned out in favor of the latter because Mr. Snake was already half dead, by appearances. He was not a cobra.

Once back in Madras we stopped at the Ghandi Mandap, a canopy-like building that serves as a prayer shelter in remembrance of him. An irreverent visitor had a transistor radio turned on while the rest of us were trying to think of Ghandi. Some Indians show poor public manners, talking loudly and pushing, for example. So ended an interesting day.

In the Y restaurant this evening, I listened to a conversation among an Englishman, an Australian, and an American. The subjects were crocodile hunting in India, wild life sanctuaries, and modes of travel in the Far East. The Australian was hoping to fetch Europe with only a few pounds in hand. He was certainly poorer than I was.

Madras, Monday, December 25

There were few choices available for celebrating Christmas Day. Attendance at St. Mary's Church was all I could do, but it was a little like Christmas at home. The congregation this morning was divided between Indians and Europeans. Fresh flowers decorated the church. Afterward I sought the vicar to ask him whether he thought the St. Thomas mission to India was truth or legend. He told me that it was a persistent legend without any historical substance. Nevertheless, it could have taken place, and the tradition might have some underlying truth.

In the afternoon and evening I joined the Theosophists, who were assembling today for their annual convention, beginning tomorrow. Only a few small groups were on hand now in the restful gardens and lawns of their world headquarters in the suburbs. The students and staff of Annie Besant High School had responsibility for the arrangements to serve meals under a specially erected coconut palm shelter.

While several curious villagers watched, I took a sea bath again at Elliot's Beach—the water fine though agitated and with a strong current. Then I looked at the library, which contains the writings of Annie Besant and other Theosophists. The society publishes monographs and articles by members and, of course, books on Theosophy.

The Theosophical Society was founded in New York in 1875. Colonel Henry Steel Olcott was the first president and Madame Helena Blavatsky the first secretary. Annie Besant was a prominent subsequent president. The society shifted its center to India, where it has become an international association of 35,000 members.

Theosophy draws on Eastern religions (as well as several ancient writers) to construct a philosophy of life that adapts to ancient spiritual doctrines of the godhead, creation, matter, and consciousness. The resemblance to Hindu ideas is evident. The society does not, however, claim to be a religion, and it does not proselytize. Its three main objects are to (1) form a nucleus of believers in the universal brotherhood of man; (2) encourage the study of comparative religion, philosophy, and science; (3) investigate the unexplained laws of nature and the powers latent in man.

One of the Theosophists I met today was an Assamese, who gave some information about his homeland. Assam is a wet region in the northeast of India. It is home to the Naga people, who have been seeking independence. As I found myself out of money again, the man from Assam offered to buy my tea and dinner. I accepted with gratitude. Then he paid for my ticket to the evening performance of classical Kathakali dance taking place at the Kalakshetra School. It was a tale from the *Mahabharata*, "Kalakeya Vadham." Men portray all parts. I watched two actors participating in a dialogue, one delivered a long speech full of grunting and moaning, while the second actor responded with facial expressions. The costumes were elaborate and makeup cleverly applied to enhance the slight facial movement. Several musicians accompanied the story on drums and cymbals. This carried on for two hours by which time I began to grow weary. At the end I was ready to conclude that I like the Bharat Natyam better, which is all movement and delightful to watch.

Madras, Tuesday, December 26

K.N. George returned from a trip and telephoned today to say I had a letter, but it contained no money, so my friend generously volunteered to lend me Rs 200. Therefore I can proceed to Pondicherry, and I can recover my radio, which I have missed while it was in hock. I paid my bill at the Y and prepared to leave. Mr. George had me to his house for a dinner of chicken salad, carrots, beans, and *chappatis*.

After dinner we walked in Egmore, which offers shops and hotel-restaurant facilities. Among other subjects, he mentioned the prevalence of smuggling here. Tourists try to bring in electronic equipment and gold; both bring high prices, the gold because the people place their assets in the metal. Import restrictions are enforced; however, tourists continue to attempt to sneak gold past customs. Foreign tourists bringing in cameras, jewelry, radios, and other saleable items have to list them and give them a value when they enter India, and are required to re-export them or pay duty when they leave. However true all this may be, I was not affected. When I spoke of my plan to visit Pondicherry, a former French enclave, he said I might stay at the Ashram of Sri Aurobindo, and so I made the arrangements.

Pondicherry, Wednesday, December 27

Pondicherry is 100 miles down the Carnatic Coast by bus. The countryside produces rice and coconuts; the two crops make a pleasing combination to the sight. Upon fetching Pondi and leaving the comfortable bus, I spied a young man, who proved to be delegated by the ashram to meet and guide visitors back to the Aurobindo community. He put me and my two bags in a pedicab and followed on his bicycle. We arrived at the dining hall, where dinner was underway. Seating was *par terre* with a metal food server placed on a low stand in front of each person. The meal consisted of a measure of boiled rice served in a large stainless steel dish, two side dishes of mixed vegetables and lentil soup, and bread. Each person received a slice of fresh lime for seasoning, plus bananas for dessert. This menu did not vary except on New Year's Day, when the rice and vegetables contained peanuts. Repetitious as it was, the food always tasted delicious and nutritious.

My guide, Babulal Saha, provided a tour of the ashram facilities this afternoon, first taking me to visit Aurobindo's *samadhi*, as the Hindus call the cremation site of a holy person. It is evidently the focus of devotions by the guru's followers—in the form of prayer, meditation, and flower offerings. It is a tranquil spot, even surrounded as it is by ashram activity.

Babulal then took me to the registry office, where I engaged to stay a short time at least, for I was curious to know more. We bicycled to the Parc à Charbon, where he showed me the dormitory and small sleeping cubicles. I chose the latter—they were monastic, clean, and well kept. The cot bed had no webbing, only boards and a thin mattress. As these quarters were directly on the shore, the surf was audible. The accommodations with meals cost $1.20 per diem.

It was deemed I should meet one of the American residents, and so my guide introduced me to Dr. Jay Holmes Smith, who had been there nine years. He was a cultivated, gentle man whose temperament may have been influenced by his long stay in India. He directed an offshoot of the ashram named World Union, which works for unity of spirit between nations, organizations, and individuals. There is a bi-monthly journal also named World Union. In the early 1940s Dr. Smith had been secretary of the Fellowship of Reconciliation, a pacifist organization which aided conscientious objectors in the war years.

We saw the library, where comfortable wicker furniture, plants, and abundant sunlight make study enjoyable. After seeing it I was more prepared to remain awhile because the community offers much nourishment to mind and spirit.

This evening a company of Calcutta actors presented a drama on the life of the Hindu theologian Ramanuja. As it was in Sanskrit, a dead language, I cannot say how much the audience understood; they must have been familiar with the story and could recognize the costumes, music, gestures, and makeup. I found the performance impressive; the man next to me—seating was *par terre*—filled me in some and also relayed additional information about the ashram, such as the daily Meditation of the Mother.

Upon Aurobindo's departure for Nirvana in 1950, the Mother became spiritual and temporal leader of the ashram community. She had arrived in Aurobindo's circle thirty-five years earlier and eventually became acknowledged by him as a yogin, or female yogi. In her resided the power to bring his ideas to fruition. Without her, said the guru, his concepts could not have borne fruit. The guru's followers continue to bestow their reverence on this French disciple of the holy man. She is the authority to whom every question or new plan is referred. The ashram guest who remains a length of time requires the Mother's blessing to be accepted.

Pondicherry, Thursday, December 28

This morning, arising before dawn, I set out from the Parc à Charbon by bicycle. Reaching the meditation place as the light of day was breaking, I found about three dozen people already gathered in the street below the empty balcony of the Mother's residence. They were quiet, their gaze directed upward where the figure was almost due to appear. Then a white-robed and hooded form emerged and cast her eyes downward at us for a minute, saying nothing. Then, eyes raised to the heavens, she held that position for several more silent minutes. Lastly, she brought her eyes down again, then backed into the house, and those present began to set forth on the day's activities. The Mother is eighty-five and she appeared pale in a white sari. I did not know what to think of this experience; surely it was different from any other I had had.

Breakfast also showed the signature of the ashram. It consisted of warm sugared milk in a bowl, with yeast bread and bananas on the side. Every morning it was the same. We could break the bread and slice the banana into the milk or consume them separately. Either way it always tasted good.

Then I walked along the sea front and stole a smoke, because the rules include a ban on smoking, drinking, talking politics, and sex. While on this walk I came upon a group of people taking a sea bath. They were coal miners and their wives on a tour of India's holy places, and while here in Pondicherry they intended to visit the *samadhi* of Sri Aurobindo. These pilgrims sought to visit more than temples and tanks.

The guru had stipulated that everyone in the ashram community would make a contribution by performing a task that helps all. Accordingly, workshops, small industries, farms, stores, and other adjuncts to the community are found. Today I joined an escorted tour to see several of them. The initial stop was at a small manufactory specializing in quality book paper. The people worked slowly and deliberately; I wondered why when they might have speeded up without taxing themselves. We were then taken to the printing plant where the many books by Aurobindo are produced. The metal shop, laundry, poultry farm, theater, and dairy rounded out the tour.

In the afternoon I visited the former European part of the city, la ville blanche, as distinguished from the Indian quarter, la ville noire. It contains regular streets of residences, old commercial buildings, and institutions presenting unembellished walls to the street punctuated by French *portails*. Most interesting is the strip along the sea containing the somewhat grand boulevard where remains the statue of Pondi's best-known French governor, Marquis Dupleix, who for a time coped effectively with the British adversary in the eighteenth century. [Later this was replaced with the figure of Ghandi.] There is a church, library, Government House, and a statue of Joan of Arc to remind people of the French regime. It was quiet in the vicinity—hardly a vehicle and very few people on the street, like a place passed by. Nevertheless the neighborhood was clean and the streets, parks, and garden surrounding the Dupleix monument were well cared for. I was reminded of France, a *station balnéaire* in the off-season. A storm-damaged pier juts into the sea and a well-built lighthouse stands next to the marine drive. Nothing of a port remains intact and one might doubt it ever existed, yet this was the principal French emporium in India.

Pondicherry, Friday, December 29

Today brings the beginning of the First Annual Convention of the Sri Aurobindo Society. Because it seemed the polite thing, I again attended the dawn Meditation of the Mother, at which no words were spoken.

The sunny comfort of the ashram library drew me as I gave most of the morning to reading several chapters of dense material on Integral Yoga and Aurobindo. His titles are "The Life Divine," "Synthesis of Yoga," "The Ideal of Human Unity," "On Yoga," and "The Human Cycle." I purchased Volume 1, containing more than 1,000 pages. It will probably remain a souvenir of my stay, for somehow I doubt if I can digest much of it. The author's writing style is good, I believe; but there is too much of it to be retained by my already overstuffed head. Aurobindo put all the forms of yoga together in one system (Integral Yoga) which, he said, is suitable for modern living and all places.

This afternoon I joined a bus trip to the rice paddies of the ashram, where the Japanese method of rice culture is practiced. It yields two crops a year and a crop of green fertilizer plowed under in two months. Then I saw the Lake Estate, the site of a projected agricultural institute to border the unspoiled lake seven miles from Pondi. The plans are ambitious.

I observed the gathering of the convention in the evening. The stage held large photographs of Aurobindo and the Mother surrounded by flowers. A recorded message from the present leader contained a suggestion on the correct distribution of wealth. It seemed to hint that members would do well to give their extra money to the ashram. I heard no distinguished speeches. I may have missed something. A talk by a representative of the ashram school gave some insights. The tenets of the institution according to Aurobindo are: (1) education centered on the individual student, (2) curriculum based on an understanding of the child's psychology and stages of development (3) atmosphere of freedom, (4) development of the personality. The school also seeks to educate for the higher life, the spiritual, and declares that qualification for diplomas is not its primary purpose.

There is a Collège de France in the town where some faculty are French and courses are taught in French. I wonder how long it will continue, for a person needs English in the India of today. However, a French-speaking individual would be equipped to live in one of the former French colonies. I met several French-speaking Vietnamese in the street who mentioned the Collège.

Pondicherry, Saturday, December 30

I visited Dr. Smith again. He told me how he came to make his residence here. It seems that he came across a book about Aurobindo in the New York Public Library and then located some people who were familiar with the holy man. Feeling inspired, he and his wife traveled to California by Greyhound bus; there they resided in a cabin on top of a mountain and studied the "Synthesis of Yoga." Both worked to save the money to come to India for one year and return should they wish. The outcome was they remained, and Dr. Smith says they intend to spend the rest of their days here. He has been a peace worker for a long time, making efforts in behalf of a group called One World Congress with whom he has traveled on peace missions.

I found the Cottage Restaurant, owned by the ashram, a pleasant place to spend a couple of hours over tea and a book. The serving area is on top of the building, where the tables are surrounded by greenery, some in flower. Other small garden plots of la ville blanche can be seen from there.

I sometimes drank coffee in a cafe of the old regime located on the south side of the square with the Dupleix statue. It had a terrace with view of the surroundings.

Pondicherry, Sunday, December 31

I began the day with attendance at the Meditation, still somewhat uneasy under the Mother's phantomly gaze. Later, as I was entering the church of Notre Dames des Anges, I encountered the two Van Sanden sisters whom I met in the street previously. They are Vietnamese and want to practice English. Then, with two Indian ashramites, we visited the church. There were Christmas decorations and a crèche. Pondi has several Catholic churches, an Anglican, and one or two small Protestant congregations.

Pondicherry, Monday, New Year's day, 1962

The sisters called at the Parc à Charbon. They are Dorothy and Lydia. Their mother is Vietnamese and their father Indian and Dutch. We sat in the pavilion next to the sea.

This afternoon the Mother wished all a Happy New Year in a *darshan* ceremony. The word means something similar to "audience"; however, there may be no audible exchange. Mere sight of the personage is sufficient for a *darshan* according to the Indian way. The people, dressed in fresh saris and dhotis, passed in front of her one by one to receive a calendar from her hand. I joined the others and received my calendar. On one side an attendant fanned her while a second person handed her the gifts one by one.

K.N. George had given me the address of a pharmacist in Pondicherry, and today in the ville noire the establishment turned up. I enquired for M. Delamourd, who was not there, so the delivery boy led me to a building site, where we found him overseeing the rebuilding of his residence-to-be. The walls were of brick, and the floors were pieced in by placing bricks between beams because all-wood construction is three times more costly, he told me. He mentioned that five masons, six laborers, and five women coolies earn a total of Rs 25 daily, about $5. The work has been underway for six months because it is difficult to find materials.

At home M. Delamourd, speaking French, introduced me to his family of four, and his wife served tea and biscuits.

This evening people in the ashram gathered in the theater to hear a recorded reading by the Mother, a passage from a poem by Aurobindo entitled "Savitri." The audience was quiet and the lights out as we listened.

Pondicherry, Tuesday, January 2

I stopped at the Bibliotheque Municipale and spoke to Mme Gaebelé, the librarian, who talked to me about Pondicherry. There is a collection of books here that tempts me to remain and browse. She showed me a case of relics taken from local excavations, particularly the Indo-Roman emporium, Arickamedou. There was a clay vessel said to have come from Arezzo, Tuscany, and other small objects such as figurines with an Italian appearance.

It could be useful to compare the different cultures resulting from the British and French presence in India. The contrast is noticeable though I have been in Pondi but a few days.

This evening I stopped at the Van Sanden residence to visit. We remained outside because evenings are comfortable, and we conversed in English, which they know better than I realized. They would like to move to France and are awaiting the results of their application.

Madras, Thursday, January 4

Today it was back to Madras for me, and I accompanied the Van Sandens on the same early bus. A pedicab called at the Parc à Charbon before dawn, Dorothy with it to guide the driver. Mrs. Van Sanden did not go, but the father did. We fetched our destination four hours later. I found the Werwies' apartment off Mount Road, the way to St. Thomas' Mount. Bertram directs the Max Müller Bhavan, the Indo-German Cultural Center, which he set up two years ago after leaving his teaching position.

Their apartment has four rooms and a pleasant veranda. The roof serves for sleeping. The Werwies have full-time help, a cook and a bearer, while the wife of one does the house cleaning. It is expensive to live here surrounded by the comforts of home; therefore Bertram receives a 65 percent supplement to his salary. He told me of the frustrations encountered in living here—blunders committed by the help, problems in getting simple things done; intense heat in the summer hot season. Madras is at 13 degrees N. latitude with June temperatures an average maximum of 100 degrees F and humid.

While my hosts were out, I stayed in to read. The bearer brought tea out to the veranda and while I went into the house a crow swooped down to raid the biscuits. I carried them with me after that, but the rascals continued to watch for a chance at them.

Lunch and dinner prepared by the cook were very good. I do not know where he acquired his skills. Only wine was lacking; lime juice is substituted. Consumption of alcoholic beverages in this climate is not advised, but we had Cointreau as a *digestif.*

When my hosts were in the United States, they enjoyed camping in the West and this evening we saw their colored slides of the trip. We also discussed their recent visit to Ceylon and I gained some useful knowledge for my upcoming journey on that island.

Madras, Friday, January 5

This morning in company with the Van Sanden family I saw the Zoo, then we had lemonade at Buhari's, a local restaurant chain. Enroute home for lunch I stopped to see the Max Müller Bhavan. The building is being enlarged and Bertram described the difficulties. For example, the contractor demanded a large sum of money in advance before he would begin. Also, nothing is completed on time and a bribe is sometimes the only way to get a job done. People work slowly. Bertram took me along on a visit to the small shop making tables for his classroom. The design was new but they did not make up a sample; and the finished pieces were insufficiently strengthened and unfit for their purpose. It seems that sometimes you cannot tell the people anything and they merely smile and say all is OK. So it was with the tablewallah.

This evening the Werwies took me to the theater, where we saw Kalidasa's *Shakuntala* in Sanskrit, for which we had an outline in the program. Kalidasa, who lived in the fifth century, is ancient India's most renowned playwright. Though the famous love story is uncomplicated and not hard to follow, it was intended for a refined audience with developed taste. The style is fresh and vigorous.

We dined at home afterward. An Indian guest revealed an interest in the United States and wanted to talk about it. We spoke of Indian bureaucracy, misappropriation of government funds, and the improved quality of manufactured goods.

Madras, Saturday, January 6

At the invitation of the Van Sandens, I accompanied them to visit a Hungarian swami who was visiting Madras. I do not know how the others learned about Sri Swami Un Omi Ananda, his spiritual name. His original appellation is Rev. Imre E. Havashy, Ph.D., L.P.T, N.D. He stays at the Catholic Center. Previously he had been in Cleveland, home to a large Hungarian community, and in California. He claims to be a philologist, among other things, able to determine the original meaning of Indian place names. Yesterday he was interviewed by the *Indian Express* which listed his accomplishments. He also claims to cure illness by diet, and this was the reason the Van Sandens wanted to consult him. At first I could not understand him; but he gradually became more comprehensible. Then the Van Sandens and I had limeade in a Mount Road restaurant. This afternoon I accompanied Mrs. Werwie on her driving practice. As traffic keeps left in India and there is a great diversity of it moving in all directions and at many speeds, it is advisable to use great care. We stopped at Spencer's, an expensive store, and also at the home of a German family, finding the parents out and children in charge of the help. We were served lime juice and snacks on the veranda.

Kanchipuram, Sunday, January 7

This morning I set out for the many-towered city Kanchipuram, thirty miles southwest of Madras by road. I had a front seat on the bus and a good view of the attractive countryside, where people and animals could be seen working or resting from their toil. We passed the natal place of the theologian Ramanuja. Historic Kanchi, as it is called, is said to be one of the seven most holy places in this land where the list is almost endless. The Pallava kings ruled from here, followed by the Cholas. Both dynasties constructed large temples with lofty *gopurams* over the gateways. They resemble elongated and truncated pyramids covered on all sides by a profusion of carving—figures of gods and people, animals and other creatures. They are characteristic of temples in the Dravidian regions of South India. Alighting from the bus, I cast my gaze about in quest of a place to begin. Fixing on a very tall *gopuram*, that belonging to the Ekambareshwara Temple, as it turned out. I set out on foot for it. As I came up to the main gateway, surmounted by the 188-foot tower, I enquired of an attendant if it was climbable. He said yes; however, I balked at paying a rupee for the privilege because there were numerous other towers in the city. One might be free. My informant offered a guided tour of the grounds and I accepted. He was, he told me, one of a hundred priests attached to this shrine. He spoke with emphasis as he leaned over toward me with his hand politely covering his mouth. He related the legend of Parvati's Penance, often depicted in art. The goddess stood on one leg, the other straight up over her head, gripped in her arms. She did it that she might marry Shiva. Then my guide showed the temple elephant tethered in the courtyard and the sacred mango tree of great age. The faithful believe its four branches represent the four Vedas and that the fruit of each has a distinctive taste. The 1,000-pillared mandapam has preserved only about 600 of its supports. A long wall encompasses the area of the temple and subsidiaries.

A short way beyond the populous area lies the old Kailasanatha Temple. It is a national monument and bears a similarity to the Shore Temple at Mahabalipuram. My guide pointed to a series of tiny meditation cells, not much larger than a kneeling man might require, hollowed out of the encircling wall. I continued to the Vaikunthaperumal Temple, which I observed from the court. It has structures resembling the cloister of a church and columns topped by lions. There is an early *mandapam* here. All of these early forms were more fully developed in later buildings.

Finally I visited the Varadarajaperumal Temple dating from the eleventh century in the Vijayanagar period. The Vijayanagar kings were the third power to arise in the Tamil region. My attention was called to the heavy chain carved from a single stone.

A day in Kanchi barely suffices for a quick look at its numerous temples. I did not see them all, partly because it took so much time walking from place to place.

After returning to the Madras and dinner at the Wervies we compared our experiences in this country.

Madras, Monday, January 8

The money I was expecting has still not appeared. Bertram loaned me enough to fetch Colombo, where Indian rupees will be cheaper than in their own land. Without the generous help of several friends, I would be in an even worse fix.

This afternoon I accompanied the Werwies on a visit to St. Thomas Mount. It is a pretty place such as you might not expect, being near the airport. Stone steps take the visitor up to the summit, which is not high but offers a good view. We found one young boy begging. He stood around quietly until Bertram gave him a coin, then went away. There may be a "thank you" but not every time.

This evening I stopped at the hotel where the Van Sandens have been staying, to say goodbye. Rev. Mr. Havashy, whom I had just met at St. Thomas Mount, walked in while I was there, the second time today that we ran into each other. The Van Sanden family returned to Pondi the next day. I do not expect to see them again.

Dinner was served late tonight because Bertram had a language class. He is studying Tamil.

Madras, Tuesday, January 9

I prepared to leave. The Wervies are storing my extra baggage, whose quantity has been increasing, and I do not require the warmer garments and blanket any longer. I called to bid K.N. George adieu and thank him for his help.

Following a light dinner at home, I went to Egmore Station to board the night train to Tiruchirappalli, or Trichinopoly (the anglicized form), or Tiruchy, or Trichy for short. For a small charge I was given a third-class berth, a shelf to sleep on while the train rolled south all night.

Trichinopoly, Wednesday, January 9

The fast mail trains generally run at night. That is the reason for traveling then. I was up before dawn and peered from the train window to see where we were stopped. I could see lights on a hill and I knew that Trichy was on a hill. I enquired of a fellow passenger if this was Trichy. He told me no, it was not. However, knowing how often misunderstandings occur in such situations, I quickly got off, for I thought the man could have been wrong, or didn't know, or did not understand my pronunciation of the name. Although it did not apply here, I have found that there is something in the Indian mind that causes them to say what they think you want to hear. I hardly ever heard the words, "I do not know." Once I could see the outline of a hill not far from the station, I was sure it was Trichinopoly and I was seeing the Rock topped by the Fort Temple. I don't know what led me here, perhaps intuition.

I set out in the dim light, picking up breakfast on the way, tea and a banana. It required only a few minutes to reach the foot of the Rock. On the opposite side, at the entrance to the stairs leading up, I encountered a young man who said he was a holy-water carrier. He accompanied me on the 438-step climb, although I did not ask him the way. The summit is reached after a steep ascent of 300 feet. The rock formation is isolated in the broad plain of the Cauvery River. It was misty at the early hour we fetched the top. This place was fought over in the wars between France and Britain for supremacy in India. When the British became established they built St. John's Church (1812) with a surrounding cemetery. I regretted that I had not the time to examine it. There is also St. Joseph's

Church and Christ Church, founded by a Danish missionary. The old city hugs the base of the Rock.

We met a group of Carnatic musicians marching outside the temple on top. They were pipers and drummers making a loud noise, probably to please the temple god. As we descended from the Rock Fort Temple, my guide began to solicit a reward for his services. I intended to give him something because he was not the ordinary street person. He had been of help and I had enjoyed the company. I was in a strange region of a strange land where I appreciated contact with an interested person. One of the many good things about being a foreigner in this country, I find, is there is always someone nearby to be interested in you, even if in many cases it is for pecuniary reasons. It may also be a human concern or simple curiosity.

Half way down we came to another temple, where a tethered elephant stood. He was beautifully decorated with paint, blanket, and sashes with bells, apparently for a planned procession.

Proceeding on down, my holy-water carrier spoke of a son whom he was trying to educate and asked me to give a few rupees for the boy. As I had to be honest, I said I could afford eight annas. He wanted a rupee. I said that we never receive everything we want and he should be satisfied with my small donation. Finally he accepted and we parted in a friendly way. I would have liked to give more and hoped he understood my predicament.

A town bus carried me three miles to Srirangam island, across a thirty-two-arched stone bridge over the Cauvery. The water surrounding the island is said to be holy, the same, I supposed, that my morning companion distributed. The island is totally taken up by the Ranganatha Swamy Temple, sacred to Vaishnavites, worshipers of Vishnu. The area covered is an astonishing mile square. The main temple is surrounded by twenty-two *gopuram* towers. The god's votaries come here for a festival every January, the Vaikunta Ekadasi days. I missed this. Seven concentric walls surround the temple, making it appear that the population resides within the temple precincts in a mutual embrace. There is a 1,000-pillared *mandapam*. Well-known sculptures of horses stand on their hind legs supporting the top story. There is much to be seen if the visitor has the time to explore.

Next I traveled two hours east by train to Tanjore, the anglicized name for Thanjavur. I had scant information on the renowned Brahadesswara Temple here; however, its fame required that I experience it, though off my route. It was built by Raja Raja Chola in the late tenth and early eleventh centuries, a time when the Romanesque style dominated in Europe. In the south, Hindu art and culture were in their glory with the Pallava and Chola kings.

There were few people present. The restrictions prevented me from seeing beyond the exterior of the temple, the galleries, and the tank. The galleries enclosing the courtyard contain remnants of high-quality frescoes. The outlines of the building with its *vimana* (tower) rising over the sanctum is pleasing, and I asked myself if this could be in part because it resembles Christian church spires. The Cholas, who had a powerful propensity for building, erected seventy-four temples in and around Tanjore. This one is called the masterpiece, as proved particularly by a stupendous eighty-ton granite cap, in one piece, hauled up the 189-foot tower. The temple builders used the same technique the Egyptians used for the pyramids—an inclined earthen plane, beginning about three and a half miles from the tower, up which the monolith was inched.

Also to be seen, although I missed it, is a large sculptured Nandi, the bull, that served as Shiva's mount, and that is frequently represented in art. I watched the people in the courtyard from my resting place in the gallery, in the shade.

Returning to the station, I met a young man from Kerala who made handpainted postcards. He showed me his work and I purchased one or two tropical scenes. They were unusual and probably saleable.

I draw nearer the southern tip of the subcontinent at Cape Comorin; however, my destination remains Ceylon. I secured my ticket and a third-class sleeping berth aboard the 9:40 Mail to Dhanushkodi. I was fortunate to get it at the last moment, since I've had so many uncomfortable train trips.

Rameshwaram and Dhanuskodi, Thursday, January 11

Rameshwaram is one of the islands in the chain of islands and two peninsulas that forms Adam's Bridge, spanning the twenty-two mile strait between India and the island of Ceylon. The name also appears to apply to the temple on the island, however the true name of that is the Ramanathaswamy Temple. I got off the train at Ramban where a spur line takes passengers the few miles to a point a short walk from the Ramanathaswamy temple. The sandy soil supports sparse vegetation and a few palm trees. The ground is sacred—every grain of sand around the temple is holy, they say. The tall, gray *gopuram* tower guides the pilgrim to his objective, which is separated from the village by a broad expanse of sand. I wondered if the area was filled with people in times of festival. Today there appeared to be few others present. An exotic location it is, distant from a settlement of any size and surrounded by sand, coral, and the sea. A sheet of clean, shallow water comes up to the building on one side. They call it a lake.

I entered the courtyard where the famous corridors skirt the interior walls, like a cloister walk. They run for a greater distance and are more substantially built than any Christian cloister I know. The pillars are elaborately sculpted, each differently.

I met again a pilgrim whom I had met on the train. Together we examined the articles offered for sale in the corridor. They had large sea shells, which were adapted for lamp shades. We walked to the lakeshore close by, where I went in briefly. Then my companion showed me the hostel where he was staying, and a young temple elephant.

This is the most visited temple in the South and compares in importance with Varanasi in the North. I count it the most interesting South Indian temple I saw, though I cannot give a precise reason. Konarak in the North is the nearest to it in overall effect. Both lie in tropical surroundings of sea, sand, and palm trees, although, to be sure, they differ completely in style.

Ramanathaswamy Temple, as seen in the name, is affiliated with Rama. He came to this place in search of his wife, Sita, whom Ravanna, the demon king of Lanka (Ceylon), had kidnapped. Rama slew Ravana, the ten-headed monster, and had to do penance for his deed. The temple is the site of the crime.

The proper celebration of these events required a second temple named Kothandaramaswamy. I did not see it.

Enquiries indicated that I should return to the quarantine center at Mandapam Camp on the Indian side of the bridge for immunization procedures, then go to the ferry station at Dhanushkodi the next day because no more trains met the ferry today.

Instead of taking this suggestion, I boarded the last train to the ferry station because I had records of my immunizations in my possession and hoped to get through. So, at the ferry station I displayed them. The people looked at my International Vaccination Certificate in several languages as though it were written in Chinese, and I was obliged to return to Mandapam Camp and there secure the required paper. I stayed overnight in the free rest house there, but I lost a day.

Colombo To Lion Rock

Tallaimannar, Friday, January 12

My travel documents were scanned by an official before I boarded the train to Danushkodi and the terminal for the Palk Strait ferry. The terminal occupies two sand dunes facing the sea. The dwellings are covered with palm thatch accenting the tropical flavor.

Muslims believe that Eden was in Ceylon and that Adam and Eve lived there after the Expulsion. They are said to be buried on Mannar Island, a sandy projection of the Ceylonese mainland, in a spot marked by a small shrine. Their offspring, Cain and Abel, are deemed to lie near the Rameshwaram station. Mannar Island is also where the mythical Vijaya, father of the Sinhalese, the island's dominant population, came ashore after leaving India with his people. The chain of islands and shoals between India and Ceylon is known as Adam's Bridge. These were also helpful to Hanuman, the Hindu god, when he crossed the twenty-two mile strait to search for Sita, as already described in connection with the Rameshwaram.

Darkness was settling on the scene as the ferry fetched Tallaimannar, where the Colombo train stood on the quai, awaiting passengers.

My second-class sleeping compartment was a big change after my experiences on the Indian Railways, and I reveled in the comfortable upper berth and lavatory shared with one other passenger.

Colombo, Saturday, January 13

It was early morning in Colombo when I found a single room at the YMCA. The pedicab driver on the short trip from the station was dissatisfied with the amount I offered and despite my effort to be gentle while remaining firm, he left feeling offended.

K.N. George in Madras had provided me with the name of Moses Karunairatnam, a lecturer at the university whom I might look up. After asking about his address at the Y, and speaking to several persons, I finally managed to reach him. A staff person at the Y drove me to the U.S. Embassy, where I was pleased to find several letters waiting. I continued by pedicab to the university; Mr. K. was expecting me. We went to the tourist office, where I found free material on the principal sights on the island, as well as postcards. Mr. K. took me to the port area, an agglomeration of modern facilities known as the Fort of Colombo, though it does not include a fort now. He pointed out the breakwater, which enabled the development of the modern port, and then left me at the Government Handicrafts Emporium. The offerings were attractive and I resolved to return when I had some money.

I visited the Department of Wildlife to find out about Ruhunu, the sanctuary I desired to visit in the southern part of the island. Colombo is uncrowded, clean, and attractive, with parks and open spaces such as Galle Face Green overlooking the Indian Ocean on one side and Parliament on the other. The city contains a group of temples, mosques, and churches which serve a diverse population. Sinhalese make up 69 percent of the population [1990 estimated], followed in decreasing order of numbers by the Tamil Hindus, Muslims, Chinese, and the Burghers, the descendants of Europeans who settled here at various times. At one time Portuguese traders controlled the country, followed by the Dutch. Then the British extended their dominion over the entire island, which prior colonials had not done. The country became independent in 1948 soon after India gained her freedom.

A superficial view seems to show a community at peace with itself; however, a closer look reveals a troubled society. At present strikes are in progress in Colombo, with the port and banks affected. Military detachments are working the port. In political life the assassination of Prime Minister S.W.R.D. Bandaranaike in 1959 was the most serious indication of danger. Now the P.M. is the victim's wife, the first woman to fill such office.

I saw the Zoological Gardens, which had been praised to me even before coming here. The collections of large cats, birds, and monkeys are very good. Many other specimens are to be seen. They are displayed in attractive surroundings—lawns, flower borders, and trees. I watched an elephant performance, which occurs every day at 5:00 p.m. Immediately after that, it began to rain hard. I took refuge in a restaurant while the rain came down in sheets with thunder and lightning. The people said it was the northeast monsoon. As it continued I joined a party in a taxi and was delivered to a bus, for the zoo is a few miles outside the city.

This evening a Y resident, Sam Nalaratnam, introduced himself, and we were soon talking on the subjects which interested me concerning the country. He provided helpful information on visiting the many points of interest on the island. We met several times while I remained in Colombo.

Colombo has good Chinese restaurants, where I enjoyed taking my meals because it was a change from the regular fare in India. At dinner today I ordered sweet and sour pork with fried rice. Supper, the light meal, I shared with Sam before attending a movie. Everything I require is within walking distance of the Y.

Colombo, Sunday, January 14

I had hoped to find the beach at Mt. Lavinia uncrowded this morning, but I found myself surrounded by bathing and sunning citizens looking like the crowd at a typical resort in Europe or America.

Later Sam, who is a Methodist, took me to his church service. His relatives were also present, one of whom brought us back to the Y. We had tea at the British Soldiers and Sailors Institute next door. Later I enjoyed a good piece of steak there. Sam advanced me a little money to tide me over until tomorrow.

Colombo, Monday, January 15

The mail held by the Embassy included three checks totaling $462, nearly the only money I had received from home since leaving Rome in August. Only $150 had arrived between then and now, but I borrowed about $100 from friends in India.

Later I visited the small museum exhibiting artifacts from the ruined Sinhalese cities of Anuradhapura and Polunnaruwa in the north.

The population of the island is 9 million and growing fast. Buddhists are 74 percent; a significant number of ethnic Sinhalese adhere to other religions. Mahinda, called Ashoka's son, was the apostle of Buddhism in Ceylon. A pretty legend describes the conversion of the Sinhalese king:

> It was on a bright, crisp morning in the year 307 B.C., when King Devanampiyatissa, yearning for the thrills of the chase, went hunting with 40,000 followers in the neighbourhood of Mihintale, a hill in the North-Central Province of Ceylon.
>
> Unknown to him, Mahinda, son of the great Indian Emperor Asoka, and a disciple of the Buddha, had already arrived at Mihintale to spread the teaching of Lord Buddha.
>
> The 'deva' or guardian spirit of Mihintale, determined to guide the king to Mahinda's presence, appeared to him in the form of a magnificent sambhur stag. Reluctant to kill such an animal without first giving it a warning, the king twanged his bow string. The stag instantly fled away with the king in hot pursuit, and when it drew near to Mahinda, vanished.
>
> Mahinda beckoned to the king. The latter, though from childhood used to command, meekly obeyed: instinct told him that he was in the presence of no ordinary man.

A few preliminary questions to test the king's intelligence and then Mahinda began to preach. (See excerpt below.) The king listened in rapt attention and so did his followers who by then had all gathered round him. Time mattered not as they listened to the disciple who preached past noon, through the shades of evening till nightfall. At the end of the sermon, the king and his followers, profoundly impressed, embraced the new faith.*

Mahinda, perhaps administering the first intelligence test, spoke as follows:

'What name does this tree bear, O King?'
'This tree is called a mango.'
'Is there yet another mango beside this?'
'There are many mango-trees.'
'And are there yet other trees besides this mango and the other mangoes?'
'There are many trees, sir; but those are trees that are not mangoes.'
'And are there, beside the mangoes and those trees which are not mangoes, yet other trees?'
'There is this mango-tree sir.'**

Colombo, Tuesday, January 16

A black market in Indian rupees exists here and a traveler like me is tempted to take advantage of the better exchange available on the street. The difference between the rate for dollars and Indian rupees in Ceylon and in India is considerable: Rs 8.75 per dollar here to Rs 4.75 in India. Therefore, the banks being on strike, I went to Thomas Cooke to exchange money and they told me about the free rate. With $40 that I got at the travel agency I was able to get Rs 350 on the street after a little asking. That is Rs 8.75 per dollar. This will make it easier to repay my Indian friends.

Then I did some shopping in a Chinese clothing store because my travel wardrobe was in need of replenishment. The equivalent of $8.50 bought me pajamas, a white dress shirt, a white summer shirt, two pairs of shorts, two briefs, and three pairs of socks. Many foreign goods are available in stores, in contrast to India where very little, if any, imports are seen. To make comparisons again, few beg-

---

* *A Travel Agent's Manual on Ceylon* issued by the Government Tourist Bureau, Sri Lanka: 1961, pp. 8-9.
** *Handbook for the Ceylon Traveller*, A Studio Times Publication, Colombo, Sri Lanka: 1974, p. 320.

gars and street people are visible in Colombo, and citizens are adequately dressed. Children are clothed. The living standard is higher and the city is less crowded than an Indian city. The economy appears good, although deteriorating.

Ratnapura, Wednesday, January 17

I concluded an enjoyable visit in Colombo and traveled by bus fifty-six miles southeast to the "City of Gems," Ratnapura. It lies only ten miles from sacred Adam's Peak, one of the island's highest mountains at 7,362 feet and the destination of pilgrims of four faiths. Buddhists believe their Lord passed here on his way to Nirvana, leaving his footprint in the rocky summit. Muslims hold that the mark is the footprint of Adam, who stood there on one foot in expiation for his disobedience. Hindus consider the peak holy by reason of its association with Shiva's dance of creation. Eastern Orthodox Christians hold the footprint to be that of St. Thomas, Apostle of India. Ratnapura is one of the pilgrims' points of departure for the ascent. Dawn is the most favorable moment to stand on the summit. This is the climbing season and I would like to have the equipment plus the knowledge to undertake it. I have never climbed a sacred mountain.

The country enroute to Ratnapura produces bananas, bamboo, coconut palm, rubber trees, and tea—altogether tropical agriculture. Upon arrival I found the rest house situated atop a small hill adjacent to the town and reached by a curving drive. Ratnapura's was one of the most comfortable and pleasant of government-operated hostelries I used. My room was well appointed with a single bed, private bath and shower, and mosquito net; all for Rs 3. It opened on the wide veranda. The staff people and food were equally good and the same held generally for the other rest houses where I stayed.

The scurry of Colombo was absent, replaced by a relaxed atmosphere among friendly people. It was enjoyable to walk about without a particular objective. The cottages were the simplest bamboo structures supporting coconut thatch; there is no need for elaborate shelter in a climate where people live and work out of doors. Women wear bright colors in clothes made of mill cloth, meaning it is imported. I had read that when the British left the country they had built up a good surplus in foreign exchange, which the new nation acquired.

Later I returned to the rest house for tea on the veranda overlooking green, hazy hills. It was gems and gemming which brought me here, though not to purchase, only to look. The region where gems are found is limited to the area surrounding Ratnapura, comprising 95 percent of the gemming fields. Ceylon has been famous for gems for more than 2,500 years. Among them are yellow sapphires, moonstones, rubies, amethysts, alexandrite, and cat's eyes. My impression was that the glorious days of gemming in Ceylon were past and that not that much remained to rejoice the gem hunter of today. Gems are still found, however, perhaps only a few of the best quality. It was interesting to look and listen as the dealers expounded on their sparkling collections contained in boxes and bags. Some sellers are ambulatory; others are fixed in small shops in front of houses. Soon I was talking gems with several sellers, at the same time meticulously avoiding the appearance of wanting to buy. And I gave attention to shops of other kinds, one of them a general store where I conversed with the proprietor while enjoying a mug of Ceylon ale. He telephoned a dealer of his acquaintance who later came to the Rest House, though I scrupulously avoided any sign that I was considering a purchase; indeed I wasn't, although the prices appeared cheap for some stones. I would have preferred to meet elsewhere; however, the visit was arranged on the telephone without me.

At the rest house a Swiss couple had returned from a day of gemming and we talked before dinner. Their name was Gubelin and they came from Lucerne. Dinner was excellent and abundant, including meat, rice, side dishes, ale, and dessert. I could not finish my plate, such was the quantity.

After this the gem dealer came and showed a group of tourmalines (the name is Sinhala in origin) and agreed to return in the morning when he would take me to a shop named the Gem Bureau.

Ratnapura, Thursday, January 18

The Gem Bureau turned out to be both museum and emporium. It showed a collection of uncut stones as well as an exhibit showing the methods of mining. There are three. (1) scraping the beds of streams, (2) sifting surface deposits, (3) pit mining. Present was a Muslim stonecutter at work. He used a hand-operated wheel because, he said, electricity would take away too much stone. The wheel is brass or lead and the grinding compound is carborundum or ash.

Then I was shown the cut stones, which looked so pretty that I chose three inexpensive examples with the intention of showing them to the Swiss gemologist, and did so at lunch. They had been gemming all morning at a nearby place named Palmadulla. He promised to test my stones in the evening using his refractometer.

After lunch I took the bus to Palmadulla, thinking it might be interesting. There was little to see in the line of gems. A young boy was washing gravel from an abandoned pit, rotating a round cane basket in the stream to remove the fine material. A seller came along to show me a large piece of clear stone, which I took to be quartzite. It was uncut and I paid Rs 4 for it.

Several hundred yards further on I came to a tea factory whose proprietor guided me through the process of refining tea. At first green leaves are wilted and dried in canvas trays in a building where air is circulated. Then the tea is ground, a process yielding several grades of the product. The tea grown in these lowlands is less pungent and so is preferred in the Middle East. Europe and America buy the high country varieties—those I will see later.

When I showed my lump of quartzite to the tea factory owner, he told me it was valueless, so I took it back, and my money was refunded without protest. The rock was too heavy in any case.

This evening Dr. Gubelin examined the three stones, finding the two cut, clear ones to be quartzite, which I had realized already, and the third a low-quality yellow sapphire. I bought them for Rs 75, about $15, mainly for the sapphire.

After supper I had a short conversation with an English guest who told me something of himself. "I plant tea," he said, and I pictured him planting tea bushes. Then he told me what his duties were. "I supervise several estates," he continued, and I saw him as the overseer of wealthy estates surrounded by tea. Finally I realized that he ran several tea plantations, not as their owner but as a manager employed by a large tea producer. Most of the high country tea and rubber plantations are still foreign owned.

Ratnapura, Friday, January 19

Upon regaining the rest house last evening I found Mr. Arulanantham awaiting me. He had my name and location from Sam in Colombo. He was a gem dealer; I told him I was not buying, but would look at his crop of gemstones if he wished. He returned this morning and took me to his home, where he placed a table in the yard and put several bottles of uncut stones on it, in water to make them more transparent, and to bring out flaws. He also had cut stones of crude workmanship. The local cutters may not be capable of fine work. We discussed his collection and he returned twice to the rest house. He seemed to want me to take stones to the United

States and told me the uncut gemstones could be exported and imported with minimum formality. Gems hold a mystique, which perhaps I was influenced by. The dealers are obliging and generous with their time.

After the gems I toured a rubber factory in the neighborhood where the manager guided me through the process of producing rubber from start to finish. The liquid sap of the rubber tree, white latex, is gathered daily by tappers, who collect an average eleven pounds, receiving more pay if they bring in excess. The pay averages $2.58 per diem, multiplied by four or five to give an idea of how much that buys here.

The raw latex is first strained and poured into a large tiled receptacle. Water is added to reduce its weight per gallon to a desired minimum; then formic acid and another chemical are added, which cause the mixture to curdle; then the foam is removed and used for another purpose. The solution stands for twelve hours or less before it coagulates. Then it is removed and passed through rollers that masticate and flatten it into long strips of tough, rubbery material. The rolling process continues in several machines until a thin sheet of white rubber results. When these large sheets are compressed together by rollers, there is complete fusion.

Mr. Arulanantham consigned fourteen stones to me for testing by Dr. Gubelin if possible. Then I had his permission to take them to Colombo, where he would meet me. Later he changed his mind, saying he was not able to meet me and it was better to have the Swiss gemologist see them, or I should buy them on the seller's assurance that they were genuine. However, I did not intend to purchase any stones without knowing what they were. Mr. Arulanantham visited me four times in all and although we didn't do any business, I could observe how the gem trade goes here and have some fascinating talks with the people.

Later this afternoon I stopped at the shop of a Muslim gem dealer named Farook, who displayed a quantity of gems. When I showed a slight interest in any one stone, he picked it up and stated a price. He certainly allowed for bargaining because when I told him his prices looked high and gave him some examples, he immediately brought them down by as much as half. This behavior did not give me much confidence in his merchandise, so I sidestepped, buying some postcards instead. I found gemming amusing; nevertheless, when it came to an actual purchase, I grew very reluctant, although some I saw were pretty and not expensive. I could not imagine a use for them or how I might carry them back with me.

The rain came again today. The people carry umbrellas.

This evening a colorful procession took place, the Duruthu Perahera, I believe, although my book says it takes place in Colombo and commemorates the Buddha's first visit to Lanka. I had not realized that he came to this island. The occasion was made colorful by costumed Kandyan dancers and musicians and several elephants in bright blankets and tassels with bells. There were fire wheels and paper figures in the procession.

Diyatalawa, Saturday, January 20

Taking an express bus to Bandarawela, I got off at the Diyatalawa road and hiked up to the village. The hill country begins here and becomes mountains farther north. The tropical climate turns subtropical and the vegetation thinner. I saw several working elephants.

Sam had given me the address of a guest house run by the Shraders, a Christian family, and I looked them up. Their bungalow bore the name "Killarney" in large letters. Mr. Shrader drove me to the post office, where I had left my bags. The country here resembles the English Lake District without the lakes, or the Derbyshire Peak District. Mr. Shrader also drove me up the road to Haputale to show me Diyatalawa from above. Although this village is distant from either level country or water, it is the site of a navy base, an army base, and even an airbase, each occupying its own hill in the vicinity.

My host was the local health inspector. I was served high tea in the English manner, and dinner in the evening featured English dishes. I had brains, peas, and potatoes. Mr. Shrader showed me his vegetable garden in which the peas grew. They were fully mature and I advised him to harvest them soon. Because he had always eaten canned peas he did not know when the fresh ones were ready to pick. The garden also contained cabbage, beans, beets, and strawberries. Concerning the last, he needed advice on the use of straw under the plant, for he had more or less dropped it on top.

The Shraders had a son recently out of college, who told me it was hard to get a job without some influence in political circles. They are Methodists; Mrs. Shrader had been an employee of the church headquarters in Colombo. The Shraders do not like the government, calling it incompetent, and referred to the strikes in Colombo. The port has been struck for six weeks.

Mr. Shrader was formerly a gem dealer. He described a test for the genuineness of a gem. If you touch the stone to the tongue and notice it remains cold, it is real. When I showed him my three stones, he said I had got my money's worth, but that's all.

Ella and Nuwara Eliya, Sunday, January 21

The Shraders have a cat and three dogs, which are clean and friendly. After a proper English breakfast and reading the English-language newspaper, I bid my hosts adieu, paying them a nominal amount. Mr. Shrader drove me to the bus. Later I realized that I should have remained longer and learned more of the country and people, while enjoying the company of this family.

Bandarawela has several hotels and a youth hostel as well as a YMCA. I passed it up to reach Ella, which I had heard was a nice area with an interesting rest house. After fetching the Ella road by bus, I walked uphill two miles to the village and found the rest house. This is the highland tea-growing country. It occupies a large area, the region from Haputale to and including Kandy and Nuwara Eliya is almost wholly tea country. The estates are on hills because tea requires good drainage; and they are strikingly neat, the bushes covering the slopes. Since all cultivation and harvest is by hand, few roads are required. Two tea estate people were aboard the bus. The aromatic tea preferred by the English comes from here, they said. In a former time Ceylon also grew good coffee. That crop was wiped out by a disease. Ceylon's agriculture is fascinating, considering the variety of important and unique crops.

A fine panorama is presented to the sight as one stands on the terrace before the Ella rest house. To the south, framed in hills, the sea is visible.

Returning to Bandarawela, I took another bus to Nuwara Eliya. The land continues its rise. It also rained steadily all the way to my destination, and me without an umbrella. Nuwara Eliya is more of England, since it was established by the British as a summer resort in the colonial period. It is 100 miles from Colombo. The island's highest peak, Pidurutalagala, 8,291 feet, is nearby, and one of the approaches to Adam's Peak begins in this vicinity, but I won't be joining those who make the pilgrimage.

The Nuwara Eliya rest house had few guests, so I was easily accommodated. It bears the name Torrington and is run by a woman whose English is good. The structure is large and musty. The floors in some places seemed to be flexing as I walked. I enjoyed a hot bath; however, it was so cold otherwise that I wrapped a blanket about me. My meal was served in the empty dining room.

Nuwara Eliya and Kandy, Monday, January 22

Continued rain prevented sightseeing. The rest house is surrounded by large conifers. Water was dripping off everything and flowing down the road. When the rain slowed, I walked into the town to visit several shops, the only activity available. I gave up and boarded the bus to Kandy. There is a train and later I learned that the trip by rail is more interesting. Nevertheless, the scenery by road was rewarding when the rain let up. We descended a long valley via Ramboda. It is all tea plantations and rocks. Many waterfalls drop over the valley's lip—it could be Lauterbrunnen in Switzerland. The trip is a long one—three to four hours by circuitous paved road with medium traffic and with a few tourists. The tea factories are similar in appearance and construction. In Kandy I found shelter at the YMCA situated on the artificial lake in the center, not far from the Temple of the Tooth.

The lake and environs present a quiet and even picturesque scene, which reminded me of places in Europe where a sheet of water is joined to the town. It is a small lake circumscribed by roadway. This is the circuit followed by the Kandy Perahera in July-August. It is the most elaborate of *peraheras* in Ceylon, still more colorful than the one I observed in Ratnapura, and includes numerous elephants in full caparison, dancers, musicians, and the Buddha's sacred tooth transported within a shrine. My first desire was to follow the road around the lake; however, the rain had started again, so I had to wait. The monks of the temple were reciting prayers and chants nearly nonstop at considerable amplification; consequently they were heard throughout that part of town. They were trying to avert the baneful effects of the conjunction of five planets on February 4. Their prayers may have been recorded. The monks would lose their voices otherwise, so continuously do they chant.

Kandy is the Buddhist spiritual center as well as the cultural capital of the country. It had been the political capital of the Ceylonese kingdom, but that ended in 1815 when the British defeated the king and took over the country. The British secured possession of the sacred tooth, which, according to Sinhalese myth, conferred the right to rule on its possessor.

Kandy is a city of 60,000. There is a United States Information Service library here, which I stepped into briefly looking for newspapers or magazines. At the Y, I encountered the same Swiss boy whom I had met in Mashad and again at Danushkodi. It's a small world even out here. His tour of India is completed and he returns home from Colombo.

Kandy, Tuesday, January 23

In the vicinity of the Temple of the Tooth are several former buildings of the Sinhalese kings, and their palace. Now they hold a collection of royal furniture and utensils—drums, arms, garments, arecanut cutters and other ethological objects. This morning I traveled to the Botanical Gardens at Peradeniya, which I found to be large and justly famous. I was impressed to see the elaborate, carefully organized plantings. The rain stopped falling and the sun came out full. At first I toured alone; then met an elderly, deaf guide and followed him. With his assistance I saw spice plants and trees: cinnamon, cloves, allspice, pepper, cardamom, nutmeg, citronella, quinine, cocoa, and others. I was shown several scented plants. Everything is labeled. The cacti collection was unexpected, and the Royal Palm avenue recalled that of Fort Meyers, Florida. Then followed the Grand Circle along whose periphery were trees planted by visiting kings, princes and prime ministers. The grove of tall bamboo made an agreeable sound as the trees rubbed together in a breeze. Then my guide pointed to a "double coconut" tree, whose fruit matures in ten years, and several Cook's pine trees from New Caledonia. The great captain used them for ship's masts. A student's garden is laid out according to plant families to aid the study of botany. The lawns were trimmed using sharpened bamboo cutters shaped to hold in the hand.

The University of Ceylon has a campus nearby. We passed it in the bus to Kandy.

I lunched at the same Chinese place I had tried last night. Then I joined a number of people who were waiting in line to offer flowers at the Tooth Shrine Room. Among them were several tourists like myself. We filed past two or more priests in saffron robes, handing our offerings to one of them, who then laid them on the altar. I had no flowers, though I had a papaya, which I offered instead. The priest accepted it with a smile directed at his colleague. The older shrine is enclosed in a modern *vihara* (monastery) and therefore I was not looking at the ancient reliquary.

Kandy's central market drew my attention this afternoon because it was well arranged and had good sanitation. I would compare it favorably with markets in Europe. It offered both ordinary and Royal coconuts. The first is usually eaten when green and the meat soft, while the Royal contains a larger quantity of milk and has an orange husk.

The following encomium to the coconut is interesting.

The coconut palm, with its slender ash-grey trunk sweeping high into the sky, crowned with a frond of fan-like waving leaves, is one of the most distinctive features of Sri Lanka's landscape. This remarkable palm has been grown here from the time of the Sinhala kings. It grows best on sandy soil near the sea, but also thrives inland at elevations of up to about 1,600 feet.

It certainly lends enchantment to the natural beauty along the sweeping coastal regions and in the midst of small valleys, hillocks and farm holdings inland.

In every sense of the word the coconut palm is the fairy godmother of the inhabitants of this country. It can be truthfully said that no single plant gives so much to man in such a variety of ways.

Let us take a look at the hut of a villager. Skillfully woven dried coconut leaves serve as a roof—call it thatch or cadjan— yet it is cool and rain-proof. The main spar of the little veranda and its supports are of coconut wood and so are the rafters. The modest fencing around the hut, too, is of dried coconut branches.

In the kitchens of village homes and the mansions of the city are utensils made of coconut shells, their designs unchanged through centuries. The village hearths are kept burning with coconut shells, dried coconut leaves, branches and withered sheaths of the coconut flower. Mats and baskets are also woven with coconut leaves and the mid-rib, the ekel, tied into little bundles or fashioned into brooms to sweep gardens.

Coconut wood is used to make furniture and the thicker portion of the coconut branch, the *pol-piththa*—used as a village bat. The young leaves, *gokkola*, pale yellow and pliant are used in weaving exquisite traditional forms and shapes to be used as ephemeral decor at ceremonials, weddings and other occasions, adding a characteristic Ceylonese touch to the setting.

The coconut palm sways supreme as a source of food and drink. The bud at the top of the stem—the *bada*—is delicious when made into a pickle. The pith of a coconut seedling, *pela pihi*, is a much sought after thirst-quencher. The younger fruits, *kurumba* and *thambili*, provide a refreshing, cool, delightful drink. The kernel of matured nuts are grated and the milk expressed, used as a medium in which almost all the tasty Sinhala curries are cooked. Coconut scrapings are made into a *pol sambol*, a hot appetiser and a palatable gravy called a *pol-hodda*, is made from spiced coconut milk.

Toddy tapped from the coconut flower is made into treacle or jaggery, a coarse brown candy. Vinegar is a by-product of toddy. From toddy is also distilled the national drink of the Island—Arrack. But toddy itself is an invigorating drink very popular along the south west coast.

The dried kernel of the coconut—copra—is finely grated and marketed as desiccated coconut which is used extensively in confectionery and cooking, mainly abroad. From copra is extracted coconut oil, used in the Island as a cooking fat and in the manufacture of soap, margarine, and hair dressings, among other things. After the oil is extracted, the residue, poonac, is used as an animal food.

Along the south coast of the Island, cottagers leave the fibrous husk to soak in pits. Later, they are beaten to extract the fibre—coir. The coir is either spun into ropes or made into doormats, brooms, brushes and a number of other utility articles, which are now used the world over.*

The fruits of this island exist in great variety; many were originally imported. Papaya, for example, is a delicious melon-like fruit often served in restaurants; it came from tropical America. The mango is an honored member of the tropical fruit category. Bananas are abundant and cheap. Pineapples and citrus fruits also are grown.

On my way home, I stopped to watch a large eight-inch chameleon near the Y. He was an attractive, green, bright-eyed and alert creature that appeared unafraid—perhaps confident that his long legs would serve him to escape if need arose.

Colombo, Wednesday, January 24

The train that returned me to Colombo was called express, though it required three hours to cover seventy-two miles. Between Kandy and the coast is a 1,600 foot drop. The mountains are not large but very irregular, steep and rocky, covered with waterfalls and verdant vegetation. Clouds hid them in part. I enjoyed the scenery from the comfortable second-class rail car, where a tea tray might be ordered if you wish.

In Colombo I visited the government Handicrafts Emporium, where quality is very good. The sterling, silver plate, tortoise shell,

---

* *Handbook for the Ceylon Traveler*, op. cit., pp. 321-322.

rosewood, ebony, copper, handloomed and carved objects such as masks are well worth the prices asked.

Then Mr. Arulanantham arrived from Ratnapura carrying the same gems I had looked at previously. After consideration I offered a price for six or seven, which he did not call sufficient; however, he allowed me to take them on my promise to have them appraised in Europe and send him more money if they were found to be more valuable than expected. This did not seem likely as all were semi-precious stones. Also, it would be a long time before I got home. [By then I had forgotten my word. I don't think he lost on the deal and I never heard from him again.]

The zoo attracted me again; this time I saw the 450-pound reticulated python. A sign said 300 persons die each year of snake bite, though more of fear than of poisonous venom.

As Colombo is a good place to shop, I bought a cheap camera. Sam and I dined at a Buhari chain restaurant, where my choice was chicken *biriyani* with rice and a pudding called *wattaleappan*. I purchased several books including two on Ceylon. The free market exchange rate makes shopping easier and the government does not appear to attempt the regulation of exchange on this level. Many dealers on the street sell rupees for hard currency.

Hikkaduwa, Friday, January 26

Today began the circuit of the island's remarkably beautiful coast by train and road, frequently touching the sea at enchanting locations. This road connects a succession of towns and villages, many of which offer the plain but suitable accommodation of a rest house.

When I arrived at the Hikkaduwa rest house a party of German tourists had preceded me. Therefore all I had was a bunk in a small side room, but it was sufficient.

The scene here is as tropical as I picture a South Pacific island to be. Soon I was swimming in the warm waters of the coral reef-protected shoreline. It was these coral gardens that brought me here. Access to them is extremely easy, as the formations begin a few yards off shore. A glass-bottomed boat is at hand, and goggles and flippers can be rented, which is what I did.

Hikkaduwa and Galle, Saturday, January 27

I spent three hours this morning in the water exploring the coral formations and watching the colorful fish and other creatures. These swim near the surface and are easy to see—at times I was swimming along with the fish. Some were fifteen or twenty inches long. So that I could stay so long in the water, I floated on my air mattress, leaving my back exposed. All this was a new experience. The price I paid was a sun-burnt back and a small scrape on my foot caused by the sharp coral. Following lunch and a rest, I continued on by bus a few miles to Galle. It is seventy-two miles down the coast from Colombo and the largest place in the southern part of the island. Galle was the maritime center before Colombo, serving as commercial emporium in the Portuguese and Dutch periods. The old Dutch wall surrounds the city center. It offers a pleasant walk along the grass-grown areaway on top. Then I met two residents of the YMCA who were eager to talk. One, a Tamil teacher from Jaffna, did not like the United States. He spoke like a Communist and his depreciation of Americans was flavored with Marxism. He accused us, in a quizzical way, of dispensing too much money to two-faced countries of the East.

I was lured into a gem shop where tortoise shell was sold, but I got away without buying. The owner told me he did not keep his business to make money but wanted to teach the trade to his sons. At least he wasn't a heartless businessman. There are two churches here, but I curtailed further sightseeing in favor of rest.

Weligama, Sunday, January 28

The sun yesterday combined with the salt water left me feeling spent, and I fell into bed upon fetching Weligama and its rest house.

Later I found myself recuperated and ready for a short swim in Weligama Bay. There are two small islands off shore named Taprobane and Parei Duwa. Coconut palms grace the scene, ending almost at water's edge where small catamarans are drawn up. Nearby is a Buddhist temple with a richly decorated interior. It is apparently not old.

Within the town I saw the colossal image of a man carved in the face of rock. His identity is not established and people have a choice of names for him.

Matara, Dondra Head, and Tangalla, Monday, January 29

I paused for a short time in Matara. At one time long ago it was famous for its spice gardens; a Dutch fort remains to indicate its former importance. Something I read later suggested that perhaps I missed more than I meant to in Matara. I do not know. The guide book described it as the "...heart of the south; throbs with hidden life; modern, yet old; a rare example of anachronism alive; visit the marketplace and feel it—modern merchandise hangs unashamedly, cheek by jowl with traditional panimul-coconut treacle packed in arecanut sheaths: the Fort, yet alive, was built centuries ago by the governor Van Eek in 1763." The Sinhalese author goes on, attempting to express his love of homeland, perhaps saddened by the changes he saw around him.

Leaving Matara behind, I came quickly to Dondra Head. It is a charming place where the sea, picturesque rocks and coastal indentations, and a good-looking lighthouse combine to make an impression on the beholder. The friendly people I encountered at Dondra Head also contributed. This is the most southerly point in Ceylon, only a few hundred miles north of the equator with no land south of it until Antarctica. The surroundings are maintained as a natural park laid out with coconut palms and walkways and including the octagonal stone-built lighthouse. The assistant keeper led me up to the lantern, explained how it functions, and described his duties in the Imperial Lighthouse Service. I signed the visitor's book after examining it awhile to learn who had preceded me in this place. There was a record of shipwrecked sailors who made a visit after their rescue.

A local man spoke to me and invited me to his home nearby. This led to an invitation to lunch offered by another local resident, which I accepted with pleasure and, perhaps, surprise. He served it himself in his modest dwelling where the family of six children and adults lived. They were adding to it to accommodate their growing number. The mother taught school. As I consumed the fish, rice, and vegetables offered, a small group of neighborhood children stood around, watching. I was tickled to be the object of all the attention. Then all of us went outside for a group photo with the shoreline as backdrop. We picked a coconut and, to please my audience, I drank the milk and ate some of the soft part. There were fourteen children in that photo, ranging from five to ten years old.

A significant *perahera* festival takes place at Dondra every year, attended by large numbers of people on pilgrimages, or merely as tourists. A small, unusual stone shrine is located near the end of Dondra Head. Although I did not see it, it is described as twenty-six feet long, constructed of finely joined stone blocks with little decoration except on the doorway. It is very old and little is known of its history or purpose. Then I left Dondra, carrying with me a pleasant memory of the place and its people.

At Tangalla on the coast farther to the east, I found another ideal seaside landscape. A rest house occupies the hilltop near the bay, and there I took tea served on old English china, slightly cracked. After a stroll in town, I walked across the headland to learn what was on the far side—pasture with scattered rocks, a few wildflowers, and a peaceful indented shoreline. The scene recalled an English coastline.

The rest house was serving venison, and though I was not hungry after eating at Dondra, I tried some. It was quite tough and the flavor was nothing to praise—too strong.

Tissamaharama, Tuesday, January 30

Several Europeans were at the rest house at Hambantota, the next bus stop, and so I enquired if any of them planned to visit Ruhunu Park by car. As an American couple were planning such an excursion, I introduced myself and asked to join them; however, they were unwilling to go along with it. Therefore I continued by bus to Tissamaharama and there checked in at the rest house. Walking across paddy fields to the town, I boarded another bus, which dropped me at the park entrance road. As I began walking in, I encountered a crowd of monkeys in the bush. They ran away. I was not in the park yet and already meeting animals. This was encouraging, but the next encounter was not reassuring. After walking about a mile, I was surprised by an elephant beginning to cross the road about 100 yards ahead. Then he stopped, faced me, and remained still. As I was afoot in a situation where it is only safe in a car, I retreated while he ambled off into the bush. The wind was blowing in the wrong direction for him to detect my odor, and elephants do not see very well. Therefore he may have heard something but did not feel threatened. Nevertheless, this meeting was sufficient to change my mind and I sought out a large tree that I could climb. No more pachyderms appeared.

I stayed where I was until a park tractor picked me up and carried me as far as the ranger's office. It was late by then. I could not find anyone visiting the reserve today. I caught a ride back to Tissa in a fish truck returning with the day's catch.

I was especially satisfied by the menu at this rest house. They turn out good meals, cheerfully served.

Tissamaharama and Kataragama, Friday, February 2

An extended family of monkeys live in the trees near the rest house. They are usually shy and one should not approach closely.

I remained indoors this morning suffering some malaise. By afternoon I felt better and went to Kataragama, inland, prompted by a chapter on the place in R.L. Spittel's book on Ceylon. It is a pilgrimage center with special character—going back far into history. People still trek here once or more yearly. The ruling deity is Skanda, before whom pilgrims make offerings of flowers and fruits; they fulfill vows and do penance in his sight for their sins. No magnificent temple exists here. The quadrangular white building with an elaborately carved main entrance holds only about 100 worshippers at a time. Inside the walls are coated with soot and camphor from oil lamps that have been burning continuously for more than 100 years. Apart from an area curtained off for the priest, this chamber is bare, in eloquent contrast to much decorated Hindu temples.

[Its purity of design, its lack of ornamentation, its air of timelessness endows the shrine with the awesome sanctity that only years of worship by millions of people could have brought to it.]*

It is remarkable that Skanda's favors are sought by Hindus, Buddhists, Christians, and Muslims. The ritual and its hold on the people makes me think that the cult of Kataragama goes back to an age before the arrival of the great religions in this region.

I stayed here into evening, when I observed, for the only instance on the trip, Hindu fire-walking. At least one man, perhaps more, walked the length of a trench filled with flaming coals as I watched. Visitors can sometimes see other acts of penance, such as silver skewers piercing a person's tongue, or hooks or spikes going through his shoulders. Such acts challenge credulity. A visitor accustomed to logical thinking wonders if they can be illusion.

Kataragama possesses a ruined *dagoba* (the same as a *stupa* in India), which is under restoration. Only the brick core remains. These Buddhist monuments endure like the pyramids, but like them they have lost their dressed stone exteriors, leaving just the mound-shaped core.

I met a saffron-robed Buddhist priest on the bus today who told me about his duties as a priest of the temple and the manner in which he is provided with his material needs, all of which are given to him, down to his umbrella.

* *Handbook for the Ceylong Traveler*, op. cit.

Kataragama is fetched by only one road, bordered by two-acre homesteads recently distributed to landless families. Small mud-and-wattle houses have been erected and the land cleared to plant vegetables. In front of many houses are small stands which display fresh produce for sale. I was told that the water supply is not adequate, and wild animals at times invade the gardens. There are several of these colonization schemes on the island; the most extensive is the Gal Oya project. The government is hoping to provide for increased population; there is also an institutionalized nostalgia directed toward a restoration of the glory of ancient times when the Sinhalese kings constructed the magnificent irrigation systems based on the great tanks (reservoirs). These were an interconnected system, later destroyed by invaders and floods. Now they are being put back in repair, although the labor required is great and progress slow.

The old kings did not simply construct a short dam across a narrow valley, but built an entirely new water system. They created the tanks by building long bunds of earth, like levees, which confined the water in great sheets. The tank at Tissa was the first one built in modern times, and it is beautiful—like a lake. It attracts birds by the thousands and many fish. The tanks are connected by channels and spillways to regulate flow.

The tank on which the rest house at Tissa is located has egrets, cranes, cormorants, ducks, and other water fowl. At the spillway were hundreds of fish trying to leap up to the tank, and I wondered why no one was fishing.

Today a tour group of Europeans arrived and took all rooms, leaving me to sleep on the veranda tonight and tomorrow. It was uncomfortable because I had grown more accustomed to comfort here. I met two young Sinhalese, one a surveyor and the other a game warden. It was interesting to hear their ideas on the jobs they do and on the country, while we drank beer. They invited me to visit them at Kataragama and offered to show me around—so too bad we didn't meet sooner.

Wild boar was served for dinner. The taste is similar to beef.

Ruhunu Park, Saturday, February 3

I am feeling out of sorts: weak, feverish, aching legs, and a former skin ailment has broken out again, making it necessary to bandage my fingers.

The visiting tourists, myself among the group, boarded six cars this afternoon and headed for Yala Park, the wildlife preserve I had tried to visit last Tuesday. Soon we arrived at the park entrance, where we divided into three two-car groups. Our trackers, the guides who accompanied us in each car, said that arrangement would make us more difficult for the animals to see, and would disturb the wildlife less than a large caravan. We scattered in different directions. Our small group arrived at an open area near a watering place. Our tracker warned everyone to stay in the car and refrain from talking. We watched a small herd of spotted deer nearby, which seemed not to object to our presence. Harder to see was the single wild boar; and then a crocodile suddenly appeared on the water's edge, opening his jaws for us. We watched these from the car, using my binoculars, which I passed around. Alert from what we had already seen, we vied with one another in sighting more wild creatures.

Continuing slowly along the track, we next encountered a herd of five elephants ahead. Seeing us, the leader trumpeted and the others looked in our direction but remained in place. Our driver expressed his concern should they cut us off by occupying the track we were following. He then drove slowly past the animals and stopped again to enable us to look back to see the giant beasts moving slowly toward us, then turning and entering the jungle. The largest was a splendid animal. I could not be sure any had tusks because foliage partly concealed them from view.

Later we saw a group of sambur, which resemble small elk. These and spotted deer are numerous in the reserve. We also saw wild water buffalo. Our tracker said these can be dangerous if disturbed.

The bird life is abundant. More than once hawks perched near us watching our movements. Several tortoise species as well as lizards and snakes are found. The terrain is not particularly interesting and large trees are few. Water for the animals is not adequate, and when the season is a dry one they venture outside the preserve, where they are in danger of being killed by poachers and irate farmers.

If our group had remained in the area toward evening we might have seen leopard; however, the time limits rendered the chances of this unlikely. These majestic hunters can be seen at Leopard Rock, where a thirty-foot rock overlooks a ground where potential prey may gather.

East of Yala and adjacent is Yala East National Park, a larger area with restricted access. The description makes a nature lover wish to see more because it sounds richer than Yala. The bird life here offers a profusion of waterfowl of every kind. The number and variety of species surpasses Florida. The only shorebird not found is the flamingo. This abundance is greatest at the tank called Kumana Villu. It is a 500-acre mangrove swamp several miles inland. Lying beyond the territory of Yala East is the Intermediate Zone and along the sea in this area you find (if you are admitted) several lagoons connected to the ocean where the bird life is exceedingly profuse. Of course I saw nothing beyond Yala Park's confines and also missed the wealth of archaeological remains in the territory. The scenery is probably very fine; rocky hills, jungle, scrub, high forest, and plains are interwoven to make a land that provides habitat to still more species, for example, fantail flycatcher and paradise flycatcher, kingfisher, blue-tailed bee eater, and they go on.

The region belonged to the Sinhalese kingdom of Ruhuna. It continued for more than 2,000 years. That is hard to believe. [I find the claim in the *Handbook for the Ceylon Traveler*, op. cit., p. 74.] Its capital was Magama, a site in a sparsely populated region where the original name still attaches to a village on highway A-4 west of Pottuvil. Wherever you venture in the Intermediate Zone, more ruins, caves, and irrigation works, now in ruins, crop up.

> Two miles north of Kiripokuna a jeep track terminates at Bambaragastalawa, perhaps the most extensive of the ruined sites in the area. The main rock capped by an unscalable peak is 368 feet high. Spread out in all directions into the surrounding jungles from its base are numerous boulders of immense size beneath most of which are drip ledged caves where monks meditated ages ago. In one large cave is a damaged recumbent image of the Buddha 18 feet in length. Scattered around are 21 caves with inscriptions. Be wary of hornets at the summit.*

Our caravan of cars reunited and returned to the Tissa rest house in time to relax before dinner. The same two lads from Kataragama were present this evening and had brought some sambur meat and arrack, the strong alcoholic liquor made from coconut palm sap. I partook of it sparingly, for I do not trust the pairing of strong drink with the tropical climate.

Diyaluma Falls, Sunday, February 4

This morning I took the bus to Wellawaya and took another bus to Diyaluma Falls. Even at 570 feet they are not the highest waterfalls in the country. Approaching on the road you head directly into

* *Handbook*, op. cit., p. 171, footnote.

the flood, then pass within a few steps of it. On my visit, black-faced monkeys cavorted in the trees near the falls, perhaps attracted by the coolness. A single working elephant, mahout astride his neck, came by and posed for a picture, the beast obedient as a dog. A passing truck returned me to Wellawaya, where I picked up the bus to Moneragala. The region traversed today is rugged, thickly covered by vegetation, and has abundant water with sparse population.

The rest house at Moneragala had space. A person there suggested an ointment to use on my hands. It was an English product sold at the local store and it soon relieved my ailment.

Today the five planets meet in Sagittarius. This is the celestial event that occasioned the chanting I heard in Kandy. A small procession of celebrants, drummers, and a single caparisoned elephant passed on the road. Today is also the anniversary of Ceylon's independence. She remains in the Commonwealth and I see portraits of the queen and royal family in homes and businesses.

Pottuvil, Tirrukavil, and Sinnamuhattuvaram, Monday, February 5

A fellow diner in a Pottuvil cafe spoke to me. He was a Tamil teacher who provided helpful information on how to proceed and what to see. Wild elephants in numbers can be seen at play on the bund near Lahugala. They throw water and slide down the flanks of the bund into the water. This is exactly what R.L. Spittel wrote of in his book. [I have not been successful in tracing this down; however, I remember his book as a most interesting description of Ceylon.] Lahugala has the largest herd of wild pachyderms in the country and they are to be seen from a safe distance at about four o'clock daily.

The teacher spoke also of the nearby Gal Oya irrigation scheme, the most ambitious of the settlements. The dam here was constructed in part with U.S. foreign aid. I did not have time to see it or the Moghul Maha Vihara, a ruin that the guide says is one of the most interesting in Ceylon.

Aurugam Bay lies close to Pottuvil, and I visited it on bicycle. The rest house faces the sea and I watched six-foot waves crash onto the beach all at once to make a deafening roar. I enjoyed a glass of ginger ale before returning to take the next bus north on the coast road. At one point the driver had to slow for monkeys ahead.

We fetched Tirrukavil on the ocean, where I paid an informal visit to Sam's brother, E.E. Gunaratnam, whom I had already met in Colombo. We conversed on a variety of subjects while sipping tea and eating biscuits and bananas. He's a Methodist minister with four churches in his care. He hailed a ride for me with the district chief of the Public Works Department. There were two other passengers, who spoke enthusiastically of a "universal church," which, one said, would be a unity of religions without merging—"like the individual flowers of a bouquet." Perhaps they were thinking of something like the World Parliament of Religions. One of the men came from southern Arabia, the second "from Purity," he said. That might be an answer to the oft-asked question, "Where are you coming from?"

They turned me over to the rest house in Sinnamuhattuvaram, where the manager was ready to turn me away because a group was taking up the facilities this evening. Then the people I arrived with spoke up and I was admitted.

There was no village—only fishermen at work in the broad lagoons. They cast their nets gracefully into the calm waters while standing in outrigger canoes.

Later the host of this evening's affair at the rest house, a member of parliament, invited me to attend the dinner so I might have something to eat. The gathering marked the opening of a new electrification scheme. The meal included boiled rice, curry, peppery-hot sauces, and vegetables. Someone present told me to take sugar to reduce the burning sensation.

Batticaloa and Kalkudah, Tuesday, February 6

The district probation officer I met at last evening's dinner invited me to lunch at his home in Kalmunai. Therefore I left the bus there and soon we were driving home in his Volkswagen. After meeting his family of five, we sat down to a meal. His wife taught school. After showing me the beach and the tennis courts and taking a family picture, I said adieu and left for Batticaloa, the next stop on my itinerary.

Even as Loch Ness is the home of the monster, Batticaloa is the home of the "Singing Fish" in its bay. No one I met understood the phenomenon—a mysterious sound heard at night when the moon is full. It is ascribed to fish of unknown species. I heard no other explanation for the charming occurrence.

By evening I had fetched Kalkudah and lodged at my usual place, a rest house.

I called informally on a local resident, Mr. S.V.O. Somanader, whom Sam had talked about. The gentleman had been a school principal and naturalist who wrote for the English-language nature magazine.

The evening meal at the rest house consisted of boar again, and fish. The electricity was off.

Polonnaruva, Wednesday, February 7

Following an English-style breakfast and a walk to palm-fringed Passakudah Bay, I rejoined Mr. Somanader for more conversation on the abundant wildlife of Ceylon. He showed some of his articles and photos and answered my questions, for example, concerning the devil bird of Ceylon. When I mentioned the "singing fish," he did not venture an opinion. He had made his own investigation in an open boat under the full moon and had dived beneath the surface.

I thanked my host and took the bus to the railhead for Polonnaruva. A dental surgeon, whom I had spoken to at the rest house, was also on the bus. He spoke of politics, saying, "Ceylon is highly blessed by nature, but the people are not very good. The government, controlled by the Sinhalese majority, is causing dissension between the several ethnic and religious communities." I have heard like statements from other sources.

The trip by self-propelled rail car took us through jungle, and, as I was seated next to the driver, I watched ahead for animals. I saw black-faced monkeys, which at times occupied the tracks. A dozen or so were on a bridge, which meant we slowed down to a crawl while they jumped clear. It seemed they felt secure sitting in the path of our machine. Further on we saw spotted deer and sambur. The quantity of wildlife to be seen is a new experience for me; at present, significant numbers of wild creatures continue to bless the land. Still, Mr. Somanather despaired for the future, telling how even here wild creatures are disappearing rapidly. Elephants, for instance, are not given adequate protection and territory when land is cleared for settlement.

We arrived at Polonnaruva and the rest house, where tea was being served. After tea I made initial acquaintance with a few of the nearby ruins, deciding that the city would be well worth exploring.

A couple of years ago, I was told, Queen Elizabeth and Prince Philip visited here and stayed at this rest house. It occupies a perfect location on the edge of the Parakrama Samudra tank overlooking the placid waters where many birds dwell.

Polonnaruva and Sigiriya, Thursday, February 8

Before my visit I knew nothing of either of the ruined cities of Ceylon. Both Polonnaruva and Anuradhapura were capitals, and both preserve interesting relics of art and architecture from their Sinhalese Buddhist past.

The Cholas and Tamils from South India conquered these places, but not much remains of their influence, or the archaeologists have not uncovered any Hindu buildings. The glory of Polonnaruva is in its *dagobas*, monolithic figures, *viharas*, *chaityas* (prayer halls), temples, and palaces. The remains possess strong monumentality and are richly decorated, marking an advanced culture. Only stonework survives; however, they also used wood. Gardens were equipped with pools and ornate baths.

The most awe-inspiring of all these remains were the monolithic stone figures of the Buddha and other personages. They are sculpted of living rock and show Buddha in the attitudes of meditating, preaching, blessing, lying down, and standing. I have read two explanations for the horizontal figure. One says he is dying and the other that he is in Nirvana. I say, why not explain it as the posture required by the absence of a rock face sufficiently lofty to permit a forty-foot figure in a standing position. There is also a gigantic standing figure with crossed arms called the Beloved Disciple Ananda.

I continued all morning, walking from ruin to ruin and also taking a bicycle to get around because it was getting hotter and the sites are far apart. A custodian loaned me his. The major part of the buildings are of the twelfth century. Five groups are found in the space of four miles, north to south. Scattered trees remain to remind the visitor of the thick jungle that stood here before the city was cleared.

My visit concluded with an after-lunch drive along the road on top of the Parakrama Samudra tank. The car which offered me the ride stopped at the colossal sculpture of King Parakrama Bahu. He stands holding a booklike object in his hands.

In Ceylon's golden age this was rich agricultural land. The kings of that time carried out the efficient irrigation schemes consisting of interconnected tanks carrying life-giving water to all areas. Later, invaders, war, and neglect followed by depopulation brought about the deterioration and final collapse of the culture.

In recent years the government has initiated the rebuilding of tanks and channels with the object of returning the land to cultivation by supplying water and settlers from the western region where there is excess population and many landless people.

Then I continued on to Sigiriya Lion Rock, fetched on the road following the confines of beautiful Minneriya tank, home to many birds. Further on, the sight of this remarkable domed formation, rising 600 feet from the surrounding terrain, can only surpass its reputation. The heat this afternoon permitted but the sighting of it from below, and the rest house staff advised making the ascent to-morrow morning.

Sigiriya, Friday, February 9

To escape the heat I set out to climb the Lion Rock before breakfast. The way up begins with steps cut in the rock. After reaching a platform the next stage consists of an inclined passage in the rock protected by an outside guard wall. Then, at the next platform, you proceed to an arrangement of iron ladders and railings—perilous looking itself—which dissuades some from going farther. The face of the rock has many cuttings made in ancient times. The present route follows the old one. At one point a lateral passage takes the climber to the Mirror Wall and Cloud Maidens. These are probably the great attractions and incentive for many to climb the rock. The Maidens are twenty-one lovely women whose torsos are painted in masterful fresco. These ladies have survived the elements for centuries, shielded only by a rock overhead that carries the rain away. Their style closely resembles that of Buddhist cave paintings of Ajanta. The Cloud Maidens wear mainly jewelry and lotus flowers, and they may be dancing. Many people might easily fall in love with them as I did. As for the Mirror Wall, I missed it. It seems to be a smooth surface on the rock face, extremely durable, on which numerous visitors have scratched comments or praise for the maidens above. These remarks have been deciphered and published.

Renewing my ascent along the iron ladders attached to the sheer rock face guarded by a low wall, I found it disquieting to have all the empty space about me. Nearing the summit, the way enters the open mouth of a lion modeled in brick, into his throat, emerging again in the open on top of the mount. Suddenly the horizon expands and relaxation is possible. The sun shines on the time-worn walls of Kasyapa's palace, scattered over the confined area. He was the regicide who stole the throne from his father in 477 A.D., but he did not last long thereafter. In his reign of a few years he was able to create this remarkable and lofty retreat. Eventually he committed suicide when his soldiers deserted.

In the still fresh morning and before the sun shone full, I poked about in the palace, finding a sculptured throne, and a small masonry tank. Before long I began the descent, crossing paths with the chief of the Department of Health and his wife. They were English and we had met before and talked about the famous Bambara bees that build nests under the edges of this rock.

After I enjoyed my English breakfast at the rest house, it was time to depart. I had to wait for the bus, which was due at noon. Meanwhile I visited the rock-cut temples of nearby Dambulla, although without a good flashlight it was impossible to see them to advantage. They contain a forty-foot reclining Buddha and other carvings. Not far from Dambulla is the Aukana Colossus, a handsome Buddha figure standing thirty-nine feet tall, carved from a living rock face. It is said to be 1,500 years old and remains in good condition, although it has been restored. The early morning sun illuminates it effectively. The bus delivered me to Anuradhapura and the rest house.

Anuradhapura, Saturday, February 10

Besides being an area of hoary ruins, Anuradhapura is a modern town served by several main roads and the railroad. To avoid the heat I began my walking tour early, using a good map of the archaeological zone distributed by the Shell Oil Company. It showed a large area occupied by excavations—so large that already I was having doubts that my energy would last until I had done justice to it all. But I set forth to do my best to see the seven *dagobas*, four tanks, sacred bodhi tree, temples, *chaityas*, palaces, *viharas* by the dozen, citadel, bridges, statues, and museum. I saw a few of the gems—the museum, the Brazen Palace—preserving a forest of stone posts difficult to explain, the bodhi tree, and the restored *dagoba* of Jetavanaramaya. The last stood 350 feet high originally and now reaches 230. Traces of pleasure gardens were present as well as ornate pools and baths. There were large sculptured figures of Buddha, which are always surprising.

The visit would have been more enjoyable if it had not been so hot, and February is a dry month. I lost my way in the vicinity of the citadel. As I sat on a stone to gain a sense of which direction to take, a man came out of a cottage to invite me in to his humble shelter. He spoke English and was a contractor who brought logs out of the jungle with oxen to be picked up by lumber trucks. He asked his wife to cut open two coconuts and together we drank their contents and ate some of the meat. It was a pleasant moment.

Then, after a walk along the panoramic road topping the bund holding Nuvara Vava tank, I arrived back at the rest house, concluding my tour.

At midnight the taxi driver awakened me for the trip to the station, where I boarded the night train to Talaimannar and India.

Again I welcomed the sleeping compartment supplied with bedding.

Talaimannar To Bombay

By train to Madurai, Sunday, February 11

I was awakened before dawn by activity around me. The passengers were leaving the train, for we had fetched Talaimannar. I quickly rolled up my bedding and joined the others on the platform, where the lines were forming before customs and immigration inspectors. As a foreign tourist I was given priority and soon found myself aboard the ferry reading a book while others required longer. Then the ferry departed and I said goodbye to Sri Lanka.

It was 7:00 p.m. before the train left Danushkodi for Madras. I traveled aboard the single rail car going to Madurai, a third-class carriage filled with people and packages. We barely crept along the sand bar leading to the mainland. It was 1:00 a.m. when I got off and climbed the stairs in Madurai station. Every retiring room was occupied, so the attendant offered me the waiting room "For European Travelers Only," which was empty. I locked the door, drew two overstuffed chairs together to make a bed, and went to sleep. This was the sole waiting room of its kind I remember in India. Every large station has separate first-, second-, and third-class waiting rooms as well as restaurants for each.

Madurai, Monday, February 12

In the morning I moved to a now empty retiring room and enjoyed a shower, then English breakfast in the refreshment room. These were cherished comforts after last night.

It was a short walk to the Meenakshi Temple, passing crowds of people and small conveyances on the way. There is a direct road from the station to the temple entrance, followed by thousands making the pilgrimage from all India. Soon I was standing before one of the four entrances to the courtyard. A *gopuram* towered above, covered with scaffolding and palm mats concealing the sculpted surface. The same was true of several of the twelve towers. Later these were to be painted in bright colors. I entered the large courtyard and soon observed the temple's easy relationship with tourists, for I was able to walk everywhere except in the sanctum. The *mandapam* hall was upheld by 985 pillars displaying an infinite number of distinct forms carved in stone. Such structures precede the main temple building; they are not lofty—between eight and twelve feet up to the superstructure. Their impressiveness also lies in the veritable forest of pillars that a large *mandapam* hall may contain. Adjacent is a group of "musical pillars," which sound pretty notes when struck.

There is also a stately tank flanked on four sides by monumental stairs that extend fully alongside the Golden Lily Pond, as it is named, and connect with a pillared portico above. This is also illuminated by night.

There is no need to leave the temple enclosure to buy bangles, saris, religious objects, or spices. These may be found in a small bazaar between the inner and outer eastern walls. A larger bazaar is located elsewhere in this large city bustling with activity.

Madurai's offerings do not extend much beyond the Meenakshi Temple except for the Tirumalai Nayak Mahal. I walked to this ruined Indo-Islamic palace with a large pillared courtyard. The usable areas are occupied by lawyers and the courts. An elderly man offered his guide services, first showing me his home-made credentials: the typewritten letter listing his qualifications and a price list. His English was limited, but I followed him up to the palace roof, where I enjoyed a good view of the many towers of the Meenakshi Temple. I gave him the stated compensation, which seemed fair, but he hoped for more and followed me for a while before giving up. Both of us remained cheerful. He was a self-appointed guide, not government licensed.

Madurai is extremely old and had trade relations with Greece and Rome, as indicated by coins found here. Seleucus, the Macedonian king who ruled from Antioch, sent an ambassador to the Mauryan court at Pataliputra in northern India. This man, Megasthenes, wrote a description of India at the time, which later writers used as a textbook on the country. Since his work was lost, it is not known if he mentioned anything concerning south India.

Madurai is sometimes called the City of Festivals. Many—large and small—take place throughout the year.

Trivandrum, Tuesday, February 13

Madurai is on the main line to Trivandrum, situated to the southwest on the Arabian Sea and near the tip of India, Cape Comorin. As I was already in the station, having slept upstairs last night, I had no difficulty in taking the early morning train for Kerala State, of which Trivandrum is capital.

Since it was a daytime train and slow, I had an all-day journey and saw many intermediate stations. There is much interesting life in them, but the countryside can become monotonous. The train was not crowded, so I was able to stretch out on the hard, upholstered second-class seats and read *Passage to India* by E.M. Forster. As I had brought no food, I relied on vendors at station stops. At lunch time I consumed a rice dish wrapped in banana leaf. At last we crossed the western Ghats and entered Kerala, where the land changed in character, becoming tropical again, recalling Ceylon. Then we fetched Trivandrum.

The first thing was to find a place to put up, but the station retiring rooms were full as was the YMCA. So far I had not lodged in an Indian hotel and had not been impressed by their appearance. I had seen several luxury hostelries in the large cities, but they are expensive. Instead of seeking further, I told the attendant to give me a retiring room when one became available, which it did later in the evening.

Trivandrum and Quilon, Wednesday, February 14

I attempted to find a student whom I met at home and who had invited me to look him up when I got here. The effort did not bring success but led me to the Padmanabhaswami Temple. Its *gopuram* is the city's most salient landmark and often photographed. The large tank nearby is well used. There were many bathers and people washing clothes along the edge. The temple has a fancy clock resembling those in clock towers. This one struck while I was present.

Then I picked up my mail at the Bharat Sevak Samaj. Then the museum and the zoo received attention. A guide at the zoo took me on a round of the place and prodded some sleeping animals so I could have a better view. As it was the hottest part of the day, I felt sorry for them because they wanted to sleep. He showed me a Russian bear named Khrushchev. A fine rhino got out of his bath and several hippos also. As for the museum, it had a gallery of modern painting. The pictures indicated a variety of influences—Indian, Chinese, Japanese, and even French. Religious and mystical themes were frequent and the great majority were objective.

At mid-afternoon I was ready to depart for Quilon by bus. As we arrived after dark, I experienced some difficulty in finding accommodations. My usual places were all occupied and it was necessary to find a hotel for the first time on the trip. The place I got was very uncomfortable, only a thin mattress placed on plain boards—no rope mesh or webbing. The bed was also too short. There were mosquitos, which I tried to keep off by using the ceiling fan, but it was hard to sleep in the draft it made. There was no outside window, as the room opened on the main salon, where people talked loudly until late evening.

Quilon and Cochin, Thursday, February 15

I enquired concerning the Communist interregnum in Kerala. Party electioneering is now taking place and national elections are scheduled. Those whom I spoke to were not party members, but may have been supporters of the Communists. They said nothing had been accomplished in the twenty-eight months the Communists were in power.

The elongated territory of Kerala, slightly smaller than Switzerland, faces the Arabian Sea and possesses several ports, which have been trading with many lands east and west for 3,000 years. Exports have included spices, tea, coffee, cocoa, rubber, and gemstones. All this contact has provided the stimulus of new ideas. It increased the numbers of Christians in Kerala. One quarter of the population is Christian in contrast to the figure for all India, which is 2 percent. The literacy rate is also high, about 70 percent.

India has a long history of contact with Christianity beginning with the traditional visit of the apostle Thomas in the first century. The traditions around St. Thomas sound true, although historians have not accepted them. According to A.L. Basham in *The Wonder That Was India*,* the Anglo-Saxon Chronicle contains an account of the visit of an English envoy of King Alfred to India in 884. The king sent rich gifts to the tomb of St. Thomas, and the royal envoy returned home safely bearing presents of jewels and spices from the local Indian king.

In the thirteenth century Marco Polo reported seeing pilgrims at the tomb of St. Thomas in Kerala as well as Nestorian Christians, who remained in the East after the Roman church declared their doctrine heretical in 431. When the Islamic conquest caused many Christians elsewhere to recant, they remained true in India. Thus the advent of the Portuguese in Kerala in 1498 came somewhat late in the story of Christianity in India. Vasco da Gama had information that Christians were established in India, and one of his purposes was to make contact with a reported Christian king in these lands. These tantalizing voices from the past cause regret that we don't know more.

As for Quilon, it is a small port with a long trading history, though it is now but an inconsiderable market town. Phoenician, Persian, Greek, Roman, Arab, and Chinese merchants gathered here in previous centuries to buy and sell with each other and the local people.

Kerala is small and does not boast of any world-class attractions; however, its waterways are uncommon. Therefore, on fetching

* Grove Press, 1959, p. 343.

Quilon I sought the next departure of one of the small passenger- and freight-carrying boats punting along the palm-lined channels. The run to Alleppey, an old port that became a backwater, requires all day, and there are nighttime trips that I might have taken had I known about them, and so bypassed the uncomfortable lodgings. After enjoying the Alleppy boat for an hour or more, I became impatient and returned to the road. There traffic was held down to a slow pace because the area is endless village.

Soon I was on the Cochin bus continuing north. At a point along our way the driver stopped and asked all of us to get off and walk across a bridge that was endangered, while the bus crossed it empty. Here was a contretemps which perhaps no one objected to.

As soon as my eyes fell on Cochin, I liked the city. For the next several days my lodging would be in the homey Mysore Cafe. The Brahmins who operated it gave me a small, clean, light room on the third floor with a view of red-tiled roofs, canal, and ships in the harbor. My foot continued to trouble me, and one of the boys brought me hot water to soak it. They were very kind and sent me to see a local ayurvedic doctor, who prescribed a medication. Nevertheless the infection lingered on. If I had seen a doctor as soon as it happened, I might have nipped it in the bud; however I was careless. The environment left it open to reinfection. It began in Ceylon when scratched on coral. The city has two aspects. One is the old character of the place—old houses, old church and synagogue, fishing nets, and calm streets. The other aspect is the one of a busy port and emporium. Cochin, Willingdon Island, and Ernakulam are knit together by small ferries crisscrossing the spacious harbor. The scene is attractive. [Macmillan's *World Gazetteer* (1955) gives the population of Cochin (not including Ernakulam) as 23,000. Webster's *Geographical Dictionary* (1980) gives the 1961 figure as 35,000. A 1981 census states 513,000 for Cochin. The latest number I found, in *The Lonely Planet Guide to India* (1990) is 800,000 for Cochin and 160,000 in Ernakulam. There seems to have been a population explosion in Cochin since I was there.]

The cafe gave me a bicycle to use in sightseeing. With it I visited the old Portuguese residential neighborhood, St. Francis Church, and the Dutch palace. Vasco da Gama was first buried in the sixteenth-century church, where his gravestone remains. It is called the oldest European church in India. The fans attached to the ceiling are operated from outside the building by boys, called *punkah wallahs*, who pull on attached ropes.

The cantilevered fishing nets along the shore are also curious, and are said to originate in China. To me they suggested giant science-fiction insects with their spindly forms and large, winglike nets prepared to swoop down into the sea and grab fish.

The remaining members of the old Jewish community live around the synagogue, which was closed when I passed. A man stuck his head out of a door to speak to me. He came from Bombay and was retired. He had chosen a good location, I thought. All the same, the majority of his coreligionists have left for Israel and other countries to live.

Marco Polo found Jews here in 1293. It is also said that some may have arrived on the ships of Solomon and again after the destruction of the Second Temple by Titus in 77 A.D. After this long history, the Jewish community of Cochin may be drawing to a close. I am not aware of any report that they ever endured persecution in India.

Mattancheri, the quarter of Cochin which includes the synagogue, also possesses the Dutch palace, built by the Portuguese as a present to the local ruler. When the Dutch took control of Cochin, it was renovated and adorned with interesting frescoes of subjects taken from Hindu scripture—the *Ramayana* mainly. These works impress some who see them; I did not find them memorable. The palace is quadrangular with central courtyard containing a small Hindu temple.

Cochin, Friday, February 16

Today I requested ocean passage leaving Bombay in mid-April and sailing to Naples. The temperature will be too hot for comfort by then, and perhaps I will have seen India sufficiently.

The Mysore Cafe provides my meals consisting of boiled rice with milk, curds, bananas, oranges, tomatoes, chappatis, and coffee—thereby I avoided hot pepper. The coffee can be very good here and is different in taste from ours.

Following supper I visited with the brothers who run the cafe. They told me how the government tries to give employment to casteless harijans in preference to high-caste people such as themselves. I already knew of organized efforts to lift the outcast citizens, such as the boys' hostel near Sompeta. One brother said he wanted to come to the United States to live and I might have asked why, but did not.

Cochin and Pondicherry, Saturday, February 17

I ferried over to Willingdon Island to see the view from the Malabar Hotel. A chair on the veranda commands a view of Cochin and its harbor. I enjoyed it while conversing with a German guest and sipping iced tea.

Content with my visit to Kerala and Cochin, I said goodbye, and fetched the train station by rickshaw and ferry. The Cochin Express departed at two o'clock for Salem. I visited with a navy man in a second-class compartment. Eleven hours later we rolled to a stop in Salem, where a branch line runs to Cuddalore. Here a wait of five hours (sleeping on the floor) was followed by an eight-hour journey by Passenger train (the slowest kind) to Cuddalore, bringing me close to Pondicherry. The scenery was not interesting, so I gave the time to reading *Passage to India* and sleeping stretched out on the hard cushions. The novel did not equal the reality around me.

After a reasonable bus trip to Pondi, I checked in at the Parc à Charbon again.

Pondicherry, Sunday, February 18

The following two weeks I rested in Pondi while tending to my foot. By exposing it to the sun as well as keeping it dry and clean, I cured the infection. I recalled having treated a case of athlete's foot successfully by the method. It helped to have everything needed close at hand.

An individual in the management of the ashram asked me if I would be interested in staying there longer in order to learn more of Aurobindo. The house, he told me, would give me a job earning enough to support life while I remained. I did not accept.

Madras, March 5

Accompanied by Jean Calmard, the French traveler whom I had met previously, also by chance, in Calcutta as well as in Puri, I departed from Pondicherry for the last time; I was sad, having met good people here and found relaxation after difficult travel.

We fetched Madras by train in sufficient time to have lunch with Bertram Werwie. This evening we attended the State Agricultural Fair.

The Y being full and since we did not have a hotel, we slept on the beach in front of the city, next to a pile of fishnets and coir rope. The temperature was pleasant and we had no disturbances of any kind. The sand was clean. Therefore we slept in comfort, while a short distance from us many street people were doing the same on pavement. It was an unusual experience.

Aboard the Bombay train, Tuesday, March 6

We awakened before dawn when the fishermen appeared. Soon Jean and I had located our train and begun the twenty-seven hour run to Bombay. The third-class accommodations consisted of tiers of bunks by night and hard seats by day. Every seat was full to over-flowing, as we rolled across the hot, dry Deccan Plateau all day.

A single meal was served the passengers today. Everyone de-trained into a trackside building, where, on the floor, places were prepared for the meal of either vegetarian or nonvegetarian dishes. The selections were served on large green leaves. After all had fin-ished and returned to their places, the train continued. This was the only repast of the kind in all my travels here. The train became hot and dirty as windows were open and sanitation failed badly.

Bombay, Wednesday, March 7

Weary after the long and confining journey, we at last rolled to a stop in Victoria Terminus in the great city of Bombay. My old friend J.C. Desai, whom I had already seen in Delhi, met us at American Express. As we needed a place to store excess baggage, he offered his office in the city center. Later Jean and I went to the suburban flat of N.V.K. Murthy, brother of a Cleveland friend who provided the introduction. Mr. Murthy gave us supper and a place to stay that night. He worked in the film industry, of which Bombay is the nucleus.

Bombay, Thursday, March 8

Jean and I found lodging in a plain Indian hotel in the Fort area a few steps from the station. There being no way to secure baggage, we left the needed articles in our room unprotected. Fortunately, nothing was disturbed. Jean, who is taking a vacation from his job in Afghanistan building a road, had made the acquaintance of a Parsi family here. They were the Narimans, proprietors of the Parsi Dairy Farm. We located them first thing because we hoped for a tour of the processing plant. When we presented ourselves, we received the kindest reception imaginable. They invited us to their apartment in one of the tall buildings on Marine Drive facing Chowpatty Beach. At the appointed time we returned to the dairy plant and were guided to their home where eight or more were gathered, perhaps in our honor for all we knew. A sumptuous dinner was served with hardly any hot pepper, so everything tasted just fine. Everyone was extremely friendly to us and welcomed the two foreigners with open arms. When darkness fell, we all attended a fair taking place on the beach in front of the building. There were bright lights, music, and many stalls selling a variety of foods and souvenirs. I do not know if it was a special celebration or an ongoing thing.

Bombay, Friday, March 9

Jean and I were given a tour of the Parsi Dairy Factory, where a variety of products are made from cow and buffalo milk. Among them are a selection of milk-based sweets of which we tasted: *gulab jamun, peda, burfi, chum-chum, bundi laddu,* and other delights. The processing is carried on in a spotless building by people dressed in white. Finished orders are delivered locally by boys who carry them on their heads, steadied by one hand.

Finally Mr. Nariman gave us a city tour by car in which we saw the triumphal arch called the Gateway to India, the Taj Mahal Hotel, and so forth. Bombay is a thronged and noisy city, more westernized than any other Indian metropolis. It has grown to its present size with the increase in foreign trade.

Elephanta Island, Saturday, March 10

We left our room in the Royal Bengal Hotel early this morning, planning to have time for Elephanta and its wonders. Fetching up the departure point near the Gateway to India, we found one of the regular boats filling up with people in holiday spirits. They carried baskets and bundles of provisions for the obligatory picnic lunch because there is little to eat on the island. The crowd reminded me of people visiting the Statue of Liberty. Before long we were moving across the broad waters. It requires an hour to reach the bare but not barren rock of Elephanta. It was low tide on our approach, a sand bar blocking further progress by our craft, so we debarked onto a long jetty. The rock is four miles in circumference and rises several hundred feet. Stairs are cut into the hard basalt and these we mounted, refusing the proffered palanquin service. The temperature was rising.

There were guides on the spot. We preferred to be without their services, although their flashlights would have been helpful, and therefore we missed some recesses. The main cave is about sixty feet deep with a low ceiling and carved pillars apparently supporting the weight above. Jean and I admired the Trimurti Shiva, who dominates the this cave.

I shall try to convey the experience of this sight by saying that after my eyes adjusted to the dimness, the very large head of Shiva (twenty feet high) became visible by the light from the cave opening. The head was carved out of the living basaltic rock in the great age of rock-cut temples (fifth to eighth century) before free-standing stone structures began to predominate. The head has three faces representing Shiva the Protector and Preserver (facing outward into the room), the Creator (on the right), and the Destroyer (on the left). The central image is best appreciated, being well lighted by natural sunlight. It is strong, fatherly, loving, just, and noble—an impressive representation of the godhead. The artist guided his chisel with consummate skill, resulting in clarity and excellent finish, all pointing to a clear idea of the god and his nature. It is regrettable that the sculptures were damaged by the Portuguese.

The lack of illumination in the cave recesses prevented further examination and we emerged into the bright sun to notice a graceful figure dipping water into a pair of copper vessels, which she carried on her head, walking away with one hand on the full receptacles. A tourist took a picture.

There were already more visitors on the island as we looked for a spot to eat and rest. In partial shade we spread out our copy of the *Hindustan Times* instead of the colorful, handwoven cotton blanket the Indians use to picnic on. It was the hottest time of day.

Later a promising-looking man came by who desired to sell us something—either service or goods, it was not clear which. I think it was anything we wanted. He was interesting and settled in with us easily, remaining until we departed. As he had not succeeded in making a sale—possibly his purpose was market research—we gave him a few annas for trying. I thought he accepted with some ruffled feelings because it made him appear to be begging. But he had given us something in exchange for our offering, and he had not made a request for money.

We had some bad luck on the returning trip. Just as our boat left the landing, the engine stopped and refused to start again. We drifted for an hour while the crew worked to restart it. We were familiar with these contretemps.

Once back in the city, we gazed at the Gateway to India and saw the lobby of the Taj Mahal Hotel. Both are mementos of the British Raj. Then we stopped to see J.C. Desai in his office. This is in a good shopping area and he took us on a short round of the shops selling handicrafts, hand looms, and objets d'art.

Our kind friend J.C. is sincerely devoted to making our stay enjoyable and interesting in every way. Since his return home from the United States, he has begun to manufacture Eagle Auto Polish. The operations as well as his residence are in the suburb of Gorgaon.

Gorgaon and the Calcutta Mail, Sunday, March 11

Jean and I located the modern electric train leaving Victoria Terminus at 9:19 this morning. After a run of half an hour, we alighted at Gorgaon station among a Sunday crowd of trippers to meet J.C. He soon appeared out of the mob scene carrying his young daughter. Both were dressed for a day of enjoyment, he in a freshly ironed, short-sleeved bush shirt and the baby in a new dress. J.C. guided us through alleys and backyards near the station to the site of his small plant, and then to his home.

The center of Gorgaon retains a village character to a large extent, although the surrounding neighborhood has evolved into a suburban community following the arrival of rails. We walked past shops, most closed, arriving at the small apartment in close proximity to its neighbors; as in similar housing in New York or London. Mrs. Desai was in her kitchen preparing dinner. She worked on the floor in an area furnished only with several shelves and a small Primus stove. It seemed very spare compared to a kitchen in our own countries. Then we sat down in the small living room, on the floor, and the food was placed before us. There were several dishes; less pepper than usual made them enjoyable. I have developed some tolerance for hot spices. The Desais are Gujaratis and their cuisine varies somewhat from others. Therefore we enquired about the unfamiliar dishes, and ate everything because it tasted good.

Then we enquired of J.C. concerning possible difficulties he might have found in starting his business. His knowledge came from study at Cleveland's Case Institute of Technology, and he compared his product with Simonize. The package described the product's merits in quaint but understandable English. There was no Hindi, so it could be exported. J.C. said that business is like a game of chess: you play and move for awhile until eventually you become a success. No details were given and he was optimistic that the numbers of cars in India would grow and so would the need for polish. He has probably chosen wisely and knows his game.

After lunch we attended a public garden party sponsored by a prominent officeholder in Bombay. We were accompanied by an Indian medical doctor and his Scottish wife. She was quiet and smiled little. I wondered if she might be the only one of her nationality in this town, or even the only European. The sponsor was a tall man who delivered a short address. Later he spoke to our group personally and described the party as a way for neighbors to meet. His intentions were noble. Families could set up tables of food for sale here and keep all the returns. Insofar as we had just finished eating lunch we could accept very little of the abundance on the tables.

Returning to the Desai residence, we discovered a snake charmer performing with a python. I held the python while J.C. snapped a picture. Then we bid adieu to our kind hosts. I think everyone enjoyed the day. J.C. saw us off again at the station.

We had already given up our room at the Royal Bengal, storing nearly everything except a few items needed for a two-day excursion. Thus lightened we could strike out for Ajanta and Ellora directly after leaving Desai; we decided to join the Calcutta Mail at a suburban station stop instead of going back to Bombay Terminus. Past experience on long-distance rail trips should have made us smarter.

Jean and I were on the platform as our train arrived, and we could see the full rail cars as they rolled past and came to a stop. More passengers were waiting to board, and they rushed to the doors in the attempt to squeeze onto the already too full carriages. This was nothing we cared to confront, and we held back. The restaurant car had stopped a short distance up from us and we headed for it, as it seemed relatively free of the crowd. Tables appeared to be open so we took our chances and got on, hoping to escape the misery of third class as well as avoid the carriers of tuberculosis and hepatitis in those close quarters.

Once we were seated, the waiter appeared and asked for our order. After some discussion Jean ordered a meal in order to satisfy them, and some time later I also did the same. I was not hungry and we prolonged the eating formality as long as we could.

Across the aisle three soldiers were finishing their refreshment. We got into a conversation in which they related how they were returning from a UN peacekeeping mission in the Congo. While telling what they had seen there, we noticed the agitation in their voices and gestures. They did not hope for prompt solutions to the conflict.

When we had ended our meal and were having a cup of tea, the headwaiter soon requested that we leave his car. We urged him to allow us to remain. Nothing worked; however, we did not offer money. The crew began turning out lights and making beds on the floor. It was hopeless and we moved at the next station stop. There being no place to sit in third class, it had to be the floor, for I had not brought my heavy metal case this time. The Indians can squat comfortably on their haunches, but we are not accustomed to holding the position.

Ajanta Caves and Aurangabad, Monday, March 12

Our train fetched Jalgaon at 4 or 5 a.m. Staggering sleepily upstairs to the upper class waiting room, we stretched out on cane-seated couches to sleep a bit. As Jean, who was up first, found the Ajanta bus about to depart, we had to forego breakfast. However, while one of us held the seats, the other made a couple of rapid sorties to pick up a few bananas and a cup of tea before departure.

The thirty-seven-mile ride to Ajanta required a couple of hours of rough going in the chock-full bus. The other passengers were local people, among them many women dressed in colorful red-printed saris and carrying loads on their heads. They gave little attention to the two foreigners among them.

We were crossing hilly, rocky country in Maharastra State, the historical Maratha region of central India. The Marathas were thwarted empire builders of the seventeenth and eighteenth centuries, whose military proficiency helped tip over the tottering Moghuls. The British retrieved the pieces instead of the Marathas.

There are large numbers of man-made cave temples in the central and eastern regions of India—about 1,200—usually in groups. Ajanta is the only one where painting is seen in such abundance and beauty.

The Ajanta caves were well apart from any human settlement that could disturb them in the long period before their discovery by British hunters in 1819. We followed a rough trail on foot for several hundred yards, reaching the horseshoe-shaped ravine where the facades of numerous caves are aligned along the cliff. No one else was present as we descended into the ravine to Cave 1. Our guide was a Department of Tourism booklet of good quality, which is distributed free of charge at tourist offices in major cities.

All twenty-nine of these man-made, chiseled out rooms were the labor of Buddhist monks who fashioned them as protected places of worship and meditation in this secluded place. We saw no defenses and believed that the region was well governed at the time monks resided here in monastic style.

India does not reward comparison with the West; although Westerners are sometimes tempted to see similarities, they often find their opinions contradicted. Even though Western art critics may compare the Ajanta painting favorably with Western wall painting, they fall far short of helping the visitor understand the creations of these nameless artists.

The earliest rock chambers were carved about 200 B.C. and the painting began about 100 A.D. It is assumed that the painters used metal mirrors to reflect the sunlight into the cave recesses. Scholars also say the high quality of the best work meant that it was done by specialists who did not reside at the site.

The caves are not numbered chronologically; Cave 1 is dated at the end of the fifth century. It is one of the best, notable for its sculpture, and especially its magnificent painting. The veranda has six carved columns suggesting that they hold up the mass of rock above. This porch leads to a square hall sixty-four feet on a side, which is again "supported" by pillars arranged in aisles. Surfaces everywhere are decorated with figures, human and animal, as well as other configurations. The shrine chamber at the rear contains a large Buddha carved, like everything else, from the living rock. He is surrounded by his first five disciples. The side walls of this *vihara* hall contain a series of monastic cells.

As we gazed around in the semidarkness, a group of visitors came in with a guide and paid for the lights to illuminate the painted walls, for it was hard to see in the corners. We tagged along with them to benefit from the light and also to hear the guide. This cave contains several masterpieces. They have been reproduced on museum walls, but that is not the same as seeing them here in their original position. There are paintings of the bodhisattva Avalokiteshvara and the bodhisattva Padmapani, whose enchanting consort appears with him and reminded me of the Cloud Maidens on Lion Rock at Sigiriya. This resemblance attests to an established style at the time, a natural, non-rigid delineation of the body by the Buddhist artists. These same characteristics are found in Hindu sculpture, as confirmed by observing any number of South Indian temples.

Every available space in this cave was once painted, including the ceiling. The largest part has flaked off, nonetheless leaving some remarkable works illustrating *jataka* fables (moral tales of Buddha's previous lives) and events in the Buddha's historical life. In Cave 1 there are peacocks and monkeys, while in other caves lions, elephants, and geese are lovingly treated.

The technique of painting was a kind of fresco. The artisan prepared a rough plaster of clay, cow dung and rice husks, then applied it to the rock, pressing it in and covering it with a coat of fine lime to make a smooth surface, which was kept moist. The outlines of the subject were applied by brush, the color added, then another wash applied, followed by refinements of hue and tone. The guidebook includes comments by a couple of European scholars on the painting. One of them, Lorenzo Cecconi, in speaking of the Padmapani, says,

> This painting in its grand outlines recalls to memory the figures of Michelangelo in the Sistine Chapel; while the clearness of the colour of the flesh, so true to nature, and the transparency of the shadows are like those of Correggio. The design and expression of the face are exceptionally surprising, in the breadth of the technique; the interpretation of the shape of the hand, made to realistic perfection, permits of a comparison with the two great artists of the Italian Renaissance.*

The professor compares these paintings, done centuries before, to Italian artists of the fifteenth century, assuming the European standard is the one by which everything is apprised.

The Waghora River below the caves appeared to be nearly dried up in this season. Each cave had once had stairs cut into the rock leading to the river's edge; however, nearly all are eroded away along with foreparts of some caves. Several caves were unfinished, especially one with a mound of uncut rock in the middle of the floor and completed cells around the sides. The occupants of that *vihara* were possibly moved into their new home before its completion.

Jean and I held to our objective of seeing as many caves as possible this morning, though the temperature in the ravine rose constantly. To escape the heat we spent little time in the open. I think we were both astonished at the wealth of subject matter in the caves, having considered Buddhism to be in the main an intellectual and moral discipline.

The guidebook of the Department of Tourism included an appreciation for the women in Ajanta:

> Having seen these cave temples the visitor will perhaps wonder at the profusion of secular themes and motifs on the walls. He may be bewildered by the uninhibited vivacity of the female figures, the famous 'Ajanta type' with well curved forms, elongated eyes, attractive mien and ample adornment. The fact was that

---

* *Ellora-Ajanta*, New Delhi, Department of Tourism, p. 53 (no date).

the artist-monks and their associates painted side by side and with equal zest the physical beauty of women and the spiritual beauty of the Bodhisattva.

'I can think of no parallel to this frank and chivalrous women-worship of Ajanta', Gladstone Solomon wrote. 'Nowhere else perhaps has Woman received such perfect and understanding homage. In spite of her obvious reality one feels at Ajanta that Woman is treated not as an individual but as a principle. She is there not female merely, but the incarnation of all the beauty of the world. Hence with all her gaiety, her charm, her *insouciance*, she never loses her dignity, and nowhere is she belittled or besmirched.'*

We encountered a French couple who were doing India in three weeks by air. They seemed fully satisfied by the experience.

By midday we were finding the ravine a true heat sink and so ended our visit. On top again, we took lunch in a very plain open-air eating establishment, the kind of place the average tourist had better avoid. We, so we believed, had developed some resistance to food poisoning by being in India so long.

We fetched Aurangabad by the bus, a torrid sixty-five mile journey. For all our discomfort we were never reluctant to pay the price to see these places. Approaching the city, I perceived it to be somehow different in feeling from other Indian cities. There were mosques, tombs, and a crenelated wall, as well as markedly less congestion. A Muslim Middle Eastern atmosphere prevailed. Emperor Aurangzeb, the last great Moghul, made his capital here in the seventeenth century.

Soon we located the guest house and were given two places in a four-bed room which might or might not be filled. If so, sharing a room is a good way to meet new people. The dining room was providing eggs, bread, butter, and tea for supper. That was all, but we accepted it in preference to going out to find better, which perhaps we might not have found after all.

Following the short meal we took bicycles for an evening tour of the town. Just two miles outside is the Bibi-ka-Maqbara, the mausoleum of Aurangzeb's wife. The structure is a bad job of counterfeiting the Taj Mahal. Even so it appears interesting. The same quality of materials is not there and we noticed much peeling paint. We also saw the *Panchakki* (water mill) where a garden, waterfall, channels, and water basins are combined into a pleasing ensemble. There are many trout to be fed. A Sufi Muslim saint's tomb is on the grounds.

* *Ellora-Ajanta*, op. cit., pp. 63-64.

[The population here has increased greatly in the years since I visited Aurangabad, from 40,000 in 1954 to 210,000 in 1990.]

There is a group of Buddhist caves near here, but we were not prepared to undertake any more.

Ellora Caves and Daulatabad, Tuesday, March 13

The well-broken-in bus carrying local people and several tourists left Aurangabad bright and early for the other famous group of man-made caves. Ellora rivals Ajanta in the quality and quantity of its art. It has always been known, being less isolated than Ajanta, and plainly visible. Still, the trip is an adventure offering few conveniences to the visitor. After the caves were vacated by the monks, they were occupied by peasants, who caused some, not great, damage to the sculptured surfaces. Their painting is all but completely lost.

The bus and taxi stand is near Cave 16, the great Kailasa. For us the appropriate starting point was Cave 1 on the north where the oldest, Buddhist *viharas* and one *chaitya* lie. We observed that everything is more spread out here and we had to walk more. Instead of the cliff at Ajanta, there is an escarpment at Ellora where the rock is cut back to make a forecourt in the open. Beyond this court a facade with a monumental door leads into the main chamber; along the side walls are chapels and cells. Their western orientation and the open forecourt toward the setting sun make these caves brighter than those we visited yesterday. They make good use of the exposure for larger, more numerous windows in the facade.

The several Buddhist chambers here are dated in the seventh century, before the Buddhist decline in India began.

Cave 5 is deep: 117 by 56 feet. Twenty-four square pillars "hold up" the roof in the observer's imagination. Rows of stone benches suggest it could have been a classroom. The rear chapel holds a Buddha figure.

We advanced to Cave 6, where an ecumenical tendency shows itself. Tolerance of another religious group is surpassed here by a switching of gods between the Buddhist and Hindu pantheons. Sarasvati, the Hindu goddess of learning, turns up. Cave 6 has a simulated timber ceiling by which it is known as the Carpenter's Cave.

Cave 10 possesses a remarkable facade, almost baroque in character. A balustrade fronts a gallery leading through a monumental portal to an interior gallery. The large round window over the portal and bas-reliefs flanking it increase the baroque effect.

Mixing of gods occurs here as well. Cave 10's titulary god is Visvakarma, who is patron saint for many Indian artisans even now and not found in the Buddhist pantheon. The guidebook explains: "This commingling of concepts, which the Mahayana system initiated, resulted finally in the absorption of Buddhism in the current of Hindu thought and its virtual extinction in the land of its birth."* Caves 11 and 12 are the culmination of the Buddhist section. They are large, three-storied evolutions with open courtyards that end in lofty facades, that of Cave 12 rising fifty feet. Each level has a pillared porch. The middle level, seventy feet wide, is divided into five aisles by forty square pillars. There are galleries of figures here, and in the shrine at the east is a Buddha with folded arms—a rare pose, the facial expression meditative, the head lowered.

Then begins the Hindu group and we need no reminder of it, so suddenly comes the change from the calm Buddhist mold. The Hindu figures show their distinctly kinetic character. Cave 14, three stories high, reveals sculptures of Durga, Vishnu, Lakshmi, Shiva and Parvati. Nandi, the Shiva bull, comes along for the first time.

In returning to Cave 16, the Kailasa, we encounter a different kind of structure. So far we have been counting caves, but this last is not a cave, although it is dug out like the others. It is a two-story Shiva temple carved out of living rock, down to the minute details on thousands of figures. The makers began in the eighth century by chipping out a trench 107 feet deep, 276 feet long, and 154 feet wide, leaving a block 150 by 100 feet in the center. By this time the throng of stonecutters had axed away 3 million cubic feet of solid rock! How many cases of silicosis did that effort cause? Walking through and around the temple, we forgot that we were not in a constructed building. It resembles a South Indian temple in many ways. The interior is accessible and given over to decoration in the form of carved figures, human and animal. The stone is reddish in color.

The Kailasa Temple is said to be the world's largest monolithic building. It is named for Shiva's Himalayan abode, Mount Kailasa, in Tibet. The temple contains a great theme of Hinduism—the in-dwelling of divine power in living and nonliving substance. The Kailasa was always in the rock escarpment, only needing to be revealed by the mind and chisel.

A fifty-foot high pavilion, the dwelling of Nandi, faces the temple; on each side rises a "flagstaff" fifty-one feet high. The flagstaffs are pillars with pleasing proportions, beautifully carved in bas-relief. They represent still another example of the Indian genius for tower-building. The decoration is restrained, in contrast to the

* *Ellora-Ajanta*, op. cit., p. 26.

treatment of figures. The remaining Hindu caves seem to fall short of the older examples at Ellora. Cave 29 is large: 150 feet wide and 18 feet high, and resembles Elephanta. It groups a series of small halls into a cross formation with three entrances, wide columns, and a pair of stone lions on guard. It is a few minutes walk from here to the five Jain caves. These we found less exciting than the others. The decoration in them is full of detail and foretells the similar work to be seen later on at Mount Abu, also Jain.

We encountered a few visitors at Ellora, foreign and Indian. A single man invited us to share his taxi on the return, and we accepted with alacrity. With him guiding us we had the opportunity to visit more places on the road to Aurangabad. First we saw an unusual Hindu temple near the caves. In place of the nearly universal temple decoration consisting of gods, people, and animals, we saw geometric shapes, scrollwork, and other nonfigurative forms covering the surfaces. It appeared an attempt to demonstrate that a Hindu building could satisfy Islamic tenets of decoration, which say that figures of humans and animals cannot be included.

Then we stopped to pay our respects at Aurangzeb's grave in Khuldabad. The name means "heavenly abode." The great Moghul left instructions that he be buried simply, with expenses defrayed by his earnings in copying out the Koran. Another source said he sewed cotton caps to cover his funeral costs. The grave is covered with earth; a marble screen now protecting it was placed there by Lord Curzon, the British viceroy. It lies on the grounds of an Islamic shrine. The town is a quiet place encircled by a protective wall placed by Aurangzeb.

Next we stopped to contemplate Daulatabad, while sipping a cup of tea and eating snacks in the open air. The outer walls that compass the medieval fortress here are formidable and extend for three miles. Besides these are inner walls and additional clever defenses and the Chand Minar, a fine Tower of Victory.

A sad story accompanies Daulatabad's history. In the 14th century, the Sultan of Delhi, Muhammed Tuqhlaq, decided one day to move his capital 700 miles south to this place, which he renamed Daulatabad, "City of Fortune." He did not first designate the new capital and then arrange for the orderly transfer of people and facilities. Rather, he compelled every citizen of the old Tuqhlaqabad— men, women, children, sick, old—and their animals to walk the distance. Many thousands never arrived. They fell by the way. The survivors were compelled to build the fort. Seventeen years later the tyrant changed his mind and removed again to Delhi, along with the suffering people. The ruins of Tuqhlaqabad still exist south of modern Delhi. They are number three in the long sequence of cities to occupy the Delhi region. The ruins could still be seen in 1961. [By 1995 they may be obliterated by the massive growth of the city.]

Daulatabad Fort, the surviving artifact, can be seen from a distance, an isolated hill surmounted by a citadel. Below were smooth slopes in stone impossible for a foe to scale, and the interior of the hill has a series of rock-hewn passages. The inner walls have iron gates fitted with elephant spikes to prevent their being forced. A large water tank is built into the solid rock, and a temple supported by 150 pillars occupies the mount. Formerly there were various palaces, which have long since fallen, leaving scant traces.

The strangest relic of the fort may be the tremendous cannon, eighteen feet long, engraved with Aurangzeb's name. The summit of the fort is reached through a dark, vertical shaft in the rock, covered by a grill on which defenders could build a fire, letting brands fall down onto the heads of anyone attempting to ascend. A small mosque completes the scene.

The view of the surrounding country from up top has to be extensive. All this, regrettably, we could not observe save from our table in the open-air tea room. It was too hot to attempt the citadel. Also, there was more ahead. Then we re-passed Bibi-ka-Maqbara, the mausoleum of Aurangzeb's wife, and entered Aurangabad.

Our kind Indian friend remained with us the balance of the day since we were taking the same train back to Bombay. By paying a brief visit to the Handicraft Emporium, we were able to see weaving in the regional *himroo* style, as well as the typical brocade-like bedspreads of nearby Sholapur. They had excellent woven bedcovers from Assam in a zigzag pattern. Because we were headed back to Bombay, I made a purchase to add to my growing collection of handwoven articles and other objects.

Before dinner at the Aurangabad rest house, an American traveler turned up in a VW, to put up at the same place. Such a vehicle might be a good way to get around here; however, it may not afford the same opportunities to meet local people. Following dinner, Jean and I and our Indian friend took the train to Manmad, a narrow-gauge feeder line. Some sleep was possible on that; however, the main-line train out of Manmad was crowded. At first we rode in a sort of caboose; chased off that, we retreated to a second-class carriage, where, later, we found places to sit. It was an uncomfortable journey back to Bombay. Nevertheless, we had our recompense—we had visited the caves.

Bombay, Wednesday, March 14

We took ourselves back to the Royal Bengal, then split up for three days of tending to individual business. I was interested in the many excellent handicrafts seen in the emporiums. The Fort area contains stores of every type and here I pursued my quest. I found, however, that the quality and variety were better in the state emporiums I had seen in other places. I concluded that goods of the quality and quantity to be sufficient for export are not likely to be available without planning. I made a few small purchases and let it go at that. My mind was not in a state to deal with business matters.

Shiv Agarwal, one of the Cleveland students whom I had met, had given me his address and an invitation to look him up here. We were both members of the International Students Group. Shiv and his wife had me home for dinner tonight, after which I remained for an evening of conversation. They have a small modern apartment in the city, where she is an M.D. and Shiv and his brother own and operate a bicycle shop. The couple intend to return to the United States this year for more training in medicine and business. The evening was enjoyable and Shiv's wife joined in the small talk.

Bombay, Thursday, March 15

My purchases made a trunk necessary, so today I took care of that. Everything not required on the final loop of the tour is to be left with J.C. I completed arrangements for ocean passage from Bombay to Naples in May, having borrowed the money for it from my uncle Chauncey, who disapproved of this trip.

Bombay is without tongas, bullock carts, sacred cows, or rickshaws. It is a modern metropolis and world business center. Calcutta and Delhi exceed it in exotic character and I like them better. The outlying sections of Bombay contain industry and *bustees* (large slums), where many of the people have only shacks without facilities of any kind. The slums exist in the shadow of expensive, high-rise apartments.

I located Shiv's store. We sipped tea served by a *chaiwallah* in real cups, no paper here, and discussed business surrounded by cycles and parts. Shiv suggested that I import ladies' shoes and handbags from his country, probably because he had a relative in the business. Nothing came of it after this afternoon's meeting. I could not concentrate my mind on it.

Bombay, Friday, March 16

Our staunch friend J.C. took Jean and me to dinner this evening before seeing us on our way to Baroda. We made a point of fetching the terminus a full hour before departure. Even so, our mail train was full and we were fortunate to find two seats by requesting that an old fellow sit up and not lie down. He was cheerful about it and we noticed that his face and his companion's were besmeared with colors. The all-India festival of Holi is now in progress, involving the throwing of colored water and powders on relatives and friends. We saw it going on in stations along our route. The white garments that many people wear make good targets.

Baroda, Saturday, March 17

As our mail train proceeded north this morning, an obliging passenger yielded his upper birth to us as he got off. Therefore Jean and I each had an hour's rest before reaching Baroda by 6 a.m. Then we slept several more hours in the first class waiting room before telephoning Guardino Dadlani, a university professor whom I had met when he was in Cleveland learning about U.S. teaching methods, probably under auspices of a Fulbright scholarship. He came to meet us. His suggestion that we put up in a station retiring room we graciously resisted, over tea, and then all of us took a tonga to the university. There we met members of the social work faculty, where Guardino teaches. [A tourist guide made favorable reference to this department, calling it innovative.]

The university of Baroda is a modern school founded in 1949, which took over a college affiliated with Bombay University. Since we saw no students, it must have been break. The faculty had time to devote to us.

As Guardino and his wife had a small billet off campus, they did not have a convenient place for us to sleep. Another faculty member, Ramdev, took us to his campus rooms; there we remained two nights, using the floor and our bedrolls. Then we were entertained at lunch by our hosts who chose a pleasant city eating place. Dining was in the open and food prepared at tableside.

The city bore its previous British-endowed name of Baroda in 1962. [It was returned to its new-old name of Vadodara in 1971. It means: In the heart of the Banyan trees. The British had a talent for mispronouncing Indian place names and substituting the result for the actual name.]

Baroda was one of the princely states before Independence, and our hosts gave us a princely opportunity to see a few of the architectural and cultural reminders of this. By horse-drawn tonga we visited the old part of the city dating from the dynastic period. The maharajahs were responsible for some noteworthy buildings, parks, and boulevards. They encouraged higher education and the arts. We followed wide, tree-lined avenues dotted with several palaces, museums, and other public buildings. The principal palace, Laxmi Vilas, was open to visitors. We saw the armory and audience chamber and the miniature steam train, which formerly carried the children of the court to school and is now available to everyone. The museum and art gallery are in the park and we briefly entered, but I was not tuned to looking at pictures, which included both European paintings and Moghul miniatures. We half suspected the Western art to be copies; however, they are genuine. These areas were not congested; the streets carried few vehicles. It made the tour easier.

Evening brought an invitation to attend a social gathering at the university. This appeared to be a pot-luck supper with a variety of excellent dishes, some of them new to us. Finally the company went up to the roof, where we sat around on a blanket and sang several songs. There seemed a lack of conviviality in the group, causing Jean and me to ask ourselves if we were responsible.

Baroda, Sunday, March 18

Ramdev, since his wife was away for this weekend, prepared breakfast himself. Jean and I lent him our assistance, as he wasn't familiar with some kitchen procedures. Guardino invited us to go for a walk in Sayaji Bagh (bagh means "garden"). Already at 10 a.m. the sun was strong and I used an umbrella for protection. We came to a vendor who was using a mechanical press to crush sugar cane. The resulting juice is flavored with lemon and ginger. Some sellers add ice as this one did, making a delicious drink costing three annas the glass. It may not be as hygienic as one would desire. The used glasses get rinsed in cold water.

Again by tonga, we trotted to the old city to visit several handicraft emporiums. The hand-woven and hand-printed bedcovers and other objects were attractive and I made a purchase. We passed the Old Palace, a more authentically Indian building than the Laxmi Vilas with its mixed styles.

Sunday dinner was hosted by Guardino and his wife at their off-campus billet. They are waiting to occupy new quarters on campus. After the hubbub of Bombay this city is a delight—quiet and well ordered. It is a smaller place, but the population is gradually swelling here also.

We learned how Guardino and his wife fled Pakistan as refugees in 1947, he wearing two suits and she three saris. They could carry nothing else. Ramdev also came over the border to India and had participated in the hostilities. He told us how the group he joined was attacked, and he mentioned the "death trains" sent across the Indo-Pak border in both directions. There was undeclared war from 1947 until early 1949. [A second war erupted in 1965 and more conflict has taken place since.] Right now there appears to be a letup in tension and there have been newspaper reports concerning the exchange of bank accounts. The Indian English-language papers report news from Pakistan.

Ramdev invited us for an afternoon swim in the university pool. This evening Jean and I dined with the dean of the social work faculty and her husband, along with Guardino and Ramdev. The meal, prepared by their old cook, had an Indo-European character. Both hosts had studied in the United States and she had worked in the social work office at New York's International House. Both teach and would like to form a local association of people who have either studied in or visited the States. Again most of them would probably be recipients of Fulbright grants.

Before 1947 and Independence, Baroda was one of the so-called self-governing princely states ruled by maharajahs and maharanees. The states occupied large and small areas in the map of British-governed India, making a political checkerboard of the subcontinent. My first experience with the princely states was in childhood. I can remember collecting postage stamps with strange names printed over regular issues of India. They posed a problem because I didn't know where to place them in my stamp album.

Much later as I began to read more and travel, the same names, Mysore, Hyderabad, Kashmir, and others, appeared again. For example, Jawaharlal Nehru talks about them in his book *The Discovery of India* (1946). They appeared to awaken dread in the great leader of the Indian Independence movement, for his first words are: "One of the major problems of India today is that of the Princes and the Indian States." He wrote this while detained in Ahmednagar Fort between 1942 and 1945, one of the nine prison terms he endured. As things turned out, however, his misgivings were scarcely warranted and the states were not obstacles to the formation of a unified India. The tragedy of partition—Pakistan, Kashmir and the whole religious issue—were not the same as the independence movement.

But my main purpose in mentioning the states is to call attention to the illustration they provide of British governing methods in India. Nehru mentions the names of twelve large princely states, including Baroda, and then says "several middling states and a few hundred small places," adding up to 601 individual units, a collection comprising a large area and population. From the British point of view, if these were governed by puppet princes who could be depended on to bend to the British officials in the Government of India, it would simplify the business of ruling. The British would save the people and money required to set up the customary government in the areas they ruled directly. In effect that is how the state system functioned—not as an indigenous authority but as a fifth-column government acting in the interest of the foreigner. In a very few instances the prince attempted to govern in a way beneficial to his people. Yet the odds were against better government because he was not responsible to the people as much as he was to the "paramount" power, the British-run Government of India. It maintained the prince in position; should he find himself in difficulty within the state, either of two things might occur. The British could declare the state "lapsed" and take it over, or they could send an army from outside to reestablish order and conditions conducive to the status quo ante. The agent or resident handled the commercial relations between the East India Company or the Government, and the princely state, and also acted as a British spy.

The period of the rise and development of the states began in the early nineteenth century and was simultaneous with the Moghul decline, the Maratha decline, and the consequent enlargement of territories under British dominion. It was 1818 that the Marathas in central India were finally reduced to accepting British dominion. The state system was utilized to facilitate that process. States became subordinate as the East India Company used the divide-and-rule principle to maintain a firm grip on the country. The treaties signed between the Company and various feudal entities left over after the collapse of Moghul and Maratha power reinforced the weakened princes, who would have disappeared from the scene if they had not been backed by the paramount power. India's old rivalries, for she had never been fully unified even in the flowering ages of the Guptas or the Moghuls, made it possible for the British to enlist Indian soldiers to police other Indians. These armies, led by British officers, served the Company's interest. The princes, subject as they were, could be relied upon to act in their own interest, and that which coincided with the Company's stake in maintaining peaceful conditions encouraging to commerce. The divide-and-rule principle was probably still more effective for British purposes because they were an outside group more interested in trade and profits than in dominion, and they had no loyalty to particular groups within Indian society. The Company was free to take sides in local disputes—helping one rival against another. When the interests of the Company were involved, the prince would usually be trusted to favor the Company over his own people because his long-term status depended more on the paramount power than on his people.

Nehru knew the direction matters were taking, and denounced the states in unmistakable terms in his book, calling them "corrupt, ineffective, uncaring, feudal, autocratic, backward, pawns, denying civil liberties, unable to support an independent economy." He thus prepared the way for the states to fade quickly away after 1947.

The Government of India was transmuted into the democratic government of free India. If the Government of India did some good things—such as establish schools, build railroads, excavate ancient archaeological sites, promote the English language as a unifying influence, and establish effective administration—they were usually confined to the regions under direct rule and not in the badly governed states, where matters generally regressed rather than improved. Nevertheless, Mysore, Travancore, and Cochin built good schools and turned out a better product than was typical in the rest of India.

The Indian Mutiny in 1857-8 provided a test for how well the state system functioned for British purposes. After it was put down, the states gained credit with the Government of India, for the good reason that many either fought alongside the British forces or stood aside and did nothing. This behavior changed some minds in Calcutta, and as a result the British began to promote the states instead of following their pre-Mutiny policy of gradual takeover and direct rule.

Ahmedabad, Monday, March 19

After our visit with members of the social work faculty, Jean and I boarded a north-bound train to Ahmedabad, Gujarat's principal city and former capital. At the end of a two-hour run we stepped down in a station pulsating with moving trains and people. We were left to our own devices until enquiry led us to an employee of the municipal bus company, who led us far across the city, over the Sabarmati River to a residential suburb where my friend Rama Rao, from Delhi, now resides. This trip was an introduction to the humming, mortally congested city that the Moghul emperor, Jahangir called the City of Dust. The neighborhood where we ended up was pleasant and the family welcomed us warmly, providing lunch and relaxation. Their new residence showed a modern, almost Californian look and was situated on a street of similar, well-built dwellings.

The Raos' two children, son Vijay and daughter Maithili, were at home because they had arrived here too late last fall to enter school. Vijay took responsibility for guiding us during our stay. This afternoon a bus tour provided an overall impression of the city. Included on this jaunt were both the new and old, although we paid more attention to the new. We saw the Civic Center designed by Le Corbusier, the park, the river, the bridges, the university, modern streets, and mosques, of which Ahmedabad has a few fine ones. After every stop to view the sights a young boy served us ice water. The high point was the Satyagraha Ashram, one of several ashrams planted by Gandhi. An ashram is a place of spiritual retreat and a residence. Satyagraha is a protest involving a fast. This one served the great leader as his headquarters during the Independence movement. It lies in an open area west of the Sabarmati and four miles north of the city. Gandhi had come to Ahmedabad to assist in resolving a serious strike by the workers in the cloth mills. The strike was kept peaceful with the cooperation of a disciplined labor force, reasonable owners, and Gandhi's nonviolent philosophy. He described the ashram as follows:

> Before I proceed to describe the progress of the labour dispute it is essential to have a peep into the Ashram....
>
> Our ideal was to have the Ashram at a safe distance both from town and village, and yet at a manageable distance from either. And we were determined, some day, to settle on ground of our own....
>
> Sjt. Punjabhi Hirachand, a merchant in Ahmedabad, had come in close contact with the Ashram, and used to serve us in a number of matters in a pure and selfless spirit. He had a wide experience of things in Ahmedabad, and he volunteered to procure us suitable land...and then [we] suggested to him [that he] find out a piece of land three or four miles to the north. He hit upon the present site. Its vicinity to the Sabarmati Central Jail was for me a special attraction. As jail-going was understood to be the normal lot of Satyagrahis, I liked this position....
>
> In about eight days the sale was executed. There was no building on the land and no tree. But its situation on the bank of the river and its solitude were great advantages.

We decided to start by living under canvas, and having a tin shed for a kitchen, till permanent houses were built.

The Ashram had been slowly growing. We were now over forty souls, men, women and children, having our meals at a common kitchen....

Our difficulties, before we had permanent living accommodation, were great. The rains were impending, and provisions had to be got from the city four miles away. The ground, which had been a waste, was infested with snakes, and it was no small risk to live with little children under such conditions. The general rule was not to kill the snakes, though I confess none of us had shed the fear of these reptiles....

During the strike of the mill-hands in Ahmedabad the foundation of the Ashram weaving shed was being laid. For the principal activity of the Ashram was then weaving. Spinning had not so far been possible for us.*

Our bus made a long stop at the ashram. First we saw the small museum of memorabilia including Gandhi's glasses, spinning and weaving implements, and a collection of photographs on the wall. Everything was spartan—no modern machines, not even a telephone that I recall, or a typewriter. The kitchen and dining room are on view. They are plain wood buildings. The other visitors, all Indians, were quiet in this place. Here began the famous Salt March.

We proceeded to see the step well called Dada Harini Vav. *Baoli* is the common name for these unusual structures peculiar to North India. In former times they were used by the people to obtain cool, fresh water. The women carried vessels down a series of stairs spaced by galleries—all in fine stone—to a small octagonal well possibly 100 feet below. The well was placed there in 1499, perhaps by a public-spirited citizen as a gift to his city. Ahmedabad has been praised for its beauty and prosperity. The *baoli* appears to belong to such a period of history. It is now a retreat from the heat of day and, when the sun is right, a place to study quietly. I descended part way into its depth.

Our tour paused to look at the Jami Masjid, the Friday Mosque, erected by the city's founder in 1424. It is an interesting blend of Hindu and Islamic styles. This Indo-Saracenic style of architecture is often seen in Ahmedabad. Ahmed Shah's ornate tomb lies next to the same mosque and contains fine perforated stone-screen windows.

Following supper we relaxed with the family at home. Maithili remained in her room during most of the time we were present, re-

* Gandhi, *Autobiography*, 1927, pp. 316-17.

covering from the flu we were told. The single family servant has been with them for years. His resting place is the veranda floor. Mrs. Rao does all cooking and serving. She is a charming, talkative woman who played the *veena* and sang for the company. The stringed instrument is placed across the folded legs of the seated performer. It sounded very pretty.

Jean and I slept in the living room on the couch and an extra cot.

Ahmedabad, Tuesday March 20

Rama Rao showed us the corn refinery where he works. It uses chopped corn from the United States, which he says is cheaper and better than Indian maize. I suspected that the real reason for relying on U.S. imports was more likely to be in the contract with the U.S. government that provided the foreign aid while at the same time helping U.S. producers by specifying that the corn came from us. The small refinery produces starch, glucose, dextrose, and animal feed. My friend does research and development.

Vijay was with us, and after the refinery visit he took us to the Gujarat State Handicrafts Emporium. Ahmedabad is a textile center, which produces cheap, machine-made cloth. The finer handwoven, hand painted, hand printed articles come from the villages and towns of Gujarat. They are irresistible. Jean and I bought several bedcovers and wall hangings. One of mine had a large figure of the Buddha as a youth, in attractive natural colors. Articles from Gujarat are some of my most interesting mementos of the trip, adding to the weight of my baggage.

After lunch and rest at home, we set forth again. The increased heat requires more exertion and leaves us preferring a midday rest period. Vijay guided us again, this time to visit the old parts of the city. The mosque of Ahmed Shah, dated 1414, was first, followed by the small Sidi Saiyad Mosque, whose remarkable perforated stone screen is a trademark of this city. It contains a tree with branches intertwined in an elaborate pattern of tendrils and leaves, purely Islamic in conception.

The Sidi Bashir Mosque with its two shaking minarets is required seeing. We ascended one shaker to find out what it was. Although we were atop a slender spire of solid stone—not a thing you usually consider shakable—it trembled, vibrated, wobbled, and quaked as if it were jelly. I do not recall the reason.

Before returning home, we stopped in the bazaars, where we found the Gandhi Khadi Bhavan. This retail store, one of a few located in large centers, sells handspun and handwoven goods (*khadi*). I had already found excellent blankets, including one of yak wool from Ladakh, in the New Delhi Khadi Bhavan. [It also had curtain material, which I later ordered after I was back in the United States.] My purchases thus far add up to more than I can carry with me, so Rama Rao has offered to send a stack of things to J.C. in Bombay for me to pick up later.

Gandhi considered the production of textiles by hand an important part of his program of Indian nationalism.

The Birth Of Khadi

....When the Satyagraha Ashram was founded at Sabarmati, we introduced a few handlooms there. But no sooner had we done this than we found ourselves up against a difficulty. All of us belonged either to the liberal professions or to business; not one of us was an artisan. We needed a weaving expert to teach us to weave before we could work the looms....But Maganlal Gandhi was not to be easily baffled. Possessed of a natural talent for mechanics, he was able fully to master the art before long, and one after another several new weavers were trained up in the Ashram.

The object that we set before ourselves was to be able to clothe ourselves entirely in cloth manufactured by our own hands. We therefore forthwith discarded the use of mill-woven cloth, and all the members of the Ashram resolved to wear hand-woven cloth made from Indian yarn only....We were not in a position immediately to manufacture all the cloth for our needs. The alternative therefore was to get our cloth supply from handloom weavers. But ready-made cloth from Indian mill-yarn was not easily obtainable either....It was after the greatest effort that we were at last able to find some weavers who condescended to weave Swadeshi yarn for cloth that they might produce....We became impatient to be able to spin our own yarn. It was clear that, until we could do this ourselves, dependence on the mills would remain. We did not feel that we could render any service to the country by continuing as agents of Indian spinning mills.

No end of difficulties again faced us. We could get neither spinning wheel nor a spinner to teach us how to spin. We were employing some wheels for filling pearns and bobbins for weaving in the Ashram. But we had no idea that these could be used as spinning wheels....

So the time passed on, and my impatience grew....But the art being confined to women and having been all but exterminated, if there was some stray spinner still surviving in some obscure corner, only a member of that sex was likely to find out her whereabouts.

...I discovered that remarkable lady Gangabehn Majmundar. She was a widow, but her enterprising spirit knew no bounds. Her education, in the accepted sense of the term, was not much. But in courage and commonsense she easily surpassed the general run of our educated women. She had already got rid of the curse of untouchability, and fearlessly moved among and served the suppressed classes. She had means of her own, and her needs were few....

Found at Last!

At last, after no end of wandering in Gujarat, Gangabehn found the spinning wheel in Vijapur in...Baroda State. Quite a number of people there had spinning wheels in their homes, but had long since consigned them to the lofts as useless lumber. They expressed to Gangabehn their readiness to resume spinning, if someone promised to provide them with a regular supply of slivers [untwisted strand of fiber], and to buy the yarn spun by them....The providing of slivers was found to be a difficult task. On my mentioning the thing to the late Umar Sobani, he solved the difficulty by immediately undertaking to send a sufficient supply of slivers from his mill. I sent to Gangabehn the slivers received from Umar Sobani, and soon yarn began to pour in at such a rate that it became quite a problem how to cope with it.

Mr. Umar Sobani's generosity was great, but still one could not go on taking advantage of it for ever. I felt ill at ease, continuously receiving slivers from him. Moreover, it seemed to me to be fundamentally wrong to use mill-slivers. If one could use mill-slivers, why not use mill-yarn as well? Surely no mills supplied slivers to the ancients? How did they make their slivers then? With these thoughts in my mind I suggested to Gangabehn to find carders who could supply slivers. She confidently undertook the task. She engaged a carder who was prepared to card cotton. He demanded thirty-five rupees, if not much more, per month. I considered no price too high at the time. She trained a few youngsters to make slivers out of the carded cotton. I begged for cotton in Bombay. Sjt. Yashvantprasad Desai at once responded. Gangabehn's enterprise thus prospered beyond expectations. She found out weavers to weave the yarn that was spun in Vijapur, and soon Vijapur Khadi gained a name for itself.

While these developments were taking place in Vijapur, the spinning wheel gained a rapid footing in the Ashram. Maganlal Gandhi, by bringing to bear all his splendid mechanical talent on the wheel made many improvements in it, and wheels and their accessories began to be manufactured at the Ashram. The first piece of Khadi manufactured in the Ashram cost 17 annas per yard. I did not hesitate to commend this very coarse Khadi at that rate to friends, who willingly paid the price.

I was laid up in bed at Bombay. But I was fit enough to make searches for the wheel there. At last I chanced upon two spinners....I was then ignorant of the economics of Khadi. I considered no price too high for securing handspun yarn. On comparing the rates paid by me with those paid in Vijapur I found that I was being cheated. The spinners refused to agree to any reduction in their rates. So I had to dispense with their services. But they served their purpose....The wheel began merrily to hum in my room, and I may say without exaggeration that its hum had no small share in restoring me to health. I am prepared to admit that its effect was more psychological than physical. But then it only shows how powerfully the physical in man react to the psychological. I too set my hand to the wheel....

In Bombay, again, the same old problem of obtaining a supply of hand-made slivers presented itself. A carder twanging his bow used to pass daily by Sjt. Revashankar's residence. I sent for him and learnt that he carded cotton for stuffing mattresses. He agreed to card cotton for slivers, but demanded a stiff price for it, which, however, I paid....Sjt. Shivji started a spinning class in Bombay. All these experiments involved considerable expenditure. But it was willingly defrayed by patriotic friends, lovers of the motherland, who had faith in Khadi. The money thus spent, in my humble opinion, was not wasted. It brought us a rich store of experience, and revealed to us the possibilities of the spinning wheel.

I now grew impatient for the exclusive adoption of Khadi for my dress. My *dhoti* was still of Indian mill cloth. The coarse

Khadi manufactured in the Ashram and at Vijapur was only 30 inches in width. I gave notice to Gangabehn that, unless she provided me with a Khadi *dhoti* of 45 inches width within a month, I would do with coarse, short Khadi *dhoti*. The ultimatum came upon her as a shock. But she proved equal to the demand made upon her. Well within the month she sent me a pair of Khadi *dhotis* of 45 inches width, and thus relieved me from what would then have been a difficult situation for me.

At about the same time Sjt. Lakshmidas brought Sjt. Ramji, the weaver, with his wife Gangabehn from Lathi to the Ashram and got Khadi *dhotis* woven at the Ashram. The part played by this couple in the spread of Khadi was by no means insignificant. They initiated a host of persons in Gujarat and also outside into the art of weaving handspun yarn. To see Gangabehn at her loom is a stirring sight. When this unlettered but self-possessed sister plies at her loom, she becomes so lost in it that it is difficult to distract her attention, and much more difficult to draw her eyes off her beloved loom.*

Mt. Abu, Wednesday, March 21

Rama Rao and Vijay drive us to the station in the ancient Ford Anglia. This they parked so they might accompany us to the train, which was due to arrive. Travelers with bags and bundles were standing in groups on the platform. The overhead fans turned slowly. Conversation hummed around us. This departure was one of many memorable ones, yet I knew it later as a particularly poignant one. Here in Ahmedabad the realization came to me that the trip was going to end. The experience of India was soon to be memory and would not be repeated. I would not again see the Rama Raos as in Delhi. They were among the people who made my journey possible, and they made India seem like coming home. I shall not ever forget them.

Our leave-taking took place in the space of minutes; however, it was extended because here trains stand long in the station. But finally the string of arriving reddish rail cars rolled to rest as boarding passengers rushed to the doors—again to encounter those getting down. After a hasty adieu, Jean and I turned to the challenge of getting on and finding a place to sit in the already near full train. We were fortunate to find two places and stowed our bags on top or underneath; then we turned to the window to see Rao and Vijay still standing where we had left them, hands raised. The windows being

* Gandhi, *Autobiography*, op. cit., pp. 260-63.

open, we could speak again before the trainmen dashed along the carriages closing doors and waving their arms at people to stand back. Then a whistle blew, the engine yanked the train, and it began to roll. The people waved more. The figures of Rama Rao and Vijay receded from us and quickly were seen no longer.

[Rao and I exchanged several letters thereafter, but life was taken up by other things and we lost regular contact. Some time afterward I learned that he had died and it all receded again.]

We had been told that Mt. Abu was a good place. It is a hill station in southern Rajasthan near Gujarat, and among these retreats it is the only one I know that is also a pilgrimage place. The light-hearted festival of Holi was still going on and therefore we stood ready, whenever moving in a station, to close our window to avoid a spray from outside. Even so we got a little. Jean remarked that the more colorful white garments might be framed and shown as modern art.

Going to Mt. Abu, a holy place, the train carried sadhus on pilgrimage. They dress in rags and are coated with ashes, hair long and scraggly, and carry a staff and, over one shoulder, a small bag. They seldom speak.

We fetched a small station in the Indian desert, Abu Road. No village appeared, but a mountain rose to the west, and at a distance we could see the Aravalli Hills. We got off to meet several pi-dogs roaming the tracks in search of a meal. A waiting bus took passengers bound for the hill station. We hoped that as we ascended the mountain we would find respite from the heat, and we did. Some way along the bus entered a wooded area and stopped to rest. Passengers could buy a cup of tea or glass of water and watch the many gray monkeys with black faces in the trees. They expected food; vendors sold folded newspaper packets of seeds which the simians aggressively demanded and threatened to steal from one another and the people.

It required an hour to reach the top, where we found an irregular, rocky plateau. We were early arrivals, before the season begins next month. We located the Municipal Rest House and moved in, the only guests. Its basicness touched us; it was only a large quadrangle lined by cubicles, each one with a door giving onto the bare courtyard and one window to the outside. Ours had two *charpoys*, nothing more, for which we were each charged two annas bed rent and shared the twelve anna room rent.

The bathroom offered a cold water spigot, squat-down latrine, and a bare concrete floor. Nights were cool and my single blanket inadequate. Near here an open-air dining place became our regular source of sustenance. The cook modified the seasoning to our taste.

We were situated near Nakki Lake, an artificial body of water on whose near side stands Mt. Abu settlement. We walked the path encircling the lake, passing unusual hollowed-out rock formations and plants in bloom. One of the stones is named Toad Rock. We wondered what here could be attributed to the English, who are credited with inventing hill stations. Perhaps they made the lake or the path we took, and they could have named Toad Rock.

We noticed several lodging places, among them one that appeared unoccupied; an elderly man dressed in white stood there. He attracted our attention and we stopped to speak. He was a Parsi who lived in one room of the house. He related how forty years earlier he had built the place and operated it ever since as a guest house. Now it was sold and he was moving to Bombay to end his days.

Then the Parsi ventured to tell us something of Mt. Abu, saying that people no longer came here as formerly. The several maharajahs' mansions are empty or adapted to other uses. The English favored this station but did not westernize things. Why Mt. Abu was losing popularity he did not say. Probably he was feeling nostalgic. Both Jean and I were glad the English had not remodeled Mt. Abu to fit their definition of a hill station. It remains an Indian place with touches of the other sojourners. [It has since come into its own again.]

Then we took supper under the trees, seated at a battered wood table. Rajendra, the proprietor's appealing little boy, gazed at us intently as we ate. He knew a bit of English and we coached him in learning more words. With darkness there was nothing to do but retire as all was dark, including our caravanserai.

Dilwara and Mt. Abu, Thursday, March 22

After an English breakfast with fried fresh tomatoes and *chappatis*, we walked three miles to the Jain temples at Dilwara. The milder temperature and lower humidity enabled us to enjoy the activity more, and the rough and rocky terrain is interesting. Mt. Abu is sacred to Jains and Hindus, and indeed the land appears more suitable for meditation and austerities than for agriculture. We did not see any crops on this plateau supporting undersize trees and sparse plants. We noticed at least two holy men seated cross-legged in stony recesses on the side of the way. As they were neither dressed in white nor completely naked, they could have been Hindu. I think the followers of both religions sometimes visit the other's sacred sites. Fetching Dilwara too soon for tourists to enter the temples, we spent the time until midday looking around and eating at the *dharmasala* (temple guest house). Since the site is secluded from large settlements and is difficult to reach and offers little accommodation, it is an onerous trip for the pilgrims who put up at the *dharmasala*.

The two temples of Vimal Vasaki and Tejpal are reputed to be the best Jain structures in all India. They were the only Jain buildings I saw adequately and measured up to their reputation, though I had seen little to compare them with. Despite their age, the interior decoration in white marble is perfectly preserved, because of the constant attention to their maintenance by stone masons. The first building is dated 1031 and the other later by 200 years. Their size is moderate. Delicate marble forms literally cover the interiors; the exteriors are plainer, which contrasts with Hindu temples. The stone is as white as Carrara marble. I saw no holy of holies, as in a Hindu temple, only a central shrine, open to all, containing an image of the first Jain to attain perfection, Adinath. The courtyard of the Vimal Vasaki Temple is bordered by fifty-two identical recesses, each containing a Buddha-like figure. These can have gemstone inlays, particularly the eyes. The entrance way has an alignment of forty-eight nonidentical marble columns intricately carved.

The Tejpal Temple, dated 1230, is full of detailed work. A marble lotus flower, lavishly carved from a single block, hangs from the center of the central dome. In detail, it might be compared to a faceted glass chandelier. The House of Elephants, as it is called, stands outside the temple and consists of a procession of marble elephants advancing to the temple entrance.

Jains cherish all life. They practice *ahimsa* (nonviolence) even as Hindus do, except Jains go as far as saving insects from accidental death. On ceremonial occasions a Jain may use a broom to sweep the ants away as he proceeds, or he may wear a mask over his mouth to protect small insects from inhalation. Jains are vegetarians and they do not practice agriculture because it entails destruction of plants and insects.

Jains are in two sects, having slightly dissimilar practices. Monks of the Digambara sect, the more ascetic group, may go naked.

Jain places of worship often contain temples in multiples, each small in size because the individual receives merit in building one. They are well maintained and open to all. Temple visitors are requested to leave leather objects outside, as belts and shoes come from animals.

This region—Gujarat and Rajasthan—has many Jains; there are 3.5 million in the country. They are prosperous, generally engaged in business, and wield much influence.

Jean and I climbed a rocky prominence where the view was good, and then climbed higher upon the rocks beyond Dilwara. This prominence also possessed a small Hindu temple and a ruined fort, plus a cave temple.

After returning to Mt. Abu settlement by bus, we walked out to Sunset Point. This we considered to be another English idea, however little changed its natural state. We found a dozen people sitting on the rocks while the sun went down, among them an English couple. They were the only foreigners we met in our stay here.

Mt. Abu, Friday, March 23

I think we felt a type of *moksha* (release from desire) at Mt. Abu. It also afforded us a temporary respite from movement. We remained another day and this morning took books to Nakki Lake to spend time relaxing.

In the afternoon, in company with an Indian family, we engaged a taxi to visit the Durga Temple. It is more than a mile and a half by road and 200 rough-hewn steps downhill to fetch it. The view over the Indian desert is spectacular. Near the temple is a small tank; monkeys are domiciled in the trees overhead. It was surprising to me to observe how adeptly the women of our party descended the steps in long saris without tripping. They did not intend to miss anything of interest.

Marwar Junction, Saturday, March 24

Our leaving Mt. Abu was tinged with sorrow due to the attractions of the place, its temperate atmosphere, and the intimation of a hard journey ahead. We are finding things and leaving them behind all the time. We were ready for the first bus and, after a pause at the monkey place, we fetched the station and were soon leaving Mt. Abu forever.

Our next goal, Udaipur, is fifty miles east as the crow flies. A road on the map cuts a significant distance off the distance by rail; I do not know why we didn't take it. Even after five or six hours traversing the Great Indian Desert we were farther from Udaipur than we were before leaving Mr. Abu. We detrained at a solitary desert station named Marwar Junction, mentioned by Rudyard Kipling in "The Man Who Would Be King." We were castaways here for the best of twenty-four hours while awaiting the branch line train down to Udaipur. It did not arrive until 2:00 a.m. the next morning.

Udaipur, Sunday, March 25

It was nearing midday as our train reached Udaipur, former capital of the old state of Udaipur (Mewar), now part of Rajasthan. We asked a *tongawallah* to take us to the tourist bungalow. He was unusually considerate and we had him back later. Meanwhile, we tried to rest and clean up in a room shared with several others who were noisy. We became involved in a minor spat with them.

We had a Tourist Department description of Udaipur, which tempted us. Also, our host in Bombay, N.V.R Murthy, had produced a promotional film on Udaipur, for which he had written the text.

The United States President's wife had been here for a visit only a few days earlier, and therefore we were inclined to follow in her steps.

Our tonga man transported us to the garden where Mrs. Kennedy had paused to admire the flowers and watch the fountains, he said. This was probably the Saheliyon ki Bari.

Then we rode along the east shore of man-made Lake Fateh Sagar, which offered good views. Stopping at the larger Lake Pichola, we visited the City Palace, but it impressed us only for size. The strings of rooms were empty. There were a few other tourists present. The building faces the water and Lake Palace so we ferried out to this picturesque Venetian apparition. Once landed and inside, it appeared we had come at the busiest stage of the building's transformation into a luxury hotel. There was limited space to walk; nevertheless the distant views were enjoyable despite the chaos. The main attractions—palaces, gardens, and scenic drives—were being fixed up by the government for use by tourists, in a renaissance of sorts. The narrow city streets and general lack of sanitation left us unimpressed.

Udaipur, Sunday, March 26

We looked into a few shops for ideas. Painted papier maché is a local metier—animals, toys, and fruit are offered and they are capable artisans in other materials. I purchased a few easy-to-carry items. Miniature painting is also highly developed here. There is an ancient school of Rajasthani painting. Small pictures on cardboard are inserted in the walls of palaces and residences. Many of them have been removed and can be purchased separately. I did not have enough money to buy a good example, but I took a damaged painting which the seller would not allow me to leave without. It showed a prancing horse with rider.

We visited a school of folk dancing and watched students practicing for a coming performance. The indigenous Rajasthani dances, brilliantly costumed, are excellent art. Then we cycled out to the east where archaeologists have uncovered an ancient city. The lower strata indicate very old occupation. Nearby we saw the picturesque cenotophs of the rulers of Udaipur, also called Mewar. Their title is Maharana.

This concluded our visit.

Chittorgarh, March 27

The bus trek across the desert from Udaipur to Chittorgarh was easy. We checked our baggage at the Chittor train station and had lunch in the quaintly furnished refreshment room. It resembled an English pub with odd hat racks.

The visit to the fort required a tonga pulled by two horses, which we arranged for beforehand. The tableland to be climbed is circled by walls, and we saw the road ascending the near side in a long, steady sweep. But before going far we paused to look around an English cemetery by the wayside. It contained several dozen well kept headstones. I do not recall the inscriptions having anything more explanatory in them than names and dates. The British never fought a battle here as far as I know.

We passed several massive gates, the view expanding as we climbed. At the topmost gate, Ram Pol, we faced an extensive field of ruins. Only two structures are intact, the Victory and Fame towers, which we recognized from pictures. The place is visited by quietness. As we walked about, we saw remains of what our guide called temples and palaces. A tank was too deep for a bath, but I went in nonetheless. Then we mounted the Tower of Victory, a real gem. The decoration—cornices, windows, and short columns—is arranged harmoniously. On top are two superimposed rooms, in the lower of which twenty-four people can stand without crowding. This chamber has a slight projection so that the whole building suggests a torch of victory. The Tower of Fame, not as tall as the Tower of Victory, was built by a Jain merchant, who dedicated it to Adinath.

Chittorgarh was once a capital and is steeped in Rajput history and legend. The events here were tragic for the defenders. On three occasions when the fort was besieged by superior forces, the Rajput warriors would not surrender and chose to put on saffron robes of martyrdom, then march out to face annihilation. The chivalric code also required the women to commit themselves to the flames in the ritual death of *sati*.

There is a legend about a beautiful princess named Padmani who was desired by the chief of the besiegers. Becoming infatuated with her after seeing her reflection in a mirror, he resolved to fight to possess her and did so to the great detriment of Chittor and its people. To lend more credibility to this story, the palace where she lived may be visited, standing apart from other buildings, and partly restored.

I found Chittor to be visited also by a sense of place. I remembered it afterward as a distinctive location.

We connected with the night train to Ajmer and were pleased to find sleeping space for the night-long ride.

Ajmer, Tuesday, March 28

Jean Calmard and I separated today, he returning to his position in West Pakistan. It has been an interesting three-and-a-half weeks of joint experiences in which we saw and did much.

Before his train, we still had time to see several of Ajmer's high points and hired bicycles to do so. First we saw the Dargah, an important Muslim pilgrimage place dedicated to Kwajah Muin ud-din Chishti. I was reminded of the shrine of the Imam at Mashad, Iran. It is an ensemble of buildings and courtyards attracting large numbers of faithful, especially on the saint's birthday and during Ramadan. We entered the first courtyard and removed our shoes; then were met by offers of guide services and requests for baksheesh. Two large caldrons stood on supports; these, we were told, received money for the upkeep of the Dargah. Another person said they contained food offerings for poor pilgrims. The Dargah itself, marble domed and surrounded by a silver platform, is in the center of the second courtyard.

The complex comprises other structures, among them mosques given by Shah Jehan and Akbar, one of them in white marble. The Moghul emperors greatly favored Ajmer, as attested by several buildings they constructed there. Akbar is said to have made the pilgrimage from Agra yearly on foot. It is 200 miles.

In cycling through the city we met a remarkable sight—a gathering of a dozen cats with their master in attendance. It is almost unknown to find pet dogs and cats in India, if my experience is meaningful. There are many mangy pi-dogs roaming around; however, no one would befriend them, and cats are almost unknown.

Ana Sagar Lake is artificial and has existed since the twelfth century, surrounded by a landscaped park, which people use for picnics. Today we saw a numerous, well-dressed company with food baskets and colorful throws, which they place on the ground for the meal.

Shah Jehan contributed the five ornamental marble pavilions which stand on the bund facing the park. The sight of these, and other beneficences, helps one to imagine another, happier country than the India of today.

It appeared too much for us to reach Taragarh Fort perched atop a steep hill; however, we fetched the partly ruined mosque of Adhai-din-ka Jhonpra on the same road. It originated as a Jain college, then was changed to a mosque by the new Muslim rulers. The principal building is placed with its back to the fort hill and is made of the same red-brown stone. I enjoyed the slender-columned prayer hall, which was added with the religion change. We climbed the two minarets, one for each of us.

The first official contact between a Moghul emperor and an English envoy took place here in 1616. The king was James I and the emperor Jehangir. The meeting could have been in the building now known as Akbar's Palace, containing a museum.

After a meal in a modern, air conditioned restaurant, Jean and I said adieu at the station. He was going to Pushkar and crossing into Pakistan. I caught a train for Jaipur, arriving at eight in the evening and finding a place at the Tourist Bungalow.

Jaipur, Wednesday, March 29

Jaipur is celebrated by the Tourist Department as the "Pink City." Mrs. Kennedy paid it a visit and saw some of the same things I did, the Wind Palace for example. This is a striking piece of architecture, though only a facade. It has become the trademark of Jaipur, photographed by one and all.

Jaipur is a planned city having wide, regularly placed main streets, and an encircling wall with seven gates. Some of the wall has disappeared for building materials. Jai Singh II was the enlightened eighteenth-century maharajah responsible, and he referred to an ancient Hindu treatise on town planning. He was an astronomer as well and built several peculiar-looking masonry observatories that measure with some accuracy. The best of these is here in Jaipur. There is also a good one in New Delhi.

This morning the City Palace drew me and I paid my Rs 3 admission—expensive by local standards—and explored the complex of structures lying around several courtyards and gardens. The main element is the Chandra Mahal with seven stories. It holds a museum comprising a textile collection, carpets, picture gallery, and armory. The State Apartments are located here, where perhaps Mrs. Kennedy stayed. I looked at everything and was not followed by the guards.

Jaipur is a good place to find handicrafts of several kinds— block prints, jewelry, ivory and marble articles, brassware, and gems. As I looked around, it was suggested that I visit the village of Sanganer to observe block printing on textiles. I went there and was shown the printing process, which uses wood blocks and natural inks. They had a cooperative society salesroom, but my cash was so low that I could not purchase anything.

Amber Fort, Thursday, March 30

My birthday. To celebrate I made the excursion out to Amber Palace, six and a half miles distant by rattling local bus. There are many hilltop forts surrounding the city; this the best because it was the center of government before Jai Singh transferred it to Jaipur on level ground in 1727. I walked up to the fort from the bus stop. The road connecting Amber and Jaipur is scenic. Old, ruined buildings stand next to it; perhaps former residences. At the top I looked back as a group of European tourists mounted painted and caparisoned elephants to ride up. The ladies and gentlemen were a sight.

Amber Palace is large and empty. It is built in Rajasthani style using cupolas, open galleries, stone screens, pointed arches, and carved stucco decoration. It overlooks a lake that sometimes picks up the reflection of the facade. I ambled slowly through strings of empty rooms without end. My enjoyment was somewhat impaired by a group of noisy people who talked between the echoing chambers.

Back in Jaipur, when I asked persons who should know if a bus goes to Delhi, they replied no; then I learned they were wrong. The Rajasthani State transport system has a bus that makes the trip in the same time as the train. In India it is sometimes an involved process to get information, and misinformation is easy to come by. When questioned on a subject on which he is not informed, an uneducated person may say nothing but the simple words "I don't know." Following this discovery, I met a Sikh who operated a truck line and he took me to his office and served tea. He invited me to ride to Delhi on one of his trucks. It sounded interesting and no more uncomfortable than the bus. I accepted. Departure was set for nine that evening. A contretemps caused it to be near 1:30 a.m.

Meanwhile we talked and talked and the train came and went. Eventually the loaded truck appeared, driven by another Sikh, this one wearing a bizarre turban and assisted by his conductor—a young boy in oily rags. I sat between them in the cab and we departed for Delhi. All of us were sleepy and dozed in turn. The boy sang to keep the driver and me awake. Other trucks were on the road. Travel perhaps was not as perilous as it appeared and we were not going fast, but we could have hit a hole or unlighted bullock cart. Every twenty or thirty miles we stopped at a check point, where our documents were presented and a road tax paid, an octroi they called it. At every stop the driver fell asleep and we let him stay for a while.

At more than one halt—eating places and rest stops—there were flocks of peacocks in the vicinity, not seen, but certainly heard. They make a piercing call. Anyone who has heard a dozen of these birds screeching together will understand. The two Sikh crewmen were good characters, friendly and generous. They insisted on paying for my supper and tea.

Delhi, Friday, March 31

The 250 miles to Delhi required ten hours. I went directly to my favorite place, the International Y where I stayed last November. There I could relax and congratulate myself for having completed the trip so far and returned to this city of good memory.

New Delhi, Saturday, April 1

After writing letters of thanks, I went to the Venkataraman home for dinner. They were eager to hear about the trip in all its aspects. A large part of the afternoon was devoted to the visit.

I put more souvenirs and extra baggage in storage.

Delhi, Monday, April 2

I was able to encash, the word for it here, a check received from the United States at Dr. Venkataraman's bank with his guarantee. After that I could again visit the Handicraft and Handlooms Emporium, the Khadi Bhavan, and other stores to buy things I had previously seen.

Jummu, Thursday, April 6

The usual traveler to the Valley of Kashmir chooses the plane rather than face the land route, but that was not my way. I had neither money nor desire to fly in. First I took the overnight train to Pathankot, a reasonably good trip with a berth. Then it worsened as

I took the bus northwards to Jummu, where the foothills of the foothills of the Himalayas begin. I passed the night at an ordinary inn in Batote, a cold and noisy place.

Srinagar, Friday, April 7

With morning the passengers climbed into the same bus and continued, the road growing worse and more precipitous. For some distance the unpaved way follows a deep valley with a rushing river far below. Then we ascended Banihal Pass with a maximum altitude of nearly 9,000 feet. [In recent years a tunnel has been driven through this pass which considerably reduces the length of mountain road traversed and permits winter use, a convenience perhaps sought by the Indian Army for use in the recurring conflict with Pakistan over Kashmir.] On the other side of the pass, the scenery quickly changes to what people come here for. An extended, verdant vale emerges below. It is under cultivation, well watered, and provided with beautiful lakes, these not appearing until we have covered more distance. The prospect from above reveals straight roads lined on both sides by trees planted by the Moghul emperors who summered here.

We found the Tourist Reception Center in Srinagar, a modern building. The name struck me wrong and the poor assistance rendered confirmed that impression. I was soon out of there and seeking my own accommodations. As it was raining hard, I had to take the first place I came to, a plain Kashmiri inn, cold and comfortless but cheap.

Srinagar, Monday, April 10

After a couple of days of waiting for better weather, it came and I looked for a more suitable place. It was in Nehru Memorial Park that a white-turbaned man spoke to me to ask if I wanted a houseboat. I was interested and said I would look at what he offered. It turned out to be one of the smaller ones, named the *Viscount*, with four rooms, beginning with a comfortably furnished living room, then a dining room, followed by two bedrooms and two small bathrooms connected by a hallway. We agreed on the price including full board and I moved in. The *Viscount* was operated by a man and his son, the younger serving and keeping house and his father cooking my meals in the kitchen boat moored alongside. My boat had a small veranda in front, while the palatial ones offer a grand sunporch.

My boat was moored along with others in a row opposite the Boulevard. Communication with the landside was by *shikara*, the

characteristic punt, which is often trimmed with a roof and
curtains.

Srinagar, Tuesday, April 11

The valley is large and mostly flat. Near the landing on the Boulevard was an agency where I hired a bicycle. To try it out I took the
road to Shalimar Bagh this morning. This is the most noted of the
several Moghul water gardens around the lakes. Shalimar consists
of four connected terraces. It was made by the emperor Jehangir,
for his empress Nur Jehan. The Moghuls loved the sound of falling
water and the flower beds, which fill out the terraces which surround the channels. It is a formal style of landscaping that fits
Moghul architecture.

On my return it was convenient to visit two other gardens,
Nishat Bagh and Chasma Shahi. A caretaker offered me a small bouquet and received a tip. In this way I collected a centerpiece for my
table. Nishat Bagh presents grand views of the mountains, and the
water from Chasma Shahi is considered beneficial in curing several
disorders. I filled my canteen. Above this garden are the ruins of a
Sufi college and astronomy school, Pari Mahal, (1650).

The houseboat meals are good-tasting European-style cooking.
After supper I stretched out under a blanket on the couch to read
and write, chewing walnuts.

Srinagar, Wednesday, April 12

The houseboat agent is also a tailor who promotes business from
his *shikara*, as others do, by calling on the houseboat resident. His
name is Salama and I told him that I would go to his shop if he
showed me some good samples.

One of the *shikara* merchants carries honey, walnuts, almonds,
and oranges—all except the last local produce. Another *shikara* is
loaded with toiletries. It comes by every morning about 7:30. Then
there is the dealer in film and postcards, who also rents cameras.
Later on, the Kashmir-grown fruit arrives: cherries, strawberries,
peaches, pears, and apples.

I stopped at the tailor shop and was measured for a topcoat and
matching hat to be made of Kashmir woolen goods. They will cost Rs
200, a little more than $40.

Srinagar, Friday, April 13

On the street yesterday a young man offered his services as a guide to the handicraft factories. The proposition did not appear too blatantly commercial and I accepted. We met near the houseboat this morning. His name was Masood Alamgir. A student, he spoke excellent English, like all Kashmiris who deal with tourists, and he possessed the social grace also characteristic here. We entered the crowded commercial quarter of Srinagar. There are no motor vehicles here; boats carry freight and people. The main artery is the Jhelum River.

Papier maché boxes, dishes, animals, and picture frames are made in quantity and meticulously painted. We saw one of the rooms where they do the work. The results are fine and the pieces not dear. I brought home several.

Walnut wood is common and the carvers turn out every kind of attractive article from tables to boxes and dishes. Later on I bought a small round table with a carved top for $10, as well as other walnut items. Everything is well finished. The Kashmiri craftsmen never produce shoddy goods.

Metalware is not as important here as it is in other places in India, although some brass is used. The greatest emphasis is probably on embroidery and woven articles such as shawls and carpets of several types. Most typical are the rugs called *numdas*. They have a felted foundation, decorated with embroidery. The result is an inexpensive and attractive small rug.

There is an industry here for the manufacture of knotted carpets, the usual method. I visited a factory. Several weavers worked on a single rug suspended on a roller. The chief weaver has the coded instructions for reproducing the design in front of him, and these he calls or chants to his fellow weavers if the design is a simple all-over one. If the design is complicated, then each weaver uses his own coded instructions.

The work is hard on eyes and body. The weavers are often children or young people. After a few years they cease the work because to continue would endanger their health as well as their eyesight. I was told that the government regulates the rug-weaving trade to prevent exploitation of the workers.

Later today Masood and I visited a *numdah* factory. The felted foundations were being formed by hand and foot. A stringed bow serves to break down the rough fiber, low grade cotton and wool, to be dropped on the floor in a space equivalent to the finished size.

Then the workers tread out the fiber with their feet until it is fully compacted and ready to be embroidered.

We also visited the Jama Masjid, the mosque of wood. Three hundred deodar pillars support the roof. Each one is a single tree. The houseboats utilize the same wood in their construction. [Deodar is a Himalayan cedar in the pine family. It is a fragrant wood, durable and light red in color, says Webster's Dictionary.]

The environs of the mosque contain ruins and graves, which share ground with the city. The fort, Hari Parbat, is near here, a landmark visible from every side. At the foot of the hill are the remains of a very ancient, large Hindu temple.

Srinagar, Friday, April 14

The weather is now warm and springlike. Today I took the *shikara* out onto Lake Dal, seeing the floating gardens—vegetables grown on floating foundations of plant matter—and the lake dwellings moored in pretty, weed-grown waters outside the city. Practice has not yet taught me to propel the *shikara* as effectively as the Kashmiris do. I cannot keep it running straight. The scene is relaxing. There is nothing to disturb the peaceful, slow movement over the waters. People gather lake grass to use as fertilizer. They harvest the long, white lotus root to slice and cook. I have had it for supper and it tastes all right.

Srinagar, Saturday, April 15

The Shah Hamdan Mosque is another wood building and, like the Jama Masjid, has burned more than once. I was able to see the carpeted interior and glass chandelier. [In later years this mosque became off-limits to non-Muslims.]

Last evening two boys called to talk about our climbing Shankaracharya hill together. The weather changed and we gave up the plan.

Srinagar, Sunday, April 16

The older of the boys, Muzdoor, joined me and Masood on another visit to the rug factories. I was careful to say that we were only looking and not seeking to purchase anything. We heard a detailed account of the method of manufacture and looked at a few finished pieces.

I went to the State Bank of India to get their help in finding and collecting a remittance of $200, which should have arrived last November. They said they would write several express letters to locate the money, and they loaned me Rs 300 because I am out of money.

Gulmarg, Monday, April 17

Gulmarg, "Meadow of Flowers," is fetched by regular bus to Tangmarg, whence the visitor may choose to walk up the steep trail to Gulmarg or take a Punjabi pony and *muzdoor* (guide). A group of saddled ponies were waiting. They are not true ponies but small and strong horses. I pretended to lift mine and drew a laugh. There was no rush of offers and the *muzdoors* had everything planned, the sequence of the mounts, and the cost. It saved a lot of time and argument. I was soon mounted. My *muzdoor* carried the equipment—two blankets, food, and binoculars. We had fair weather and a muddy, steep trail to climb, passing through a deodar forest. It was not cold. As we gained altitude, snow appeared and warm sunshine. The *muzdoor* would not take his pony across snowbanks because, he said, he could break a leg. I dismounted and walked where I could. My unsuitable footwear did not allow me to get far and I settled on a bench in front of a closed lodge. All of the hotels and guest accommodations were closed now. It was between seasons.

Gulmarg, according to the guidebook, has many attractive walks and views; however, I could not see much but a distant range of snow peaks in part concealed by the deodars. The altitude here is about 8,000 feet. I reclined in my blankets on the bench, enjoying the solitude and the snowscape around me, until time to return. The English developed Gulmarg. It remains unspoiled, apparently.

On the return bus we stopped when someone called out after sighting Nanga Parbat. It is the ninth highest mountain in the Himalayas at 26,600 feet. The summit, all white, illuminated by the sun, hangs in the sky ninety miles to the northwest, a beautiful, exciting sight. It was climbed first by a German team in the early 1950s.

Pahalgam, Wednesday, April 19

The bus tour requires a full day to see Pahalgam and several intermediate points of interest. Near Avantipur, in a valley surrounded by snow-capped mountains. I saw the excavation of an ancient Hindu temple. Then came Islambad, where there is a natural spring surrounded by several small temples, followed by Achabal Bagh. This Moghul garden was planned by Shah Jehan's daughter and the empress Nur Jehan enjoyed it. Kokarnag is another garden, this one known for roses. I began to be sated, but it was not over yet. Martand remained, site of a well-known temple excavation from the eighth century. I saw the spring here, not the ruins.

It was raining on our arrival at Pahalgam. I walked up to the meadow with a Kuwaiti passenger from the bus. That which we were able to see of Pahalgam was disappointing, yet we may have overlooked the best places. The village was under tourist development.

Srinagar, Saturday, April 22

Today was an occasion to enjoy more of Kashmir's particular charm by taking an all-day *shikara* trip, starting at the *Viscount*, passing the Jhelum's plant-grown backwaters to Nagin Lake. I was piloted on this excursion by the bearer—I wish I knew his name.

We looked at the new Hazratbal, Mosque of the Prophet's Hair. It is an impressive building. Nasim Bagh, a ruined garden, attracted some curiosity, then Char Chinar island. The name means "four chinars" (specie of tree). It was either at this or another tiny island that we moored for lunch, this in a box brought from the *Viscount*. Another, large boat was also moored there. It was owned by the local merchant of souvenirs, Subhana the Worst. I had spoken with him already at his store in Srinagar. He invited us to hear the musicians in still another boat also tied up there. He was evidently paying them. The island was so small that nothing else could have found space. After hearing the concert we were on our way again across Dal Lake to visit the same gardens that I had visited several days earlier. Then it was back to the houseboat after an interesting trip.

The Kuwaiti from the bus to Pahalgam had taken the large houseboat down the line from mine. He invited me and an American woman who showed up, to have tea on his boat.

The final few days in Kashmir were easy going and I had time to enjoy them before preparing to leave the country. I disposed of my radio and binoculars for a good price. That gave me money to spend on local wares. It was difficult to resist these and I collected too many. I purchased three *gubbas*, or rugs made by covering a jute foundation with stitches (chain or cross). They makes an attractive wall hanging, resembling needlepoint. I acquired two covered baskets to carry my purchases. A fur hat and gloves, a floor lamp in sections that screw together, and other smaller articles went to increase the amount of my baggage.

The Road to Jummu, Saturday, April 29

Yesterday Masood helped me transfer my baggage to the Tourist Reception Center. It was a crisp, clear morning in the valley as the bus sped along the tree-lined road to Banihal, gateway to Kashmir. There were a few military vehicles visible. They appeared out of place in this peaceful spot.

This trip was nearly a repetition of the one that brought me to Kashmir. Again I spent the night in a rest house where, to save cash, I shared a room with others.

Jummu and Pathankot, Sunday, April 30

Rain. For unknown reasons, the bus did not leave Jummu until afternoon. When the rain ceased, I wandered about and looked at the bazaar, purchasing two handmade brass kitchen utensils to take home, and sharing a papaya with a cow. She liked the peel.

Then our bus returned with the baggage reloaded. I hoped the handling would not damage my souvenirs; nevertheless, a papier maché lamp base became broken. It was a mistake to purchase such a fragile thing, but it was pretty.

Later we fetched Pathankot and I was able to get a third-class berth.

Delhi and Chandigarh, Monday, May 1

After arriving in Delhi and cleaning up in the first class waiting room, I was ready to take everything unneeded to the Venkataraman residence. As often happens, a bitter argument over compensation ensued. I required two coolies to carry all out to the street and a motorcycle rickshaw. The price always triples when they see a foreigner.

My credit was good because I had made a payment on the amount I owed to Dr. Venkataraman. Therefore, he loaned me another Rs 150 because I was down to a few again.

Then I relaxed at the Y until it was time to take the bus to Chandigarh. After getting underway, I learned that this bus required a reservation, and I, being without one, caused a new contretemps. When boarding the conductor motioned me to take a seat, never mentioning a reservation, but when he checked the tickets and learned that I was without a reserved seat, even though no one was standing, it caused a big fuss. The driver said a reservation was essential and reversed the bus to go back. This so upset the passengers that they began to shriek. Some of them were probably members of parliament in Chandigarh. The hubbub made an impression and our driver again changed direction and we were on our way.

The trip needed six hours, meaning an arrival in late evening. I was directed to a good, modern hotel and a pleasant single room. A good supper followed.

Chandigarh is a new city designed by the contemporary French architect Le Corbusier, who also worked in Ahmedabad.

Chandigarh and Simla, Tuesday, May 2

At the Time of Partition in 1947 the old Punjab capital, Lahore, went to Pakistan, leaving Indian Punjab without a capital of its own. Therefore Chandigarh was created from the ground up. Street plan, government buildings, residential and market quarters, and parks are all new. The density of building is low; there are large empty areas, and moving around requires time and effort.

To avoid the heat I left the hotel early and went to the government quarter to see the Assembly and Secretariat buildings, both Le Corbusier designs. From in front of the Governor's Residence, I asked directions of a passerby. He was an assemblyman and we shared a cycle rickshaw to fetch the legislative buildings, where he gave me a brief tour of the Assembly. Then we stopped in the lunch room for refreshment. A colleague happened by and I listened to their conversation until it was time to return and pick up my bag. This ended my visit; the Secretariat was closed.

Still seeking to avoid the increasing heat, I decided to go to Simla. The road to this hill station begins to rise at Kalka, the same town where the narrow-gauge train begins its winding, tunneled climb. The road and the tracks often encounter each other. After three hours, the top finally came. Darkness had fallen, making it harder to find a lodging. A crowd of eager coolies pressed around the passengers, giving special attention to the two Europeans—I and a woman. One said he would guide me to an inn and I accepted. We climbed on foot in near darkness until he announced that we had reached the place. After I saw the room, a single which looked good, the man asked for Rs 5—for ten minutes' work. He would also receive something from the innkeeper. I objected and tried various stratagems to make him come down—doubt, humor, annoyance, and trying to give him less, which he would not take. Finally, after I had unpacked and was ready to wash, he was still standing there. I turned him about and, facing him to the door, delivered a swift blow with my knee out the door. This astonished him and he departed a small distance. His answer was to stand outside, peering in at the window, until the manager came to intervene and it was agreed to pay him, probably about Rs 1, for the service. I could have carried my bag myself.

Late though it was, I was given supper in my room.

Simla and Kufri, Wednesday, May 3

As Simla was the summer capital of British India and notable for the social life it offered, it became the most famous of the hill stations. Everyone who was able to moved up to Simla and other refuges from the heat of summer in the plains.

Kipling placed some stories here—"The Phantom Rickshaw" for one. The following extract contains names of several Simla landmarks.

> Nothing would please her save a canter round Jakko. With my nerves still unstrung from the previous night I feebly protested against the notion, suggesting Observatory Hill, Jutogh, the Boileaugunge road—anything rather than the Jakko round. Kitty was angry and a little hurt: so I yielded from fear of provoking further misunderstanding, and we set out together towards Chota Simla. We walked a greater part of the way, and, according to our custom, cantered from a mile or so below the Convent to the stretch of level road by the Sanjowlie Reservoir. The wretched horses appeared to fly, and my heart beat quicker and quicker as we neared the crest of the ascent. My mind had been full of Mrs. Wessington all the afternoon; and every inch of the Jakko road bore witness to our old-time walks and talks....*

I emerged this morning and quickly found the Mall. This broad promenade wends along the contour of the ridge where Simla stands, connecting a maze of narrow lanes. The Mall is flanked by substantial buildings, residences, and shops. There are social clubs and churches. There is an English flavor; indeed, until World War I, Indians were not permitted to live here.

It was cloudy. Nothing appeared to be happening around me as I walked the length of the Mall. Few people. The hills—the Jakko most conspicuous—are forested. Trails are available for walkers.

As I wanted a place to stay for several days, the Tourist Office offered a choice of several rest houses. I chose the Winter Sports Club in Kufri. A phone call by the manager resulted in a reservation. It was ten miles from Simla on the Narkanda Road, which goes on to Tibet. It was raining as I arrived, but the building was solid and comfortable; the room was warm and equipped with a real bed and fireplace.

I wanted to do nothing for several days and not have to look for a place to stay or eat. The cook brought my meals to the room—a choice of Indian or European cooking. Both were good, and I enjoyed stew, vegetables, potatoes, and dessert.

*A.L. Burt, ed. *The Phantom Rickshaw and Other Tales.* New York, n.d.

Kufri, Thursday to Saturday, May 4-6

The earliest passage I could get from Bombay is on the 23rd, and therefore I have more than two weeks to wait. Three days here in Kufri allowed reading, writing, and walking in the immediate surroundings, the terrain being too uneven for more adventurous trips. I could see a grove of conifers above the road and found the way to reach it. An attractive guest house occupied only by a caretaker was hidden in the trees. It was a prettier location than mine. Rain threatened regularly and the sun never came out full all the time I stayed here.

Buses passed on the main road at frequent intervals. Today I boarded one to discover its destination; however, after a few miles it stopped without apparent reason. I hitched a ride on a truck, which also stopped; however, I now saw the reason: a small rockslide was blocking the road.

It was here that I observed a herd of goats, each carrying a burden strapped to its back—perhaps twenty pounds of salt or grain. They were not impeded by their packs and it looked like an efficient conveyance. [In later reading I came across the following in Kipling's short story entitled "The Miracle of Purum Bhagat": "And he met the Thibetan herdsmen with their dogs and flocks of sheep, each with a little bag of borax on their back."] Tibetans, easy to pick out, were working on the road, including women who deposited their young children on the side under trees for shelter, within their mother's sight.

By bus to Dehra Dun, Sunday, May 7

Leaving Kufri and returning to Simla involved delay. Buses were passing the Sports Club, but everything was full and I wondered if all the movement had something to do with the landslide I had seen yesterday. Finally an empty bus picked me up. All day and all night I traveled, sitting up all the time, arriving at Dehra Dun the next morning at eight.

Mussoorie, Monday, May 8

Still searching for cooler weather conditions, I chose Mussoorie, a hill station twenty-two miles from Dehra, because it is easy of access and overlooks the plains. I found it attractive from the start. The bus stand is on Mall Road. It is like the Simla Mall but more open to breezes. At each end are bazaars—Library and Kulri. They might be compared to a shopping mall in the west.

Mussoorie also was established by the British and preserves much of that period, including buildings and schools. It is a harmonious town, light in spirit and friendly, in contrast to Simla, where I sensed a certain stuffiness. Here also motor vehicles cannot pass beyond the Mall, making the place quiet and clean. The lanes are narrow and sloping. Rickshaws are pulled and pushed by two or more men.

I began to seek a lodging place and soon found a small apartment where I was assigned a cot bed by the manager, Mr. Gupta. I told him how I was getting along on little money and could not pay well, so he gave me the bed for a reasonable amount. The room had three beds, all of which were occupied at night. Mr. Gupta also had a sporting goods shop on the Mall and one of his friends ran a sewing machine store.

There are Anglo-Indians living in Mussoorie, one of whom stopped on the street to speak to me. He was an elderly man. We walked down the lane to his house but did not enter. He spoke of his ancestors, pointing to a large house, which, he said, once belonged to his relatives, who were important here. We took tea together.

I continued to think well of Mussoorie, which seemed an eminently livable place. During my stay, clouds moved in, usually, after the middle of the day, with rainstorms and strong winds. The elements impressed me and broke my umbrella, the same one that had been given to me in Ceylon. A Mr. Fixit made repairs for thirty cents. Umbrella stores are an institution here. The tourist can find quality merchandise in Mussoorie shops. My own buying was over, and I was caught in a rupee squeeze. My diet was beginning to be affected. [In a place where disease is prevalent, I needed good nutrition, and, in fact, soon after returning to the United States I came down with pleurisy. No T.B. was diagnosed, but I was hospitalized for weeks. For years thereafter I received annual chest x-rays. I was fortunate.]

Mussoorie, Tuesday, May 9

The high ground here contains buildings once used as a military hospital under the Raj. Now they are used for secret purposes by the Indian government and I was not permitted inside the gate.

Two men wearing pajamas and riding a Vespa motorscooter stopped to say hello. We walked together, meeting a single American man on the way. He told us he was a missionary and visiting his daughter enrolled in one of the local schools.

Then I encountered a man on the road who desired to tell me something of the pilgrimage places in the Himalayas. He offered the thought that I might direct my steps to Badrinath, to the shrines to Vishnu and Shiva, and he drew me a map of the route to follow. It is a long distance from Mussoorie, and a large part of it by foot. The scenery is said to be excellent and rest houses are found along the route. I lacked nearly everything that such a trek would require, but it sounded good. The first article to acquire might be one of the carved walking sticks sold here in Mussoorie.

Rishikesh and Hardwar, Wednesday, May 10

Today is the final day of sightseeing in India. Mr. Gupta, now almost a friend, saw me off on the bus and gave me the present of a notebook. It was nice to stay at his place, a real house, resembling a Bed and Breakfast in the West.

Back in Dehra Dun, I talked to a supervisor of buses, who told me that in twenty years India would overtake the United States economically. I offered no comment. [Thirty years later it appears that he was more correct than a visitor would have predicted then. India has, after all, an extensive, consuming middle class now.]

Rishikesh is a few miles from Dehra. I wanted to see the holy place where the Ganga flows out of the Himalayan foothills into the plains. I walked to the water's edge and saw that it flows rapidly here and is deep and narrow as well. No one was in the flood. A few groups of holy men were nearby. I think I expected more of this locale. [Later in the 1960s the Beatles came to Rishikesh to see their guru, Maharishi Mahesh Yogi. Their trip ushered in more development in the shape of ashrams and *dharmasalas*.]

Another few miles downriver I came to Hardwar, a clean city on a clean river full of hungry trout, which people fed. This city may be compared with Banaras in some ways. Both are major places of pilgrimage on the Ganga, with ghats. Banaras is much concerned with death rites, Hardwar with joy and life. This attitude is suggested by the ceremony of Arti, which I attended, standing on the bridge. Just at sunset the people launch many small, grass-woven and flower-filled boats into the rapidly flowing stream. Each has a short candle burning in it and looks pretty bobbing along. It lasts briefly. Hardwar is a religious Coney Island. I don't intend to be critical. There are large numbers of people—some of them there to have a good time. There are shops selling everything imaginable in the religious and secular categories. There are also holy men, and around Hardwar are large empty spaces where they may camp. Every twelve years the festival of Kumbh Mela takes place at Hardwar. It draws millions and makes it the greatest of religious gatherings, probably, in the world. It is a rotating festival, occurring in one of four locations every three years.

The Delhi train rolled to a stop. It was already full in spite of starting at Dehra. No chance of lying down tonight; everything was overflowing and passengers were stuffed in the top luggage racks or sprawled on the floor, but I had my metal case to sit on. A man spoke up, demanding that some of the prostrate men get up and yield the space to women who had no seats. He was an astrologer and talked a great deal. He offered me snuff and when I sneezed everyone around laughed. They seemed in good spirits.

The chaos encourages ticketless travelers, as they are called. Conductors cannot make rounds to check passengers in such a cattle car. The ticketless will climb through the windows on the track side to get around ticket takers on the platform side. If one is caught, he must pay double fare. Crawling through the window is an accepted way of entrance and egress when the train is swarming.

Delhi, Thursday, May 11

I have eight days in Delhi before I have to get going again. The heat is now an obstacle to activity. There is no air conditioning in the Y, only ceiling fans. I spend as much of the day as possible in the British Council Library—the Anglo-Indian cultural organization. I arrive at opening time and stay until closing at seven. During the two hour closing at midday I return to the Y for dinner and rest. At night I carry my *charpoy* out to the courtyard under the stars and require no other blanket or shirt, it being hot everywhere.

The Y offered occasional cultural events. One of these was a magic show presented by a family of performers. India is famous for street entertainment, going well beyond snake charmers.

On the Bombay train, Friday, May 19

Today I collected everything at the Venkataraman place and repacked it at the Y, making seven pieces. I managed to move it all to the station, where the Bombay train departed at 3:20 this afternoon. I had the benefit of a third-class sleeper reservation purchased well in advance. The temperature stood at about 105 degrees F and the seasonal *loo*, a hot, dry wind, was blowing in from the west. In stations, travelers can buy earthenware bottles of water. Their porosity cools the contents slightly. The journey continued for twenty-nine hours. There are air conditioned cars on some trains, accompanied by a quadrupling of the fare.

Bombay, Saturday, May 20

We fetched Bombay Terminus at 8:30 p.m. It being too late to look for a place to stay, I requested a retiring room. They were all taken and I asked permission to use the first-class waiting room, which was granted after some haggling with the attendant. After showering I slept well all night on a couch.

Bombay, Sunday, May 21

With a few scarce annas I was able to secure help in taking everything out of the station to the taxi. J.C.'s office was not yet open, so I borrowed from his bearer to pay the taxi. Then I proceeded to repack everything for the third time. It was important to consolidate it into the fewest possible packages. I wound up with two trunks, two baskets, the metal case, the round table from Kashmir, and one other package. J.C. had given me the trunk which I had bought for his use in Cleveland several years ago. It went back with me.

I collected my ticket for tourist-class passage to Naples on the *Sydney*. I found a place at the Y for my remaining two nights. Another small loan from J.C. tided me over until my final departure.

I made another call on Shiv Agarwal at the cycle store. He served cokes rather than tea this time. He mentioned his plans to return to Cleveland in September to take up his old job at East End Neighborhood House. He gave no particulars of this or reasons for going.

I attended a movie one of these evenings. It featured Alfred Hitchcock's *Psycho*, evidently popular among movie goers here.

Bombay, Monday, May 22

I carried the better part of my baggage to the pier. It weighed in at nearly 200 pounds. If it had gone over I would have been charged.

Sailing from Bombay, Tuesday, May 23

Up early this morning. After collecting the last baggage at J.C.'s and asking his bearer to pay the taxi, I reported to the ship and stowed my things in the stateroom. Near the dock I had left some laundry to be done, but I lacked the money to pay for it. The proprietor forgave the debt and I had my shirts for a going away present. I often thanked the existence of a common language.

J.C. came to the pier to say farewell. He carried some flowers to wish me bon voyage and we had a good hour together. Many were the visitors on board. I overheard an Indian mother give her son complete instructions for the voyage. Then they asked visitors to leave and soon the ship cast off its moorings and began to move away from the pier. The people on shore grew small and vanished. I was soon lured inside the ship to escape the heat of midday. Before long we were on the main and encountering a swell that left some seasick.

The passenger list was diverse. The ship had come from Down Under and was carrying Australian immigrants returning to Europe to visit. There were also Indian students and professionals aboard. I was the only non-Indian in my cabin of six berths.

At sea, Monday, May 29

The six days out of Bombay could be considered one long day given to crossing the Arabian Sea to the Gulf of Aden. Shipboard life centered on deck. There was a small swimming pool. I remained largely to myself, reading, but met several fellow passengers. There was a well-educated Spaniard returning from Australia to his country. After a year he had decided not to settle there. There was a Polish couple returning to their native land to visit. They owned a rooming house in Australia. We played chess. The fare was very plain, most of it canned, but I could not complain having survived Indian meals for so long. Being an Italian ship, the *Sydney* also served ordinary table wine. In trying it I feared I had lost my taste for wine, but the enjoyment returned once I was back in Italy and better was at hand.

There were three doctors at my table—Dutch, British and Maylayan. They had been working in the east. Then we had an Italian who lived in Bombay, working as a ladies' hairdresser. He cut my hair for nothing.

Aussie beer was cheap, but I had no money to purchase it. Never mind. Tea and sweet bread were served every afternoon. The Italian crew did not do the service in correct English style. They served it on an assembly line and if you missed your tea call you were out of it. The *Sydney* was not the *Queen Mary*.

We sailed through the Gulf of Aden and into the Red Sea. Three more days were required to fetch Port Suez.

Suez Canal and Port Said, Thursday, June 1

It was a Middle Eastern bazaar on deck this morning. Every available inch of space was occupied by colorfully robed merchants selling souvenirs—the things anyone might buy and take home to display in the living room. They offered embroidered garments, leather goods, cushions, metalware, sandals, luggage, jewelry and toys, and more. There were heads of Nefertiti and pyramids and sphinxes in alabaster.

We waited several hours before proceeding into the canal in a long line of ships, each keeping about one third of a mile between it and the one ahead, moving slowing, an exciting sight for the passengers. Children waved from the edge of the sand bank on the sides of the narrow passage, or ditch, through the desert. The procession continued all day long, at midday passing the anchored file of southbound ships. The canal is surrounded by uninhabited desert. It appeared that it had been widened in some places. A railroad track parallels the channel. Walls prevent erosion of the canal's edges by the wake of passing ships.

It was becoming dark when we came to Port Said and anchored. Then a floating gangway was brought out to enable passengers to debark and visit the town this evening. I joined them for a brief observation and land walk.

A group of passengers rejoined the ship after a rapid trip from Suez into Cairo and out to Giza. We sailed for Naples this evening.

Six months have run out since arriving in India and the time to return home is here. Even though it be too soon to attempt a reckoning, if that can ever be, every day of the extended visit has brought new wonders. The trip has not been easy, but it is what I chose, with all the sacrifice. I doubt that I shall ever be the same afterward because the experience is such a profound one.

Glossary

A

Ahimsa—nonviolence, harmlessness
Anna—one-sixteenth of the pre-metric rupee
Ashram—spiritual college cum retreat
Ayurvedic—Indian natural and herbal medicine

B

Bagh—garden
Baksheesh—tip, bribe, or donation
Banyan—Indian fig tree
Baoli—well, particularly a step well with landings and galleries
Bazaar—market area
Bearer—butler, servant
Betel—nut of the betel tree, chewed as a mild intoxicant
Bhagavad Gita—Krishna's lessons to Arjuna, part of the Mahabharata
Bidi—small, hand-rolled tobacco leaf
Bodhisattva—a potential Buddha, a saint
Bo tree—*ficus religiosa*, the tree under which the Buddha attained enlightenment
Brahmin—a member of the priestly caste, the highest Indian caste
Bund—embankment or dyke
Bustee—slum areas of Calcutta
Byzantine—pertaining to the Eastern Roman Empire and its culture

C

Cantonment—administrative and military area of a town during the era of the Raj town
Caste—a hereditary social class, station in life
Chaitya—Buddhist temple, meditation hall
Chappati—unleavened Indian bread
Charpoy—Indian rope bed
Curd—yoghurt

D

Dacoit—robber, particularly an armed robber
Dagoba—see **pagoda**
Dargah—shrine or place of burial of a Muslim saint
Darshan—offering or audience with someone, usually a guru
Darwaza—gateway or door

Devadasi—temple dancer

Dhal—lentil soup, what most of India lives on

Dharma—Hindu-Buddhist moral code

Dharmasala—religious guest house

Dhobi—person who washes clothes (female—**Dhobin**)

Dhoti—a man's garment, like a **lunghi**, but the cloth is pulled up between the legs

Digambara—"sky-clad," followers of a Jain sect who extend their disdain for worldly goods to include not wearing clothes

Diwan—principal officer in a princely state, royal court, or council

Diwan-i-Am—Hall of Public Audience

Diwan-i-Khas—Hall of Private Audience

Dravidian—a member of one of the aboriginal races of India, pushed south by the Indo-Europeans and now mixed with them. The Dravidian languages include Tamil, Malayalam, Telugu, and Kannada

Durbar—royal court

Durga—same as Kali, a terrible manifestation of **Parvati**.

F

Fakir—accurately, a Muslim who has taken a vow of poverty, but also applied to Hindu ascetics such as **sadhus**.

G

Ganesh—god of wisdom and prosperity, elephant-headed son of **Shiva** and **Parvati**, probably the most popular god in the whole Hindu pantheon

Ganga—Ganges River

Ghat—steps or landing on a river

Godown—warehouse

Guru—spiritual teacher

H

Hanuman—monkey god

Harijan—literally "Children of God," the name Mahatma Gandhi gave to the untouchables

Hinayana—small-vehicle Buddhism as practiced in Ceylon, Burma, Thailand, and Cambodia

Hittite—ancient people of Asia Minor and Syria, 1700-700 B.C.

Hookah—water pipe for smoking tobacco

I

Imam—Muslim religious leader

J

Jainism—a religion founded by Mahavira in the sixth century B.C. preaching solicitude for all life

Jatakas—tales from the Buddha's various lives

Juggernauts—huge, extravagantly decorated temple "cars" dragged through the streets during Hindu festivals

K

Kali—**Parvati's** terrible form

Karma—fate

Khadi—homespun cloth

Krishna—**Vishnu's** eighth incarnation, often colored blue

L

Lingam—phallic symbol, symbol of **Shiva**

Lunghi—man's garment like a sarong

M

Mahabharata—one of the two major Hindu epics

Mahal—house or palace

Maharaja—Hindu king.

Mahatma—literally "great soul"

Mahayana—large-vehicle Buddhism as practiced in China, Korea, and Japan

Mahout—elephant rider or master

Maidan—open place or square

Mandapam—pillared pavilion in front of a temple

Mandir—temple

Mantra—prayer formula or chant

Maratha—war-like central Indian people

Masjid—mosque; Jami Masjid is the Friday Mosque, or main mosque

Math—a Hindu monastery

Mela—a fair or religious festival

Memsahib—European married lady, from "madam-sahib"

Mihrab—niche in the wall to which Muslims look when praying in order to face Mecca

Moghul (Mughal)—the Muslim dynasty of Indian emperors, from Babur to Aurangzeb

Moksha—release from all material desires

Monsoon—rainy season, from around June to October, when it rains virtually every day

Mughal—see **Moghul**

Muezzin—one who calls Muslims to prayer from the minaret

N

Nandi—bull, steed of **Shiva**, representations usually found at Shiva temples

Nirvana—the ultimate aim of Buddhist existence, a state where one leaves the cycle of existence and does not have to suffer further rebirths

Numda—Rajasthani rug

O

Ottoman—a Turkish dynasty whose dominion centered in Anatolia and into southeastern Europe and around the eastern Mediterranean, Egypt, North Africa; it peaked in the sixteenth century

Ouzo—a colorless Greek cordial flavored with anise seed

P

Pagoda—Buddhist religious monument composed of a solid hemisphere containing relics of the Buddha—also known as a dagoba or stupa

Palanquin—boxlike vehicle carried on poles on four men's shoulders; the occupant sits inside on a seat

Pan—betel nut plus additives for chewing

Pandit—teacher or wise man

Parsi—a member of the Zoroastrian religion in India

Parvati—consort of **Shiva**

Peepul—fig tree, especially a **bo tree**

Puja—prayer performed before a god's image

Pukkah—proper, very much a Raj-era term

Punkah—cloth fan, swung by pulling a cord

Purdah—seclusion in which Muslim women are kept

R

Raga—any of several conventional patterns of melody and rhythm that form the basis for freely interpreted compositions

Raj—rule of sovereignty, but specifically applied to the period of British rule in India

Raja—king

Rama—incarnation of **Vishnu** and hero of the *Ramayana*.

Ramadan—Muslim holiday; a period of daily fasting from sunrise to sunset

Ramayana—the story of **Rama** and Sita, his wife, and their conflict with Ravana, one of India's most best-known legends, retold in various forms throughout almost all Southeast Asia

Rath—temple chariot, or car, used in religious festivals

Raths—rock-cut Dravidian temples at Mahabalipuram

Retsina—a Greek wine flavored with resin

Rickshaw—two-wheeled vehicle in which one or two passengers are pulled; only in Calcutta and one or two hill stations do the old man-powered rickshaws still exist; in towns they are now generally bicycle-rickshaws

S

Sadhu—a celibate Hindu holy man

Sahib—"lord," title applied to any gentleman and most Europeans

Samadhi—the place where a holy man was cremated, usually venerated as a shrine

Sati—"honorable woman," what a woman becomes if she throws herself on her husband's funeral pyre, a practice banned a century ago

Seljuk—a Turkish dynasty; its culture or people

Satyagraha—nonviolent protest involving a fast, popularized by Gandhi; from Sanskrit, literally "insistence on truth"

Serai—place for accommodation of travelers, specifically a caravanserai where camel caravans once stopped

Shikar—hunting expedition

Shikara—gondola-like boat used on Dal Lake in Kashmir

Shiva (Siva)—God of the Hindu Trinity—the destructive and creative aspect

Stupa—Buddhist sacred mound

Sufi—ascetic Muslim mystic

Swami—title given to initiated monks, meaning "lord of the self"

Sweeper—lowest-caste servant, who performs the most menial of tasks

T

Tank—artificial water-storage lake

Thali—traditional south Indian vegetarian meal—the name derives from the "thali" plate the food is served on

Thug—follower of thuggee, religious-inspired ritual murderers in the nineteenth century

Tonga—two-wheeled horse or pony carriage

Trimurti—three-faced **Shiva** image

U

Untouchable—lowest caste for whom the most menial tasks are reserved; the name derives from the belief that higher castes risk defilement if they touch one.

Upanishads—ancient Vedic Scripture, the last part of the **Vedas**

V

Vedas—the four most ancient Hindu Scriptures

Vihara—a Buddhist monastery

Vimana—principal part of a Hindu temple

Vishnu—the Preserver of mankind in the Hindu Trinity

Wallah—person involved with a specific thing; the term can be added onto almost anything—thus dhobi-wallah (clothes washer), taxi-wallah (taxi driver)

Y

Yatra—pilgrimage

Z

Zamindar—landowner

Glossary adapted from *The Lonely Planet Guide to India*, 1992 edition.

Further Reading

Agrawala, V.S. *Sarnath*, 2nd edition. Departmant of Archeology, New Delhi, 1957.

Akbar, M.J. *Nehru: The Making of India*. New York: Viking Press, 1988.

Sri Aurobindo. *On Yoga I: The Synthesis of Yoga*. Sri Aurobindo Ashram Press, Pondicherry, India, 1957.

Basham, A.L. *The Wonder That Was India*. New York: Oxford University Press, 1984.

Benares (leaflet). Indian State Railways. Printed by the Times of India, Bombay, n.d.

Blunt, Wilfred. *Splendors of Islam*. New York: Viking Press, 1976.

Byron, Robert. *The Road to Oxiana*. London: Oxford University Press, 1982.

Collins, Larry and Dominique Lapierre. *Freedom at Midnight*. New York: Simon & Schuster, 1975.

Ellis, Royston. *India By Rail*. Edison, New Jersey: Hunter Publishing, 1993.

Ellora-Ajanta (booklet). Department of Tourism, Government of India. New Delhi, n.d.

Fischer, Louis. *Gandhi*. Newmarket: 1982.

Forster, E.M. *A Passage to India*. New York: Harcourt Brace Jovanovich, 1924.

Gandhi, M.K. *Experiments in Truth* (autobiography). Ahmedabad: Navajivan Publishing House, 1927.

A Handbook for the Ceylon Traveler. Colombo: Studio Times, 1974.

Iran. Victoria, Australia: Lonely Planet Publications, 1992.

Kipling, Rudyard. *The Jungle Book and The Second Jungle Book.* New York: Doubleday, Page and Co., 1923.

_____. "Plain Tales from the Hills," "The Phantom Rickshaw," and other writings.

Lapierre, Dominique. *City of Joy* (Calcutta). New York: Doubleday, 1985.

Lloyd, Seton. *Ancient Turkey: A Traveler's History of Anatolia.* University of California Press, n.d.

McGowan, William. *Only Man is Vile: The Tragedy of Sri Lanka.* New York: Farrar Straus and Giroux, 1992.

Mehta, Ved. *A Portrait of India.* New York: Farrar, Straus and Giroux, 1967.

Moorhouse, Geoffrey. *India Britannica.* New York: Harper and Row, 1983.

Moraes, Frank and Edward Howe, eds. *India.* Introduction by John Kenneth Galbraith. New York: McGraw-Hill, 1974.

Nehru, Jawaharlal. *The Discovery of India.* New York: Asia House, 1946.

Rice, Edward. *The Ganges, A Personal Encounter.* New York: Four Winds Press, 1974.

Theroux, Paul and Steve McCurry. *The Imperial Way.* Boston: Houghton Mifflin, 1985.

A Travel Agent's Manual of Ceylon. Colombo: Government Tourist Bureau, 1961.

Turkey. Hawthorne, Victoria, Australia: Lonely Planet Publications, 1985.

Williams, Gwyn. *Eastern Turkey: A Guide and History.* London: Faber and Faber, 1972.

Wolpert, Stanley. *India.* University of California Press, 1991.

_____. *A New History of India.* New York: Oxford University Press, 1977.